"May this book become your mirror and your catalyst. May your organizations become places of collective savoring, where strategy dances with soul, and purpose becomes a living song. And may we all learn, as Sankar and Wasu have shown, not just to lead change but, with everyone involved, *including ourselvesas change-makers*–to *Drench* in it."

– Dr David L. Cooperrider

I0130609

Organizational Transformation through Appreciative Inquiry

This book offers a pivotal concept, model, and tool called "Drench" that meets the need within organizational transformation to internalize, abide, and sustain the insights, learning, and the energy for change generated during an Appreciative Inquiry (Ai) or any other organization development (OD) process.

Drench is an active, non-action (state of presence) that helps an organization celebrate the discovery of strengths, soak in the dream of transformation, and allow the future to emerge. It facilitates a shift in the organizational consciousness and helps develop a belief in its ability to sustain the transformation. Bringing together field experiences, conceptual understanding, and practical tools, and with a foreword by Dr. David Cooperrider, this book introduces Drench as an addition to the existing 5-D model of Ai. The book is divided into three parts: the first part introduces Drench in the context of organizational transformation through Ai; the second part consists of case studies from our experiences of facilitating organizational transformation; the third part offers a set of practical tools and models that can be combined in a logical as well as intuitive way for deeper results.

Challenging conventional notions of change and development by providing a helpful set of concepts, models and a toolbox for organizational transformation, this is a useful book for change consultants, facilitators and coaches who use OD and/or Ai for transformation.

Sankarasubramanyan Ramamoorthy, MA, has 37 years of professional experience in human resources development, consulting, organization development (OD), and applied behavioural science. Sankar is the International Director in the Board of NTL (www.ntl.org) and the Director of Changeworks (www. changeworksindia.com), a consulting organization based in Mumbai, India. Sankar is a past president and professional member of the Indian Society for Applied Behavioural Science (www.isabs.org). Sankar has hands-on experience in OD, people process implementation, personal growth, leadership and team development, executive coaching, and Appreciative Inquiry (Ai)-based interventions. He is a Routledge author having published his book *T- Group*

Facilitation – Theory and Practise of Applied Behavioural Science. He has also published two other books and many articles in peer-reviewed journals.

Wasundhara Joshi MSc, MD, is a paediatrician, change facilitator, OD consultant, coach, and yoga student and practitioner. She is the Director of Changeworks (www.changeworksindia.com). She is a professional member of ISABS (www.isabs.org) and certified in change facilitation, transformational coaching, appreciative coaching, and holds an MSc in Yoga. She is a faculty, and mentor for Level 2 training of coaches (PCC). She specializes in the use of Ai as a method for both coaching and organization change. She is engaged in the field of OD through Ai, leadership development, personal growth, and executive coaching for the past two decades. She has published many articles in the field in peer-reviewed journals.

Organizational Transformation through Appreciative Inquiry

Experiences and Reflections
on Drenching Processes

Sankarasubramanyan Ramamoorthy
and Wasundhara Joshi

Routledge
Taylor & Francis Group

LONDON AND NEW YORK

Designed cover image: Getty Images @nicholashan

First published 2026
by Routledge
4 Park Square, Milton Park, Abingdon, Oxon OX14 4RN

and by Routledge
605 Third Avenue, New York, NY 10158

Routledge is an imprint of the Taylor & Francis Group, an informa business

British Library Cataloguing-in-Publication Data
A catalogue record for this book is available from the British Library

ISBN: 9781032884912 (hbk)
ISBN: 9781032884899 (pbk)
ISBN: 9781003538059 (ebk)

DOI: 10.4324/9781003538059

Typeset in Optima
by Newgen Publishing UK

Dedicated to Sharad Sakorkar
a dear friend and colleague who walked the
path with us

Contents

Foreword

I feel like I've struck gold when I encounter fresh and enlightening Appreciative Inquiry (Ai) practices and theories, such as those revealed by Sankarasubramanyan Ramamoorthy and Wasundrhara Joshi in their "Silver Jubilee" of work together – and their new book. It's a masterful volume. It's a gift for everyone interested in organization development (OD), change leadership, and the kinds of *depth* organizational *transformations* that serve to bring out the life-giving best in people, heighten group unity and collaboration, and help the community of change-makers to savor and saturate themselves in their new organizational dreams and most generative designs.

Right from the start, the "Sankar and Wasu" express it: "This book is a celebration of our work together in the vast field of Appreciative Inquiry and our gratitude to the field and its people for adding so much to our lives."

I too, right from the start, want to thank the authors for the opportunity to learn from them and, in this foreword, to be given the privilege to shine a light on three significant achievements inside this volume (and you will find many more!)

First, this book brings to life, in lucid writing, the vast background and rapidly growing literature on Ai (the other "AI") from the past 40 years. And what they do is *not cheapen it* with over-simplifying one-liners, like "AI is simply a *strengths-based* approach to OD and change", or "Ai is all about positivity." As Sankar and Wasu write, "the so called 'positive' focus is only apparent. The real focus in AI is on *life-giving forces* and that which gives energy and vitality to systems ... it is the choice to inquire into what is life."

Indeed, Ai is a life-centric, whole-system, and collaborative *inquiry-and-change* process that seeks everything that gives life to organizations, communities, and nature's "more than human" systems when they are most alive, creative, relationally healthy, and fertile. It's part of the paradigm shift from the Age of Enlightenment's mechanistic-machine metaphors to what's now being called the Age of Enlivenment's worldview.[1] Here, the fundamental dimension of existence is the miracle of life: *it's about aliveness. It's about that one unifying thread that is intrinsic to all human and biological processes and to the cosmos as a bio-geochemical whole.*[2]

In Ai, our basic assumptions or metaphors matter. From the earliest articulation of the idea of Ai over four decades ago, Ai posited that human systems are not inert machines or mechanistic and broken down "problems-to-be-solved."[3] That kind of metaphor often leads us, it's been shown, to pervasive deficit-inclined interventions with less than favourable results.[4] Instead, Ai chooses to embrace "the mystery and miracle of life on this planet" whereby human organizations, as living systems, are viewed as relationally alive and intrinsically embedded in our "universe of strengths."

As Einstein once remarked, "There are only two ways to live your life. One is as though nothing is a miracle. The other is as if everything is a miracle."

Indeed, the authors quote Einstein in numerous passages, and I will return to this, especially the authors' courage and sensitivity to the *spiritual,* in their writing on the relationship between Ai's deeper worldview and Indic philosophy. In these days, too many scientists and scholars view it as an insult if they are accused of being drawn towards mysticism or a reuniting of the sacred and secular, especially if they are making the argument that the experience of the mystical or life-as-a-mystery is a legitimate knowledge method, that is, it is something that can consciously be harnessed in the service of creating generative knowledge of consequence.

The second inspiration I want to underscore is that the entire volume is written with a deep sense of humanity and humility, and provides us with an artful blend of real-life stories from the field, along with "how-to-do-it" guides and theory. I personally love the "living proof" – all the vivid examples – and the expansive range of settings the authors write about, for example: global engineering firms; huge public health systems; technology firms in the banking industry; maternity homes; and one of the largest Ai projects ever in India. Indeed, the authors have worked with over 50+ organizations, have trained 500+ OD practitioners and change makers, and have published their advances in AI widely in the *Organization Development Review*, the *International Journal of Appreciative Inquiry, The AI Practitioner,* and more.

And now to the book's central innovation. It's about a different theory of change. Its not just about the discovery of strengths in a system. In Ai, we often speak of the universe of strengths. These are meant and taken as not just human strengths but every relevant resource available to us *across the entire systemic strengths' spectrum,* outside and inside the enterprise, including all relevant and available social and cultural assets, technical and economic ones, psychological and spiritual strengths, best practices, ecological strengths, the strengths of moral models, enlivening values, and our greatest collective dreams and images of possibility. In some writings, this combination is collectively referred to as the positive core of a system.[5] The concept of the positive core is defined as "all past, present, *and future* capacities, as well as all the greatest good that *is* possible."

Moreover, the authors go further and delve deeper. They argue that the study of life-giving or optimal states does not just signal optimal states. Ai is not just about some study and technical feedback report of the positive core of a system to be recorded and filed away. The bigger story is that these optimal states or strengths *can be strengthened*. In other words, strengths don't just perform, let's say, like an orchestra performs. Strengths do more than perform – *they transform*. And their transformative power can be elevated, magnified, and intensified. How? By helping human systems and individual beings DRENCH themselves and each other in their vital discoveries, dreams, and the vast and powerful concentrated version of the "positive core" of all past, present, *and* future capacities and dreams.

Drenching is a new model in the Ai cycle to help people and their organizations to attend to, intensify, and amplify *the positive core of a system* in liminal and embodied ways – through narrative richness and story, ritual, generative metaphor creation, inspired symbolism, celebration and song, powerful practices of mindfulness, moments of stillness, activating deeply personal questions, and embracing something of a soul consciousness as in "yes, this is the soul of our organization" that brings life to our organization and each individual in a kind of *conscious co-elevation*. Drenching, propose the authors, involves pausing, saturating, savouring, embodying, and soaking, for example, in the most potent dreams that bring an organization into a state of communitas, that is, deepened group unity and collaboration. It cultivates inclusion, reinforces emotional resonance and full engagement, and humanizes the real-time change process. For example, it helps people see the union of organizational transformation *and* personal transformation, whereby people experience the whole of it: "I too must be the change I want to see in this organization."

To be sure, all such congruent and significant transformations are emotionally demanding. And in liminality terms – where an individual, group, or culture is in that state of "in-betwixt and between" – that's precisely where drenching provides the kind of energy to leap into the new, the better, and the possible. It's a leap that is not without fear. But it is one that cultivates the trust and social–psychological–spiritual capacity that brings with it more hope, inspiration, meaning, and joy. It's about absorbing the sensory richness of each stage in Ai. It's about collective flow and allowing inward, upward, and outward momentum to take hold.[6] It's about building the new and eclipsing the old while keeping the most precious system-wide threads of continuity. Drenching, in this sense, isn't just about self-indulgence. It's about ignition. It's about building *communities of appreciation* and the gift of new eyes. It enables a saturation spiral for *transformational change*.

May this book become your mirror and your catalyst. May your organizations become places of collective savouring, where strategy dances with soul, and purpose becomes a living song. And may we all learn, as Sankar and Wasu have shown, not just to lead change but, with everyone involved, *including ourselves as change-makers* – to *Drench* in it.

David L. Cooperrider, PhD
Distinguished University Professor and the
Covia Professorship in Appreciative Inquiry
Case Western Reserve University Department of Organization Behavior
Honorary Chair of the Cooperrider Center for Appreciative Inquiry,
Champlain College

Notes

1 Cooperrider, D. L., Godwin, L. (special issue editors). (2024). Appreciative inquiry as a research method for qualitative research and prospective theory building for the age of enlivenment. *The International Journal of Appreciative Inquiry: The AI Practitioner.* 26, 1. 3–106. ISBN 978-1-907549-58-8 dx.doi.org/10.12781/978-1-907549-58-8

2 Weber, A. (2008). *Enlivenment: Toward a Poetics for the Anthropocene.* Cambridge, MA: MIT Press.

3 Cooperrider, D. (1986). *Appreciative Inquiry: Toward a Methodology for Understanding and Enhancing Organizational Innovation.* [Doctoral dissertation at Case Western Reserve University]. Also see: Cooperrider, D., Srivastva, S. (1987). "Appreciative inquiry into organizational life". In R. Woodman, R. W. and Pasmore, W. A. (Eds.). *Research in Organizational Change and Development*, vol 1. Leeds, UK: Emerald.

4 Nohira, N., Beer, M. (2000). Cracking the code of change. *Harvard Business Review.* May–June. https://hbr.org/2000/05/cracking-the-code-of-change. Also see McKinsey Report on the 70% rate of change management failure: www.mckinsey.com/capabilities/transformation/our-insights/common-pitfalls-in-transformations-a-conversation-with-jon-garcia

5 Cooperrider, D. L., Whitney, D. (1999). "Appreciative inquiry: A positive revolution in change" in Holman (Ed.). *The Change Handbook.* San Francisco, CA: Berrett-Kohler Publications. Also see: Cooperrider, D. L. (2005). "Foreword to appreciative intelligence" in Thachenkery, T. (Ed.). *Appreciative Intelligence.* San Francisco, CA: Berrett-Koehler Publishers.

6 Fredrickson, B. L., Joiner, T. (2002). "Positive emotions trigger upward spirals toward emotional well-being". *Psychological Science.* 13, 2. 172–175. https://doi.org/10.1111/1467-9280.00431. Also see: Robson, L. (2015). *The Language of Life-Giving Connection: The Emotional Tone of Language that Fosters Flourishing* [Doctoral dissertation]. Case Western Reserve University.

Preface

This book has been a dream from the time one of us ventured into the Appreciative Inquiry (Ai) world in 1995 attending a workshop by Jane Watkins as part of the 50th anniversary of NTL Institute at Bethel, ME. The other attended a workshop in 1999 by some members of UNICEF who introduced this model for their work in India. Both of us got hooked to the elegance of the model and to the principles. These principles not only became guiding force in our lives but also brought us together as a couple!

We have been consultants for Ai-based organizational transformation for many organizations in India from the year 2000. We have also trained more than a few hundred Ai practitioners in India, coached many more using the Ai principles, presented and published papers in Ai global conferences and in the *Ai Practitioner* and *OD Review*. We are celebrating with this book as our silver jubilee present to ourselves.

In 2019, we presented the concept of Drench at the Ai global conference in Nice, France (we are using Ai as a short form of Appreciative Inquiry). One of the people who attended our session was Gervase Bushe. He told us that we should publish this work since he saw it as a significant contribution to the field. Our article was accepted and published by *OD Review* in 2019 and in 2023, Routledge approached us to write a book. We have given more than a year in putting together our experiences and reflections on organizational transformation using Ai with a focus on Drench.

The Drench that we described in 2019 has grown, matured, and encompasses all the stages of Ai while retaining its identity as a sixth stage. We are convinced that drenching at different stages and staying drenched after the Dream stage is what makes Ai into an organization transformation process. We will share the basis of our conviction through our experiences, stories, reflections, and conceptualization thereof. In order to learn any subject and be convinced about one's knowledge, it requires three steps – understanding, contemplation, and practice. We hope this book will offer you the first two and energize you to practice and internalize this learning.

This book is divided into three sections. The first section is metaphorically called stepping into the water. We have imagined the reader starting tentatively into this field, wetting their toes, and preparing for the dive. This section introduces the three important topics of inquiry in this book: (a) Organizational transformation, (b) Ai and (c) Drench, a crucial step for organizational transformation. These chapters provide the contextual and conceptual base for the book. They also introduce the various nuanced colours that form the background, including the historical context, the principles that drive transformation, Ai and Drench, as well as the different perspectives offered by others in the field.

The second section is called Drenching Experiences where the reader dives and discovers different facets of drenching and staying drenched in the Ai process. There are six chapters and they are all stories from our work. They describe a variety of experiences of facilitating Ai processes and stressing Drench in all stages to enable organization transformation. The fourth chapter is called "Develop Appreciative Eye for Transformation" and this tells the story of a series of Ai Summits that we did for a large engineering conglomerate in India where we explored the core values of the group. The transformation we experienced in the system was the opening of the appreciative eye – to see opportunities in addition to problems, to appreciate others for who they are, and to see the future manifesting in the present (to see the mighty oak in the acorn). In this chapter drenching in the discovery stage through storytelling and retelling process is the main focus.

The fifth chapter called "Revere Diversity" is focused on an organizational transformation project anchored on Diversity, Equity and Inclusion (DEI) for an international NGO in India. This story also helps the reader to understand why Ai is highly appropriate as the philosophy and method for DEI-based organization transformation. This chapter tells the story of a long-term drenching process i between the dream and design.

The sixth chapter is called "Embrace the Dream" and we describe stories from three diverse organizations – one working on biodiversity, another a low-cost health facility, and the third a pharma company. The common thread among these three stories are the process of drenching in the dream by being completely open and thus allowing the future to emerge and manifest as a vision, a value and as a roadmap for success.

The seventh chapter called "Nurture Use of 'Us'" is a fascinating story of how collaboration between us and the internal OD consultants group contributed to the project of collaboration between two groups in the client organization. This story illustrates how we need to drench into what we aim to deliver for the client in the project. The story is told by one of us who was the external consultant and two of the internal consultants, Nidhi Malhotra and Srividya Natarajan. Each one of us talks about how we learned to work together with the other and how the trust we developed spilled over to the two business groups we worked with which helped them to live the collaboration of their dream.

The eighth chapter called "Pause within: Co-creating the Research Vision" is a story contributed by a dear colleague Dr. Lalitha Iyer about her work with the research department of a large university. This story brings out how researchers need to take a pause, drench and look at themselves, their work, and the system within which they produce research. This ceasing within enabled the group to envision the future of research in that university.

The ninth chapter is called "Honour the View" describes one of the largest public health project we facilitated called the City Initiative for Newborn Health in the city of Mumbai, Maharashtra. This included a randomized control trial using Ai with pre and post indicators for assessing impact. This work is continuing over the past decade and has been extended to many more cities in the state of Maharashtra.

The section summary reflects what we would typically do in an Ai summit during the story telling. We ask the group to once again soak into the stories, savour their lingering sweetness, appreciate oneself and others for being a witness to the moment, and then identify the themes that contributed to the stories and hence discover the gold nuggets that seem to lie just beneath them. We attempt the same with all the stories from the six chapters. We have gone one step further to create a model for the Drench processes that emerged f.

Section 3 of the book has three chapters. The first chapter is a collection of methods, tools, and exercise that we have used in our work. This chapter is our gift to the readers and practitioners of Ai. We offer all the methods we have learned and used in our work at all the stages of the 6-D cycle including some tips and the impact we have seen. We plan to open this chapter for our colleagues and ask them to contribute more so that we have an abundance of resources to drench oneself in.

The second chapter in this section is an exploration of the spirit and Ai, and the spirit of Ai through an Indic lens. We have learned spiritual practices in Advaita Vedanta and Ashtanga yoga, and many other Indian philosophies ranging from Buddhism to Samkhya and the Bhakti traditions. We experience Ai as a deeply spiritual practice and see various linkages, especially with reference to the Drench for transformation. We hope that some of our readers will also see linkages in the wisdom traditions that they are familiar with and bring those too into Ai practice.

The third and last chapter is a collage of stories that describe how we have drenched in the field of Ai, what we have learned, shared, and how we have transformed ourselves as individuals and as professionals in the field. We also write about how drenching in Ai changed our life. It has deepened our relationship, nad given it many more dimensions. It has helped us value the diversity that we bring nurturing the best in each other. This is our celebration of our work together in the vast field of Ai and our gratitude to the field and people for adding so much to our lives.

"In Closing" is a series of conversations that we have had with some of our friends, colleagues, and clients about their stories, perspectives, and dreams about Ai for organization transformation and the power of drench in enabling and energizing the same. This chapter is also a way by which we have included more voicesto add to the richness of the field.

The book is structured like the 6-D model. It starts with the definition, then tells stories of discovery, dream, and drench, and the designs we offer; and finally the destiny that awaits us just around the corner. We welcome readers to read from anywhere or just take in sections of it. We would be equally delighted if you drench into the book from cover to cover and walk with us through the journey of transformation from define to destiny.

Regards
Wasundhara and Sankar, July 2025

Acknowledgements

None of this would have been possible without the birth of Ai. David Cooperrider and Suresh Srivastava will forever have our gratitude for developing Appreciative Inquiry. they have inspired us to live it, not just practise it. We are overjoyed and grateful that David Cooperrider graciously and promptly agreed to write the graceful foreword. It affirms our belief in our work. None of this work would have been possible without our clients. They gave us the opportunity to learn, experiment, practice, and contributed to our growth in the field. We have worked with more than 50 organizations and 500+ individuals using Appreciative Inquiry(Ai) during the past 25 years. While it is difficult to name everyone, some names stand out and we want to express our gratitude to them.

Dr. Armida Fernandez, the doyen of maternal and child health movement (now palliative care as well) in India, was the first to recognize the immense power of Ai and encouraged us to bring it to the public health system in the city of Mumbai when she was the Dean of Sion Hospital. She started SNEHA, an NGO, and that led us to work with the City Initiative for Neonatal Health project. This is one of the largest Ai project in India covering 4 big hospitals, 10+ maternity homes, 20+ health posts, and more than 3,000 health workers, doctors, nurses, support staff, administrative staff, social workers, and municipal officials.

Cheryl Francisconi and Namrata Jha helped us to stretch this work internationally, work with diverse groups in Bihar and Addis Ababa, and strengthen our scholarship and practice.

Sunil Jha, CHRO of ACG Global, gave us the opportunity to facilitate a large organization transformation experience involving more than 5,000+ people and 6 group companies in the corporate sector. We also published our work in Ai practitioner with Sunil and Priya Vasudevan. We also thank Nikita Panchal for her lovely poetry that we have used in this book.

Sneh, Pratim, and Mathew from Keystone Foundation became our friends by accident and they gave us the opportunity to work with Adivasi's (forest dwellers in the western ghats) and helped us to learn that having an appreciative eye is natural and easy to cultivate.

Sundeep and Garima offered us a chance to work with a startup venture wanting to build their vision, mission, and values around the principles of Ai. They attended our workshop and were convinced about the idea of seeing health as a possibility rather than as a problem.

Dr. Lalitha Iyer has presented a unique experience of working with a university system using Ai and a very different way of Drenching. Her chapter adds to the richness of this book. She also helped with the editing and indexing of this book for which we are very grateful.

Srividya Natarajan and Nidhi Malhotra collaborated with us in writing the Chapter on "Use of 'Us'" based on a real experience of working together in a complex AI assignment.

Dr. K.K Verma, the Director of The Academy of HRD, gave us the first opportunity to teach Ai to the world, showcase our work and publish them. The academy published a book and produced a teaching video on Ai with us as the main teachers.

Dr. Tojo Thatchenkery has been an inspiration, mentor, companion, and friend in our Ai journey. He appreciated our work and encouraged us to write more, including this book.

We also thank Mac Odell who inspired us to take Ai to community development.

Our sincere gratitude to all of them. Our gratitude also to all our clients, participants, and our readers who encouraged us to continue our scholarship and practice in this field.

Lastly, thanks to our immediate families for   encouraging and supporting us. us. Some were curious enough to attend the workshops and others gave us the space to do our thing.

Wasundhara and Sankar, July 2025.

Section 1

Stepping into the Water

Chapter 1

Organizational Transformation

"Extraordinary things begin to happen when we dare to bring all of who we are to work. Could we invent a more powerful, more soulful, more meaningful way to work together, if only we change our belief system? as human beings, we are not problems waiting to be solved, but potential waiting to unfold."

Fredrick Laloux

Introduction

We were facilitating a vision and strategy workshop for the top three levels of leadership of a banking applications technology organization in India. The first day was spent on identifying their strengths as an organization, opportunities in the market, the shared dreams of the members of leadership, and shaping the vision for the future. We started the second day by asking everyone

DOI: 10.4324/9781003538059-2

to write a personal story of their life in this organization three years into the future. They had to visualize themselves three years from now and look into the past towards this day and trace their journey. We told them that their story will be about their personal transformations that aided the organization and the organization transformations that impacted them personally.

There was some initial reluctance to get into the activity. Some of them couldn't see the connection between transformation of self and the organization. Some people got it immediately. Soon everyone got so engrossed in the activity that we had to wean them away saying that the time was up to present their stories. An intensely emotional sharing followed where participants spoke about beliefs that they let go, relationships that they built, new learning they acquired and innovations they brought to their way of working. The penny dropped when one of them said "As I wrote my story of the future, I realized that all that I wrote needs to happen today, now." They realized that organization transformation is not something they will watch as observers. They are active participants in the process and only when they do, the organization transforms.

This was a big eye-opener for us too, as consultants. When we work with a system, facilitating transformation, we won't be successful unless we transform our view of the system we work with.

Let us now dive deep into organizational transformation.

Organizational Transformation

All transformations are not the same. We have this stereotypical idea when we hear the word transformation. The image of a beautiful butterfly emerging from a sticky-gooey mass called the pupa. It is an image of a metamorphosis, a miraculous event where what existed before and what emerged are diametrically different in how they look and act.

Another transformation that is a less dramatic but an everyday occurrence is the transformation of a lump of wheat dough to a fluffy loaf of bread when kneaded with some yeast, left overnight and baked in an oven.

This transformation is partly natural (due to the interaction between the dough and the yeast), partly due to conditions like the temperature in the oven, the quality of wheat, water, yeast, etc., and partly due to the human intervention, the knowledge, and skill of the baker.

The outcome of both these transformations is similar. We have a new entity (the butterfly or a loaf of bread) that is fundamentally different from the previous entity in form and function. The butterfly is a feast to our eyes and the bread is a source of nutrition. In both cases, the transformation is irreversible – the butterfly will never go back to being a pupa and the bread will never become dough again.

A similar view of transformation can be considered when a baby grows up to be an adult. The form, appearance, and the functions of an adult will be different from the baby. Here nature and nurture both play an important role in the quality of the outcome of this transformation. We may have mature or immature adults as a consequence.

Transformation in human systems, specifically in our organizations, follows a more complex process. There are natural processes, human interventions, and the character of the organization; each of which plays a role in this process. The third element – character – is a complex element comprising of identity, purpose, culture, and leadership. Similar to human development from baby to adulthood, organizations can transform to be ethical or rogue, caring or to be insensitive, diverse or parochial, etc.

Lastly and perhaps more importantly, organizational transformation is very unlike the previous three examples. The transformed entity also carries some aspects and characters of the previous version, unlike in the case of a butterfly or a loaf of bread that are bereft of the previous character. This makes organizational transformation more complex and perhaps more interesting as well. Transformation in an organization may not create impact across the whole system hence a critical mass required for that change is not reached. One can say that the "inflection point" required for organizational transformation is often difficult to reach and hence requires long and sustained efforts.

This chapter begins by defining organizational transformation, exploring triggers for transformation in organizations, and reviews both external and internal trends that can trigger such a process. The key concepts around organizational transformation are then taken up, compared, and contrasted. This will be followed by conceptual inputs around incremental, planned, and emergent change that organizations experience. The chapter concludes by introducing various transformation models and why Ai is perhaps one of the most comprehensive and effective of them all.

Understanding Organizational Transformation

A review of literature on organization change, development, and transformation throws up many definitions. They range from changing corporate culture, restructuring, changing mission, vision and values, business strategy, digital transformation, and so on. Many terms like "second-order change", "quantum change", "large- scale change", "strategic change", etc., are used by many authors in several studies. We believe that organizational transformation is all of the above and much more.

Organizational transformation is a portfolio of interdependent change initiatives that lead to changes at three levels – at the level of doing, at the level of learning and at the level of being. For example, organizations can transform some of the practices and establish new ones. They can also acquire new knowledge and skills for developing new products, dealing with competition, and so on. At the level of being, organizations can drop certain values and worldviews that are unhelpful in the current world and embrace new ones. As one can see, transformation at the level of being is more sustainable and impactful as compared to knowing, which in turn is more sustainable than transformation in doing.

While change management is generally focused on a particular "problem" or an "opportunity", transformation addresses the very core and identity of an organization. Change is an answer to an existing situation that needs to be addressed. Changes are generally small, incremental, and adaptive. Change can be an event or long term when organizations address needs that evolve over time.

Transformation can be an organic process triggered by the changes in any of the following: age of the organization, new leadership, diversity of the workforce, changing nature of businesses and the impact of competition and socio-economic and political environment. Organization transformation can also be based on a clear intention, vision, and strategy of leadership.

Transformations have a larger scale and scope than adaptive changes. Because of their scale, these changes often take a substantial amount of time and energy to enact. Transformational changes are often pursued in response to internal or external forces or triggers such as the emergence of a disruptive new competitor or supply chain issues because of lack of collaboration between departments.

In our view, scale, scope, or outcomes don't define organizational transformation. It is defined by the shifts in core beliefs, values, and organizational worldview. We also see organizational transformation as a second and third order of change as opposed to first-order change (Bartunek and Moch, 1987).

Bartunek and Moch say that most change initiatives in organizations are of the first order since they focus on solving problems so that established patterns can function more effectively. A second-order change is about bringing in a new pattern, paradigm or schema of working and phasing out the old. In the third order of change, the organizational members themselves develop the capability to identify and change their own schema that they deem fit for the current reality of the organization (Table 1.1).

Additionally, a second order of change could be creating a new way of seeing the existing things without making any changes to them per se like the famous quote from Marcel Proust "The real voyage of discovery is not seeking new landscapes, but seeing the same land with new eyes"

An example of a first-order change is re-organization. Here the organization changes some of the reporting relationships between functions and distributes tasks across functions for better co-ordination, communication, and better accountability. A second order will be restructuring where the entire organogram is changed and a more centralized or decentralized way of operating the organization is created. In restructuring, some of the functions

Table 1.1 Orders of Change

First Order	Second Order	Third Order
Focus on behavior change. Requires learning	Focus on attitude change. Requires unlearning	People decide the focus for change. Collective mindset needs change
Incremental change	Fundamental change	Fundamental change with people engagement
Less resistance since they don't change beliefs	More resistance since people needs to think anew	Allow people to take ownership of change
Change individuals to fix the system	Change the system and individuals will change	Change is in the interaction between system and people

maybe completely eliminated and people might lose jobs in comparison to a reorganization of departments/ functions. The third order of change is based on the principles of organization development (OD), where members of the organization restructure themselves dynamically and organically based on changing requirements within and from the outside environment. Here people will voluntarily decide even to close a department and re-assign people to other units or offer voluntary termination based on needs of the situation.

During the pandemic, the authors had the opportunity to see all the different orders of changes with one of our clients. When the pandemic happened, the top management panicked and fired one-third of their employees within the first three months. This was a first-order change with no change in the operating paradigm except for reducing headcount. After six months, they discovered new ways of continuing operations in a limited way and restructured themselves. They called back some of the employees whom they had fired. This was a second-order change with a new schema of operating. However, the resultant changes led to low morale and voluntary exits. We were then invited to work with the organization and we facilitated a process of organizational transformation where all the employees participated and contributed to how the new and changed organization should be. We adopted an OD process and used Ai as a basis for the same. The organizational purpose got redefined and so were some of the business strategies and operating methods. In addition, people voluntarily offered to take salary cuts to preserve the jobs of their colleagues. They also saw that some jobs will be required once the pandemic was lifted and decided as a strategy to hold the people in those jobs and continue to pay them salaries. This worked well for them as these functions were crucial in the organization's revival when the pandemic-based restrictions were lifted.

External Triggers for Transformation

Leading an organization is never easy in the best of times. Today, it is becoming extremely complex considering that things once considered stable are changing overnight and completely blindsiding us. In 2019 no one would have predicted that the next two years would be mayhem for the entire world with more than a million deaths, countries shutting its borders, organizations downing shutters and every congregation of people from a roadside football match to the Olympics cancelled. The rapidity and the scale of impact were more than what the world was capable of handling. Such Black Swan events like the COVID pandemic that have high-impact and are difficult to predict were rare events or interspersed in time and intensity. Not so anymore. In a rapidly changing world such black swan events are becoming more and more common and can change the fortunes of an organization in a day. The rate of change is increasing and the periods of stability in between change and disruptions is decreasing.

COVID transformed the world irreversibly and brought in new practices like work from home and virtual meetings. Organizations that learned the science and art of online sale of products and services succeeded and those that relied exclusively on physical outlets failed. A very significant change that was brought in through the pandemic is that of the virtual organization that doesn't have a building, assigned offices, and employees congregating at the same place. It created a new breed of employees who say that they work for an organization but never saw an office, and never met the people they work with.

Leaders today are expected to deal with pandemics, wars, supply chain issues, artificial intelligence (AI), economic recession, increased competition all at the same time and are expected to overcome all of them. Organizations have also become flat and gone are the days when the leader could issue and order and expect things to get done. Leaders' need to enlist people, inspire and engage them in the process of organizational transformation.

The Directors of the McKinsey Institute in their book *No Ordinary Disruption* (2016) identified four forces that are transforming global economy. According to them, they are (a) the rise of emerging markets; (b) the accelerating impact of technology on the natural forces of market competition; (c) aging population, and (d) accelerating flows of trade, capital, people, and data. They write that "A radically different world is forming. The operating system of the world is being rewritten as we speak. It doesn't come out in a flashy new release. It evolves, unfolds and often explodes."

We asked ChatGPT to list the megatrends for organizations for 2025 and beyond and it covered the following:

1 Generative AI, automation and robotics along with issues around cybersecurity, digital identity, etc.

2   Consumer spending and rewarding themselves with experiences reaching an all-time high.
3   Climate change is becoming a norm and impacting people's lives. Focus on renewable sources of energy continues but is not keeping pace with climate change.
4   Population is still growing; people are living longer and the world is getting more aged. Fertility rates are decreasing and will impact availability of people for jobs, especially in the developed world in the long term.
5   Inequalities are also rising in the world and more than 71% of the people live in countries of high economic and social inequity.

One can see some similarities between the McKinsey research and the ChatGPT output. This also begs the question whether we are getting into a world where there is no difference between people who do decades of research to reach some conclusions versus someone who types in a question to an AI system and comes up with similar conclusions. Today we could write a similar book with ChatGPT and not use our own intelligence, experience, and insights, and offer that to the world. This is already impacting educational institutions and even the film industry where one finds it difficult to differentiate between creative or intellectual work of an individual and that is generated by an AI program.

The impact of the pandemic and its social, economic, and psychological fallouts on organizations are still being understood. They have. in turn created a sense of urgency for organizations to invest in long term digitization, building organizational resilience and risk management. Julie Hodges (2016) in her book *Managing and Leading People in Organizational Change* writes "There is an acceleration in the need to ensure that the thinking, work and change in organizations is designed with the threat of a herd of elephants in mind." The herd of elephants is unpredictable and they maybe just around the next corner.

In a developing country like India the challenges of organizational transformation are also due to changes in institutional frameworks. Business environment was completely controlled by the Government till the 1990s and the liberalization process began subsequently. Organizations that enjoyed monopoly status during those times had to undergo transformation to survive and thrive in a competitive world. Even today, there are significantly more controls on business in India as compared to some developed countries. This also creates a different schema for multinationals when they operate in India.

"… institution-level change produces new value commitments inside the firm, often with the help of new leadership. Those with new value commitments and new capabilities scan the available organizational templates, choose an alternative that is more appropriate, and change the organizational appropriately…" writes Newman (2000) in her article on organizational transformation during institutional upheaval.

Internal Triggers for Transformation

Internal triggers of transformation could range from leadership changes, mergers and acquisitions, cultural shifts, changes in organizational demographics, the increasing diversity, and lack of teamwork and collaboration across different groups. Big data and AI are also driving change within the organizations today in a big way. Digital transformation is a buzz word in the industry.

Growth is another driver for transformation. Growth is a must for survival of the fittest in the business world and growth comes with many challenges including better talent acquisition, customer service, product innovation, and a culture of care.

Resources are precious in organizations especially financial resources. Allocating financial resources appropriately for needed investments and saving cash where possible will also necessitate transformation projects for restructuring operations, retrenching staff, and improving operational efficiency and productivity.

Lastly, change from a traditional family leadership to a professional leadership is an important opportunity for organizational transformation. Many organizations have made the mistake of bringing professionals to lead the organization but continued to operate in a family based environment. t.

All the triggers mentioned previously also present opportunities to redefine strategies and processes, align teams, and build a more diverse and inclusive culture. Hence triggers can be seen from an appreciative lens as opportunities for transformation to a more vibrant and vital living system.

"Something is broken about how we manage organizations today. There is a sense of tiredness and lack of meaning to all the processes" writes Frederic Laloux in his book *Reinventing Organizations* (2014). He takes an evolutionary and historical view of organizations and opines that every time humanity has shifted to a new stage of consciousness, we have reinvented a more radical and productive organization that meets the needs for that change.

Changing organizational consciousness as an internal trigger for transformation has been an area of personal interest to the authors. Organizations, like individuals, have an awareness side and a shadow side. Both sides are characterized by needs, wants, attitudes, beliefs, values, and motivations corresponding to the level of growth and maturity of the organization. More mature the organization is, the larger will be the frame of awareness and it will lead to better corporate governance, ethical practices and inclusive environment. Alternatively, when the shadow side is larger/ stronger, the organization will be exploitative of people, resources, and the environment for meeting selfish ends. Transformation from the shadow side of organizations can be triggered by events or by leadership reflection on the being of the organization.

Ashok Malhotra (2018) wrote the book *Indian Managers and Organizations: Boons and Burdens* wherein he postulates a model called the Existential Universe Mapper (EUM) to map the organization's identity flowing from an "existential universe" in which the organization operates. Inspired by Clare Graves' work on the framework of evolution, this model helps to map organization's identity reflecting its business philosophy, outlook towards employees, stakeholders, and society at large.

Based on this model an organization identity can exist in six different universes. The first one   being CLAN, where the organization lays premium on security and stability. The next universe is called ARENA, then CLOCKWORK, NETWORK, ECOLOGICAL and ending with HOLISTIC universe characterized by an organization that is ambitious, efficient, caring and ethical symbolizing sustained, and dignified growth. The model doesn't place an organization in a particular universe and highlights the dynamics and interplay within an organization as it operates in multiple universes.

Examining an organization's tendencies and developing a common aspiration of the universes that one wants to embrace will be a positive internal trigger for transformation.

To summarize, leaders need to be aware of the forces of transformation impacting their system on a consistent basis. Leaders who are aware of and anticipate these forces see them as opportunities rather than threats. They are more likely to respond by preparing the organization's readiness to change rather than react in a way that could be counterproductive. "External and internal drivers do not by themselves bring about change and transformation but create the need for change" (Hodges, 2016).

Planned and Emergent Models

Now that we have understood organizational transformation and the external and internal triggers for the same, we will take an overview of the models that help us to navigate the process of transformation.

These models differ in their construct based on the paradigm or lens used to view organizations. In the machine paradigm, organizations are seen as instruments designed to achieve specific goals. Goal specificity, formal structures, plans and a rational approach to problem-solving are characteristics of organizations when viewed from this paradigm. A planned approach to transformation is in line with this way of thinking.

When organizations are seen as organic, living systems, they are seen as open systems that interact with the environment and function to thrive as a system. Vitality, fluidity, energy, and flow are seen as characteristics of organizations when viewed from this paradigm. Here change is seen as giving a new life or energy to that system. A more emergent model of transformation is desired in this way of thinking.

Table 1.2 Planned and Emergent Transformation Models

Planned Transformation	Emergent Transformation
Organizations are machines and they can be fixed when broken	Organizations are living beings and strengthening the system is more important than dealing with the problem
Mostly driven from top of the organization	Can emerge at any level of the organization
Structured and organized approach to change with clear timelines.	Mostly open-ended, spontaneous and flowing nature, though a pattern might be present
Mostly linear with clear focus on specific areas and with clear targets	Mostly non-linear or wholistic and encompasses every aspect of organization life.
The change process is supported by data and logic	The change process is supported by stories and emotions
Diagnostic and change models like Weisbord's six-box, McKinsey's 7S and Six Sigma, LEAN etc.	Conversational models like Appreciative Inquiry, World Café, Complex Adaptive Systems etc.

A comparison between a planned and emergent model is given in Table 1.2. We would like the readers to view the above not as polarized positions but rather as a continuum. The two paradigms co-exist in any organization and it is for the leadership to bring these to the awareness of the organization, locate the energies for transformation present in these beliefs and choose an appropriate model or combination thereof that will work in the current context.

We wrote about the differences between transformation and change in the section "Understanding Organizational Transformation". We will now introduce another term called Organization development (OD). OD is a discipline consisting of theories and practices that provide the knowledge, skills and values required for anyone engaged in executing the processes of change and transformation. OD as a field can be traced back to the work of Kurt Lewin and his associates at the Research Center for Group Dynamics in 1946. OD is variously defined and we would like to offer one of the definitions that is relevant for our book. Richard Beckhard (1969) in his book *Organization Development – Strategies and Models* defines OD as "an effort that is planned, organization-wide, managed from the top to Increase organization effectiveness and health through planned interventions in the organization's "processes," using behavioural-science knowledge".

The classical or diagnostic OD approaches are aligned with the planned approach to system wide transformation using various models and tools for diagnosis and interventions. In the past decade, "Dialogic OD" as formulated by Gervase Bushe and Robert Marshak (2015) has become more popular. Dialogic OD is a name given to many emergent transformation models that are conversational and interactive. Generally diagnostic OD separates the object of diagnosis from the subject, i.e. the leader or the diagnostician. By contrast, dialogic processes take the perspective that organizations are meaning-making systems, where leaders are a part of the process of discovering new futures. Inquiry is no longer a focus on objective facts, instead it becomes a focus on narrative and the shared meanings given to events.

The conventional approaches used for planned transformation are theoretically sound and have been tried and tested in different environments in the past. However, their effectiveness in the rapidly changing environment is questionable. Emergent models offer more flexibility and are more agile in adapting to changing conditions and therefore more suited to second and third order changes in an organization.

Dialogic OD

Gervase Bushe (2015) stated:

> This generic model of Dialogic OD rests on the assumption that change occurs when the day to day thinking of community members has altered their day to day decisions and actions, which leads to a change in the culture of the community that entrenches those new ways of thinking.

Dialogic OD is founded on social constructionism (Gergen, 1990) where it is believed that reality is socially constructed, there are multiple realities and reality involves power and political processes. The truth is immanent and emerges from the dialogues that happen in that community. Dialogic OD essentially involves three processes. These are narratives, reframing and generative images. Narratives are how we tell our story about who we are, reframing helps to change the language that we use to describe ourselves and generative images create our collective dream of the future.

Dialogic OD assumes maturity among organizational leaders and participants of the dialogue. It also requires an expert facilitator who can hold a safe container for genuine and sometimes difficult dialogues to happen and walk the thin line between order and chaos. There are many organization transformation approaches and tools that meet the criteria of Dialogic OD according to Gervase Bushe and Robert Marshak (2015). The popular ones are Open Space Technology (Owen, 2008), Future Search (Weisbord and Janoff, 2010), World Café (Brown and Isaccs, 2005), and Ai (Cooperrider and Shrivastava, 1987).

This book is primarily about our experiences around the application of Ai, one of the most effective and popular models within Dialogic OD.

"Will Organizational Transformation Really Work for Us?"

While none of you will have any dispute about our statements about the external and internal challenges faced by organizations, some of you will ask the question "does this mean we have to undergo organization transformation? Will it work for us?"

There are sceptics amongst management gurus like John Kotter (1995) who said that 70% of all organizational transformation initiatives fail. There are many reasons cited for that . However, we believe that no organization transformation will be total success or failure and the results will be somewhere in between. There is a Kanter's law which states that "In the middle, everything looks like a failure."

Ai can be a powerful tool for organizational transformation as pointed out by Gervase Bushe and Aniq Kassam (2005) in their article "When is appreciative inquiry transformational" (*JABS*, June 2005). Bushe wrote:

> Highly consistent differences between the transformational cases and the others led the authors to conclude that two qualities of appreciative inquiry that are different from conventional organizational development and change management prescriptions are key to Ai's transformative potential: (a) a focus on changing how people think instead of what people do and (b) a focus on supporting self-organizing change processes that flow from new ideas.

The constructs that Bushe concluded in his article are also supported by our own experiences of using Ai for the past twenty five years. We might add one more element to Bushe's two qualities mentioned above and that is the profound individual transformation that Ai brings in and aids in the collective transformation of systems. Individual transformation, especially for leaders can have a cascading effect. When leaders internalize the appreciative worldview of "catching people doing this right" and an internal view of building on one's strengths, they release locked up energies in people bringing hope and anticipation for the future.

Organizational transformation can be a long and hard process and it is easy to give up in the middle. Developing an appreciative mindset helps to stay committed and hopeful. Sometimes, transformation happens, people behave differently but they don't recognize it and it is challenging to convince them that they have changed. Transformation means letting go of the past and embracing the new. Appreciative mindset helps to celebrate the past and let it go, leading to acceptance of change.

We believe that it is an imperative for today's organizations to reinvent themselves to be relevant in the marketplace. Hence organizational transformation is a given. The leadership should build the passion and the capacity for sustained transformation and resilience for the long haul. Ai has the core philosophy, models and tools to engage with any system or community to locate the energy for change. We will take a deeper look at Ai in the next chapter.

References

Bartunek, J. (1987). *First-Order, Second-Order, and Third-Order Change and Organization Development Interventions: A Cognitive Approach.* JABS.

Beckhard, R. (1969). *Organization Development: Strategies and Models.* Boston, MA: Addison-Wesley.

Brown, J., Isaccs, D. (2015). *World Cafe – Shaping Our Futures through Conversations.* New York: Berret-Koehler.

Bushe, G., Marshak, R. (2015). *Dialogic Organization Development.* CA: Berrett-Koehler

Bushe, G., Kassam, A. (2005). When is appreciative inquiry transformational? A meta-case analysis. *The Journal of Applied Behavioral Science.* 41. 161–181. 10.1177/0021886304270337.

Cooperrider, D. L., Srivastva, S. (1987). "Appreciative inquiry in organizational life" in Woodman, R. W. and Pasmore, W. A. (Eds.). *Research in Organizational Change And Development.* Stamford, CT: JAI Press. 1. 129–169

Dobbs, R., Manyika, J., Woetzel, J. (2016). *No Ordinary Disruption – Four Global Forces Breaking All the Trends.* Public Affairs.

Gergen, K., (1990). *An Invitation to Social Construction.* Newcastle upon Tyne, UK: Sage.

Hodges, J. (2016). *Managing and Leading People through Organizational Change.* New York: KoganPage.

Kotter, J. (1995). Leading change – Why transformation efforts fail. *Harvard Business Review.* https://hbr.org/1995/05/leading-change-why-transformation-efforts-fail-2

Laloux, F. (2014). *Reinventing Organizations: A Guide to Creating Organizations Inspired by the Next Stage of Human Consciousness.* Brussels: Nelson Parker.

Malhotra, A. (2018). *Indian Managers and Organizations: Boons and Burdens.* Abingdon, UK: Routledge.

Newman, K. (2000). Organization transformation during institutional upheaval. *Academy of Management Review,* 25. 602.

Owen, H. (2008). *Open Space Technology – A Users Guide.* New York: Berret-Koehler.

Weisbord, M., Janoff, S. (2010). *Future Search -Getting the Whole System in the Room.* New York: Berret-Koehler.

Chapter 2

Appreciative Inquiry

Key Points

1. Understanding Appreciative Inquiry as a philosophy and as a method for organization transformation.
2. Differences between Ai and other change models
3. Learning how Appreciative inquiry is applied for organizational transformation.
4. Introduction to the 6-D model of Appreciative Inquiry including "Drench" as the 6th D.
5. Our experiences when Appreciative Inquiry works

"The miracle of life... is a root metaphor for human science that is more powerful than 'the world as a problem-to-be-solved"

David L. Cooperrider

Introduction

In 2000, we were engaged with the public health system in the city of Mumbai, India as part of a Citywide Initiative on Neonatal Health (CINH) project. We worked with hospitals and health delivery institutions run by the Mumbai Municipal Corporation as part of this project. We conducted many focus groups to diagnose the issues around neonatal health and mortality. We asked the question "What are the issues and problems in the system that lead to neonatal mortality?". We got many responses. In the second part of the focus group, we asked "What actions can we take to overcome some of these issues?". We again got many actions that could help in changing the situation. Then we asked, "Who will do it?" and people just looked at each other or pointed upwards indicating the authorities! They were willing to identify

DOI: 10.4324/9781003538059-3

issues but not willing to take responsibility to fix them. While the participants liked these sessions, we were losing hope that anything will be done.

When we debriefed our experience of the meeting, we realized that the way people responded depended on the question/s we asked. Since we asked a question about a problem, they brought out all the problems and its solutions. However, this process ended up in blaming the system for the problems and they were not ready to be part of the problem or the solution. The emphasis is about the question that one asks the system. The answer or response will depend on the question that is asked. Hence we decided to change the questions for the next focus group meeting.

In the next focus group meeting, we changed the question and asked, "Tell me the story of a time when we were able to save our small babies?". People shared many stories and there were heightened emotions in the room. In the second half of the session, we asked "How can we save all our babies and make them healthy?". Again, many suggestions were made. Then we asked the crucial question "Who will do it?". This time all the hands went up! People enthusiastically teamed up to address several suggestions. Two interesting shifts happened this time: a) people saw their strengths in changing the system in the past and b) People became hopeful that things will change. We also became hopeful that things will change!

Over the next couple of years, the people who attended our sessions actually implemented many of the changes they had suggested during the intervention stage of this project and helped transform the health system for new born babies. More importantly, there was a transformation in the people themselves. Instead of complaining against the authorities for their inaction, they started taking initiatives in doing things that were helpful to save one more new born baby.

This was one of our initial experiences with Appreciative Inquiry and it transformed us as well. It opened our eyes to the possibilities this approach can offer to organizational transformation.

What Is Appreciative Inquiry (Ai)?

We are using the shortform "Ai" to indicate Appreciative Inquiry and to distinguish it from the other popular "AI" i.e. Artificial Intelligence!

Appreciative Inquiry (Ai) was developed as a philosophy and a model to understand organizations through work done by David Cooperider and Suresh Shrivastava from the Case Western Reserve University (1987).

Gervase Bushe (2014) writes in the article on Foundations of Appreciative Inquiry :

David Cooperrider and Frank Barrett, another student working under Srivastva, were engaged in an organization development (OD) project where the standard action research feedback process was being met with a high level of conflict and hostility. During a meeting amongst the three and Ron Fry (a professor), the emotional baggage from their experience led them to argue with each other. As that dynamic became more uncomfortable – and unusual – Srivastva said, 'I wonder if what is going on now is a consequence of the questions we are asking?' At that moment a 'light bulb' went off – the power of questions, the deficit nature of most questions, questions beginning the change, inquiry as the engine of change – and Appreciative Inquiry was born. Cooperrider and Barrett went off and reconceptualized everything they were doing with that client. They engaged the managers in an inquiry into the best practices in another organization which completely changed the dynamics in the system and led to major improvements (Barrett and Cooperrider, 1990). Concurrently, Cooperrider did a survey-based, empirical study on the impact of inquiry on social systems, which solidified his views and became his doctoral dissertation on Appreciative Inquiry (Cooperrider, 1986).

Here are some excerpts from story of the "discovery" of Appreciative Inquiry as articulated by the aicommons.champlian.edu which is a bit different from the story told by Gervase Bushe:

> The birthplace and co-founding of Ai happened in the doctoral program in Organizational Behavior at Case Western Reserve University in the collaboration between David Cooperrider and Suresh Srivastva in 1980. As a young 24-year-old doctoral student David Cooperrider was involved doing a conventional diagnosis or an organizational analysis of "what's wrong with the human side of the Organization?" In gathering his data, he becomes amazed by the level of positive cooperation, innovation and egalitarian governance he sees in the organization. Suresh Srivastva, Cooperrider's advisor notices David's excitement and suggests going further with the excitement-making it the focus... The Cleveland clinic became the first large site where a conscious decision to use an inquiry focusing on life-giving factors forms the basis for an organizational analysis. The term "Appreciative Inquiry" was first written about in an analytic footnote in the feedback report of "emergent themes" by David Cooperrider and Suresh Srivastva for the Board of Governors of the Cleveland Clinic.

David Cooperrider, one of the founders of Ai says that

> More than a method or technique, the appreciative mode of inquiry is a means of living with, being with and directly participating in the life of a human system in a way that compels one to inquire into the deeper life-generating essentials and potentials of organizational existence.

The publication of the article "Appreciative Inquiry in Organizational Life" by David Cooperrider and Suresh Srivastav (1987) shifted Ai from being a theory to a way of understanding and transforming organizations and communities.

> Action-research has become increasingly rationalized and enculturated to the point where it risks becoming little more than a crude empiricism imprisoned in a deficiency mode of thought. In its conventional form action research has largely failed as an instrument for advancing social knowledge of consequence and has not, therefore, achieved its potential as a vehicle for human development and social-organizational transformation. While the literature consistently signals the worth of action research as a managerial tool for problem-solving ("first-order" incremental change), it is conspicuously quiet concerning reports of discontinuous change of the "second order" where organizational paradigms, norms, ideologies, or values are transformed in fundamental ways.

Table 2.1 comes from this article and is used to describe some of the distinctions between Ai and traditional approaches to organizational development.

Appreciative Inquiry is groundbreaking, going beyond the problem or deficit focus that was the prevalent model for change in those days. Appreciative Inquiry is based on the concept of *multiple realities* and *generativity* as articulated by Kenneth Gergen in his theory of social construction (1992). The appreciative approach involves collaborative inquiry, based on dialogues, to collect and celebrate the good news stories of a community – those stories that enhance cultural identity, spirit and vision. Appreciative Inquiry is a strategy for purposeful change that identifies the best of "what is" to pursue dreams of "what could be." It is a co-operative search for the strengths, passions and life-giving forces that are found within every system – those factors that hold the potential for inspired positive change.

Table 2.1 Problem-Solving and Appreciative Inquiry

Problem-Solving	*Appreciative inquiry*
1. "Felt Need," identification of Problem	1. Appreciating & Valuing the Best of "What Is"
2. Analysis of Causes	2. Envisioning "What Might Be"
3. Analysis & Possible Solutions	3. Dialoguing "What Should Be"
4. Action Planning (Treatment)	4. Designing "What Will Be"
Basic Assumption: An Organization is a Problem to be Solved	**Basic Assumption:** An Organization is a Mystery to be Embraced

Principles of Appreciative Inquiry

Appreciative Inquiry as a process is very simple and straightforward. The philosophy behind this process is also very simple, yet profound. Life is a constantly emerging organic process that amazes us with its richness, colours, texture and simplicity as well. Life is a mystery to be unravelled rather than a problem to be solved. Naturally, all life forms, whether they are people, communities or organizations will gravitate towards the energies that are growth oriented and life giving. What is required is to trust that natural flow and not work against it.

The "mechanistic" and "analytical" paradigm views living systems as inanimate and approaches them as something that can be broken into parts, corrected and re-assembled. But people, communities and organizations are living organisms and require to be viewed through an "organic" and "holistic" view and paradigm. They are more than the sum of their parts! This is an important AI perspective.

Another important aspect of AI philosophy is captured in the statement "what you believe is what you see". Life is holistic – it is a myriad of all emotions and life states. If we chose to split this whole, you will obviously see what you are looking for!

David Cooperrider and Suresh Srivastava developed the core principles of Appreciative Inquiry in the early 1990s, which described the basic tenets of the underlying Ai philosophy. Many principles were added by other authors and practitioners. We have used the essence of five principles as stated by Gervase Bushe (2013) in his article on Appreciative Inquiry Model for Kessler's Encyclopedia of Management Theory.

1. The *constructionist principle* proposes that what we believe to be true determines what we do, and thought and action emerge from relationships. Through the language and discourse of day to day interactions, people co-construct the social reality of the organizations they inhabit. The purpose of inquiry is to stimulate new ideas, stories and new images of reality that generate new possibilities for action.
2. The *principle of simultaneity* proposes that as we inquire into human systems we create the seeds for change. The things people think and talk about, what they discover and learn, are implicit in the questions asked. Questions are never neutral, they are fateful, and social systems move in the direction of the questions they most persistently and passionately discuss.
3. The *poetic principle* proposes that organizational life is expressed in the stories people tell each other every day, and the story of the organization is constantly being co-authored. The words and topics chosen for inquiry have an impact far beyond just the words themselves. They invoke sentiments, understanding, and meaning. In all phases of the

inquiry, effort is put into using words that point to, and enliven the best in people.

4. The *anticipatory principle* posits that what we do today is guided by our image of the future. Human systems are forever projecting ahead of themselves a horizon of expectation that brings the future powerfully into the present as a mobilizing agent. Appreciative Inquiry uses artful creation of positive imagery on a collective basis to refashion anticipatory reality.

5. The *positive principle* proposes that momentum and sustainable change requires positive affect and social bonding. Sentiments like hope, excitement, inspiration, camaraderie and joy increase creativity, bring openness to new ideas and people, and increase cognitive flexibility. They also promote the strong connections and relationships between people, particularly between groups in conflict, required for collective inquiry and change.

Appreciative Inquiry Models

While Ai did not have an original model to work with organizations, some of the practitioners developed models that they built based on their own experiences of using Appreciative Inquiry. There are many models and we will look at two popular models – the 5D Model and the SOAR model. We will also introduce "Drench" which is a 6th D that these authors have added to the 5D model. The concept of Drench will be articulated in the next chapter and in some of the subsequent chapters we share our stories and experiences of using Drench in our work on organizational transformation.

The 5-D Model is perhaps the most popular model for Ai. There is no clarity about how this Appreciative Inquiry model came into being. According to the website, Appreciativeinquiry.chaplain.edu, Suresh Srivatsava, David Cooperrider, and Ron Fry worked with the health systems in Romania as part of the Social Innovations in Global Management Project, 1989 (SIGMA) and generated a 3-D model that had "discovery, dream and destiny". The 3-Ds were transformed to 4-Ds, adding the "design" phase during the Global Excellence in Management Initiative (GEM) project done in the 1990s. According to *aicommons.champlain.edu*, Rob and Kim Voyle transformed the 4-D into a 5-D model for organization development adding "Define" as the starting point of the model. They also acknowledge the contributions of Bernard Mohr in the development of the model.

Appreciative Inquiry practitioners all over the world have embraced this 5-D model as the most practical and energizing approach to applying Appreciative Inquiry for individual, organizational, and societal change initiatives.

We (Ramamoorthy and Joshi, 2019) have proposed another D called *"Drench"* between Dream and Design where the system can soak in the possibility of what the future holds in the moment before venturing to actually build the same (Figure 2.1).

Applying A.I.
6-D Model

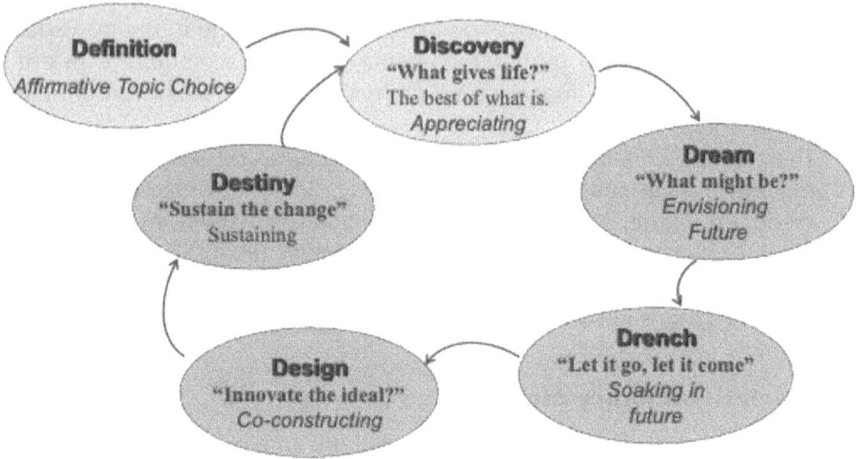

Definition
Affirmative Topic Choice

Discovery
"What gives life?"
The best of what is.
Appreciating

Dream
"What might be?"
Envisioning
Future

Destiny
"Sustain the change"
Sustaining

Drench
"Let it go, let it come"
Soaking in
future

Design
"Innovate the ideal?"
Co-constructing

Figure 2.1 6-D Model.

Source: Authors' creation based on existing 5-D model).

1) **Define**- identify the focus of inquiry. We ask the question "What is the generative topic that we want to focus on together?"
   Clients more often than not, approach us with problems and the task of the Consultant is to help them "reframe" the problem statement into a possibility that the client really desires. The 5-D starts with the premise that *what we want to focus on becomes our reality.* Hence, we do not focus on the problem. The Define phase clarifies the project's purpose and content and the desired future.

2) **Discover** – share stories and identify themes when the system was at its best. Here we ask the question "Tell me a story of a time when we were at our best?"
   The purpose is to "inquire" into that topic by recounting stories of when they experienced the topic of inquiry, when it worked at its best. This is called discovery since It operates on the assumption that what we want already exists in the client system and is just waiting to be discovered.

3) **Dream** – visualize a possibility when the system can be always at its best. The question we ask here is "How will we be as an organization when we are always at our best?"
   The Dream in Appreciative Inquiry is an amplification of the themes from the story; Imagine how it will be when we are at our best all the time,

how we can be as an organization? The Dream is stated as a provocative proposition stated in present tense.

4) **Drench** – Suspending action and staying in the present. Here we ask the question "What do we let go and let come in?"

Drench is a process of holding together the discoveries of the past and the dream of the future in the present. There is a tendency to quickly get into action after developing a compelling dream for the future. Soaking/ drenching in the future will allow the future to come into the present.

5) **Design** – Build the scaffolding of a system that will bring the dream to the present. Here we ask the question "What and how it should be when we live the dream?"

Design is a process of dialogue and brainstorming to determine how the future can be brought into the present. While the discovery and dream stages are divergent, design is the beginning of convergence to specifics.

6) *Deliver* – live that system in the here and now and sustain that process into the future. Here we ask the question "How do we continue to live this way all the time?"

The last stage of the 6-D cycle is Delivery (some of us like to call it the more poetic "Destiny"). The Delivery phase outputs are a set of action plans that are set into motion that the system believes will take it towards the desired future. While the above is a general understanding of the 6-D model, different practitioners implement this differently and also customize it to the requirements of the situation.

SOAR Model

SOAR stands for Strengths, Opportunities, Aspirations and Results was developed by Jacqueline Stavros, David Cooperrider and Lyn Kelley in 2007 when they published a paper by the same name. It was also published in the *Change Handbook* (2007). SOAR is a tool that is specifically used for strategic planning workshops using appreciative inquiry (Table 2.2). We have found this a very valuable model for working with organizational purpose, mission, vision and values.

Table 2.2 SOAR

Strategic Inquiry	*Strengths:* what are our greatest assets?	*Opportunities:* What are our best opportunities?
Appreciative Intent	*Aspirations:* What do we want to be in the future?	*Results:* What are the measurable results to be achieved?

Source: Stavros and Hinrichs (2009).

What Is Different about Appreciative Inquiry?

In our two decades of consulting experience, we have witnessed four fundamental transformations in leadership thinking in organizations that auger well for Appreciative Inquiry: These are a) from one truth to multiple realities b) from problems to possibilities b) from analytical to systems thinking and c) from "emotions have no place" to valuing emotions as integral to change process.

Multiple Realities

Some years ago, we had a meeting with the CEO of an organization wherein the CEO gave us a rundown of all the problems and issues facing them, which departments are working in silos, who amongst his direct reports are collaborative and so on. After having heard all this, we proposed to the CEO that we would like to meet with his direct reports and get their perspectives as well. The CEO looked shocked and said "They will tell you their stories, but I'm telling you the truth". We politely disagreed with him and said "you are sharing *your* truth and others have their truths as well. There could be multiple truths in an organization and it depends on the person who is perceiving it". The CEO reluctantly agreed to our suggestion. His eyes opened when he heard the stories from his own team members and understood how they perceived the organization was very different from his own. Over time, he also became open and appreciative of that fact that there are multiple perspectives and it is ok to have them.

Meaning is socially constructed and is subject to change. The social construction of reality is a theory originally proposed by Berger and Luckmann (1966) that people create their own understanding of reality through their interactions with others. This includes our world view and how we interact with the world. People's perception of reality influences how they act within that reality. Berger and Luckmann called this "habituation". This concept was further worked on by Gergen (1990) who opined that we derive our conceptions of what is real, rational, good etc. through our relationships. Gergen's work had a major influence on the development of Appreciative Inquiry and its applications.

We see many leaders today valuing diversity of thought and proactively suggesting to us that we should meet many people and help them understand why there are multiple realities. Acceptance of diverse views that are sometimes polar opposites of one's own is slowly being seen as positive and opening up possibilities.

Possibilities Approach

For every hundred times that we have been approached   by clients asking for our services to intervene in an organization situation,   ninety-nine of those instances are t client/s wanting help in solving a problem or a suite of problems. They believe that our facilitation, consultation, coaching etc. will help in understanding and addressing the problems. In the last two decades of our practice, our first engagement is always to get the client to reframe the problem/s into possibilities and shift the energies towards an anticipated future rather than drain energies by a forensic examination of the past. Appreciative Inquiry is one of the best methods for reframing.

Problem-solving approaches generally have one best solution and someone who is an expert in the area is the best person to analyse the problem and suggest asolution. Solutions, when offered by experts are well received by others since they value the expertise. Solutions get implemented when there is an edict to do so from top leadership. Since expertise is "more and more knowledge about less and less", the expert who finds solutions to a particular problem will have limited or no expertise about other parts of the system (like a Urologist who specializes in kidney diseases has no knowledge about the heart). Problem-solving is achieved through analytical thinking – breaking the problem into its components as against systems thinking, which is to view the whole. Analytical thinking isolates variables that impact the problem identified whereas systems thinking brings in more dependent variables and increases the complexity of the task of problem-solving.

Problem-solving can also be called as the first-order change (see Chapter 1 for details) and can be best applied to technical problems. However the same cannot be applied to adaptive challenges that require a different way of thinking.

In contrast to technical problems, adaptive challenges are second-order changes that don't have a single best solution. In fact the word "solution" itself is not used for adaptive challenges. Adaptive challenges require changes in beliefs, values and approaches to work. People working with adaptive challenges will have multiple perspectives in defining the issues themselves and in the various possibilities that are available to address them. Adaptive challenges require all voices to be heard and need a systemic view.

Most organizational "problems" are adaptive challenges and not technical problems. For example, growing customer complaints is not a problem to be solved. There is no one way this problem will be defined and there is no one solution to the problem. Secondly, it is difficult to isolate the variables that cause this problem since it is systemic in nature with many dependent variables.

Thatchenkery and Metzker (2006) in their book Appreciative Intelligence highlights this quality of seeing the mighty oak in an acorn as a quality of Appreciative Leadership. They say "Appreciative Intelligence is the ability to reframe a given situation, to appreciate its positive aspects, and to see how the future unfolds from the generative aspects of the current situation". In order for Appreciative Inquiry to be an organizational transformational process, leaders need to have Appreciative Intelligence. In our experience, a combination of appreciative intelligence along with emotional intelligence enables appreciative leaders to be open to transforming themselves as part of organizational transformation.

Systems Thinking

Systems approach is to see an organization as a set of inter-related and inter-dependent parts that exhibit properties and behaviour that individual parts do not. It is to see the whole with its parts and not just the parts. There are times when we see the parts and miss the whole. We remember an instance when we facilitated a team to bring a more collaborative environment in the work-place. While we focussed on the team, we missed seeing their dependencies with other teams within the organization that contributed to the climate of collaboration.

Peter Senge (1990) defines systems thinking as a "framework for seeing interrelationships rather than things, for seeing patterns of change rather than static snapshots". Unlike analytical thinking which is focussed on the com-ponents, systems thinking is focussed on the relationships, interactions and impact of one component on another and on the overall system. Now we can add the element of "living" to systems and we change the paradigm from mechanical systems to organic systems. Mechanical systems are machines that are closed systems with limited interactions with the environment. Living systems in contrast are constantly interacting, impacting and getting impacted by the environment. Systems thinking is an important requirement for trans-formation whereas analytical thinking is essential for problem-solving.

In order to get a systems view, we need to bring all voices into the room. Appreciative Inquiry based organization transformation projects bring together senior management and the employees. This approach ensures that the whole system is in the room and all views about the system are sought and received. .

Emotions Are Integral to the Process

We have seen some of our clients advocating clear thinking devoid of any emotions when we embark on a change process. It was believed that emo-tions are the opposites of cognition and being emotional means clouded cog-nition. There is now a realization among many of our clients that emotions are an integral part of any experience and an organization will be at heightened emotions during a transformation process. All transformations necessarily need passion and without that everything will be clear intellectually but lack energy and vitality.

Emotions are generally seen as an individual phenomenon. However, Parkinson and Simons (2009) and many others point out that emotions are a social contagion and they impact organization climate and the social construction of the change, resulting in driving or derailing an organizational transformation process. Appreciative interviews conducted during the discovery process generate a contagion of positive emotions that provide the energy for transformation.

Conversations where stories are told about the peak experiences of the organization and about personal experiences when people were at their best bring strong emotions into play. Sharing and listening to these stories also bring hope, trust and strengthen relationships at work. We recently worked with a group where we noticed on the first day that interactions were mostly logical, fact based and devoid of any feelings. While there seemed to be an understanding of how the future needs to be, there was no energy around it. On the second day, we asked them to represent their future in the form of a collage of pictures. The entire group got together, took out pictures from magazines, posted them on a large newsprint and built a collage. When the activity progressed, one could hear and see emotions getting expressed, people laughing together, singing, hugging and living out the world in the here and now that they were envisioning the day before. The expression of emotions enabled the group's alignment to the dream and unleashed the energy for transformation.

The four transformations in organizations that we have experienced in our practice viz. multiple realities, possibilities, systems thinking and valuing emotions are important pillars for organizational transformation. They are also aligned with the principles of Appreciative Inquiry that were enumerated earlier in this chapter.

Criticism of Appreciative Inquiry

Appreciative Inquiry has it's skeptics in many academicians, practitioners and authors. These criticisms are based on how, at which level one perceives this philosophy and the model as a tool for organizational transformation. Hence we have classified the criticisms and our own observations at three levels:

1. Appreciative Inquiry at the practice level:

One of the biggest criticisms about Ai is the apparent focus on the "positive" and hence the "negative" gets ignored or is not allowed space to be present in the discourse. Focus on positive stories and experiences can marginalize participants who have negative organizational experiences. Pratt (2002) highlighted that participants couldn't inquire appreciatively in systems when they had unexpressed resentments. Her case study and reflections suggest that until unspoken resentments are surfaced and expressed, participants will find Appreciative Inquiry invalidating.

We suggest that the so called "positive" focus is only apparent. The real focus and Ai is on the life giving forces which give energy and vitality to systems. However, some practitioners see it as the opposite of a problem-solving, deficit focus which they call as "negative". We do recognize this issue and we do not see any "positive" and "negative" when we frame our questions for inquiry. We use the terms "life giving", "peak" "important" experiences that one would like to tell stories about. We also clarify that negative and positive are labels and we don't want to label experiences in this manner. We would like participants to share stories from when they felt alive, vibrant and experienced vitality around. feeling absolutely alive, vibrant etc. can arise from an experience of accomplishment, or anger and confrontation as well.

Cooperrider and Fry (2020) confirm our thinking when they write "AI is not about being or thinking positively or negatively. Its call is to transcend this polarity. It is not about positive verses negative experience, *it is the choice to inquire into what is life."*

Another criticism at the practice level is the social construction of the words "appreciative" and "inquiry". In many societies like in India, the word "appreciate" means "to say nice things" and not necessarily "to value" as it is perceived in the West. The word "inquire" is associated with the word "inquiry" that has connotations of "finding who or what is responsible for a failure".

We often flip the word "appreciative inquiry" which is a noun to a verb "inquiring appreciatively". This highlights the process of inquiry and takes it away from being a noun or 'thing'. It puts the accent on acknowledging "what is" without any judgements of praise or blame.

Drew and Wallis (2014) brought in some of the practical issues on the use of Ai for organizational transformation by raising the following concerns. Appreciative Inquiry can be resource intensive, needs involvement of geographically distributed stakeholders, takes considerable time and needs a supportive and open environment. Drew and Wallis (2014) argue that careful planning becomes important when we consider using AI in specific contexts.

2. **Appreciative Inquiry at the Principle level:**

Johnson (2013) addressed the dilemma Ai faces when dealing with problems. Ai sees problem-solving as a deficit discourse and differentiates itself from that by defining itself as a change management approach that doesn't focus on problems. This generates an either/or polarity with problem-solving approach that goes against the principle of social construction of reality that is one of the basis of Ai.

In our practice, we go by our sensing of the client system. In case we do see a strong need for addressing issues, we allow them to do that and then ask the question "and what next?" Or bring attention to the fact that "Despite all these issues, the system still exists, it has life, vibrancy. Can we explore that?". In the Indian context, we believe in embracing the good with the bad, the problems with the possibilities and the light with the shadows. Hence we don't experience these polarities so much in our practice as compared to when we do this work with some of our clients in the west.

Further, one of the Ai principles is "wholeness" and to us it also means honouring the whole selves of people which includes the appreciative and the cynical self.

3. **Appreciative Inquiry at the Paradigm level:**

Some of the biggest criticisms of Ai is around how when one set of beliefs are given space for expression, the others tend to go into the shadow. Fitzgerald (2010) writes " reflexive awareness of Ai-Shadow relationships creates the space to appreciate and embrace all that is human. Holistic appreciation is the most significant part of Ai, not appreciation as positive, but rather as honouring."

As stated above as a criticism of Ai in practice, a focus on the positive creates a polarization between the positive and negative and censures all that is perceived negative. This censure creates a shadow of unspeakable material that not only impacts the discourse but also the implementation of decisions taken in an Ai summit. Fitzgerald continues to say that such censoring and delegitimizing some of the cognitions, emotions, and behaviours shapes the organization culture.

One of the practices that we follow diligently is to ask the question "what is the unsaid here?" during conversations. This legitimizes the space to hear contrarian views that could be suppressed.

Cooperrider (2018) writes about three levels of AI, from the least to the most profound. The least level is what he calls as "Appreciative Inquiry into the Extraordinary". Here the focus is on positive deviance that takes us above the average and opens our appreciative eye. The next level is "Appreciative Inquiry into the Ordinary". Here the focus is to see life giving/ changing dynamics in seemingly ordinary and insignificant events in a system. The most profound level is "Appreciative Inquiry into the tragedy". This inquiry gives us the ability to see the silver lining, to see possibilities even in desperate situations and to summon our better humanity. It is our resilience in the midst of tragedy. Cooperrider and Fry (2020) quote several leaders like Martin Luther King, Mandela, Gandhi, Helen Keller and Vicktor Frankel and his work "Man's search for Meaning" as examples of how leaders can focus on how we overcome suffering rather than the suffering itself.

References

Berger, P., Luckmann, T. (1966). *The Social Construction of Reality*. New York: Anchor Books.
Bushe, G. (2014). Foundations of Appreciative Inquiry. *AI Practitioner*. 14, 1. 8–20.

Cooperrider, D. L. (2018). "Appreciative resilience" in McArthur-Blair, J. and Cockell, J. (Eds.). *Building Resilience with Appreciative Inquiry*. New York: Berrett-Koehler. 3–15.

Cooperrider, D. L., Barrett, F., Srivastva, S. (1995) "Social construction and appreciative inquiry: A journey in organizational theory" in Hosking, D., Dachler, P., and Gergen, K. (Eds.). *Management and Organization: Relational Alternatives to Individualism*. Wiltshire, UK: Avebury Press. 157–200.

Cooperrider, D. L., Fry, R. (2020). Appreciative inquiry in a pandemic: An improbable pairing. *Journal of Applied Behavioural Science*. 56, 3. https://doi.org/10.1177/0021886320936265

Cooperrider, D. L., Srivastva, S. (1987). "Appreciative inquiry in organizational life" in Woodman, R. W. and Pasmore, W. A. (Eds.). *Research in Organizational Change And Development*. Stamford: JAI Press. 1. 129–169

Drew, S., Joseph, L. W. (2014). The use of appreciative inquiry in the practices of large-scale organisational change: A review and critique. *Journal of General Management*, 39, 4. 3–26. https://doi.org/10.1177/030630701403900402.

Fitzgerald, S., Oliver, C., Hoxsey, J. C. (2010). Authors' response to commentaries on "Appreciative inquiry as a shadow process". *Journal of Management Inquiry*. 19, 3. 242–244.

Gergen, K. (1990). *An Invitation to Social Construction*. London: Sage, 1990.

Gergen, K. J. (1992). "Organization theory in the postmodern era" in Reed, M., and Hughes, M. (Eds.), *Rethinking Organization: New Directions in Organization Theory and Analysis*. London: Sage. 207–226.

Johnson, P. (2013) Transcending the polarity of light and shadow in appreciative inquiry: An appreciative exploration of practice. *Advances in Appreciative Inquiry*. 4. 189–207. 10.1108/S1475-9152(2013)0000004007.

Parkinson, B., Simons, G. (2009). Affecting others: Social appraisal and emotion contagion in everyday decision-making. *Personality and Social Psychology Bulletin*. 35. 1071–1084.

Pratt, C. (2002). "Creating Unity from Competing Integrities: A Case Study in Appreciative Inquiry methodology" in Fry, R., Barrett, F., Seiling, J. and Whitney, D. (Eds.). *Appreciative Inquiry and Organizational Transformation: Reports from the Field*. London, UK: Bloomsbury.

Ramamoorthy, S., Joshi, W. (2019). Drench-living the dream before action. *Organization Development Review*. 51, 3. 50–56.

Senge, P. (1990). *The Fifth Discipline, the Art and Practice of the Learning Organization*. NY: Doubleday/Currency.

Stavros, J., Cooperrider, D., Kelley, D. L. (2007). "SOAR: A new approach to strategic planning" in Holman, P. et al.(Eds), *The Change Handbook: The Definitive Resource on Today's Best Methods for Engaging Whole Systems*. New York: Berrett-Koehler. 375–380

Stravos, J., Hinrichs, G. (2009). *The Thin Book of SOAR*. London, UK: Thin Book Publishing.

Thatchenkery, T., Metzker, C. (2006). *Appreciative Intelligence: Seeing the Mighty Oak in the Acorn*. New York: Berrett-Koehler.

Chapter 3

DRENCH

A Crucial Step in Organizational Transformation

Key points
1. Introduction to the concept of Drench 2. Our earlier and newer perspectives on Drench 3. Towards a new Drench Model 4. Way forward

"We shape the clay into a pot. However, it is not the pot, but the emptiness inside that help us to hold whatever we want in the pot"

Tao Te Ching

Introduction

We are practitioners of Appreciative Inquiry in organizational transformation projects and/or as facilitators of Ai summits and as coaches for leaders for the past 25 years. We had some highly successful and impactful assignments and some others where we felt a sense of incompletion and a wish for more.

In 2018 we received the announcement of the global Ai conference in Nice, France and we wanted to present a paper at the same. We spent time reflecting on what more could be added to strengthen the Ai process based on our experiences. We specifically looked at experiences when we felt Ai was transformational and when it wasn't. We started seeing a pattern of processes that emerged or were initiated by us that were critical in shifting the energy for change in a very powerful way. In most cases we saw those processes as non-action, a pause, a deep silence and calmness before actions surfaced again. In some cases, they were specific activities that participants did in a session with a significant difference. The activities were all focused inwards,

DOI: 10.4324/9781003538059-4

towards them rather than the organization. We saw them as inner journeys to prepare and become ready to bring the future to the present. We could see alignment with what Bushe (2005) wrote "Ai is transformational when it focuses on changing how people think rather than what people do". One of us saw the image of someone standing in the rain, soaking wet and welcoming more drenching in the rain. We called this process "Drench".

We wrote a short abstract and sent it to the conference organizers and forgot all about it. We then received a mail accepting our abstract and inviting us to offer a workshop! We had no option other than to drench ourselves into the concept that was germinating within us. Our workshop attracted 30+ people and something told us that we had stumbled on something new and important for the Ai practice. Many participants told us during and at the end of the workshop that they have also experienced this drench though they didn't have a name or the language to express it. They were happy that we discovered that. This motivated us to write and publish a paper called "Drench – living the dream before action" in the summer of 2019 issue of Organization Development Review (ODR, Vol.51, Number 3, 2019).

This chapter is a rewrite of our article with deeper understanding and more experiences with Drench processes. We stumbled upon Drench in an intuitive way, then made more sense of it and now we take more intentional steps forward with it to build the theory. We have also expanded and deepened our conceptual base, especially in Indic philosophy and in spiritual practices. We now draw from these concepts as well to build the theory for this step.

The Concept of Drench

In the 2018 article, we conceptualized Drench as an additional stage in the 5-D process and called it the 6th stage. We positioned it between the Dream and Design stages. We had proposed that between the expansive and possibility infused phase of discovery and dream, and the action-oriented converging phase of design and destiny/delivery, there needs to be a pause, a time of inaction before the action, a sixth D. There is a need to completely *Drench* in the dream to let the new imagined world soak into the system, to embody the same and only then move into action to generate ways to live the dream. This phase of *inaction* is an important determinant to the quality of the actions in the design and delivery phases that ensue.

Drenching is to soak in the Dream. Drenching is standing in the rain and allowing raindrops to seep into each pore of our skin, it is allowing the magnificent sunrise to embrace our whole being with the golden light as the dream emerges. To Drench is to stay in the energy of the dream, to *"just be"* and suspend all actions. Drench is counter intuitive. In a world that applauds fast and decisive action, Drench proposes inaction. In a world

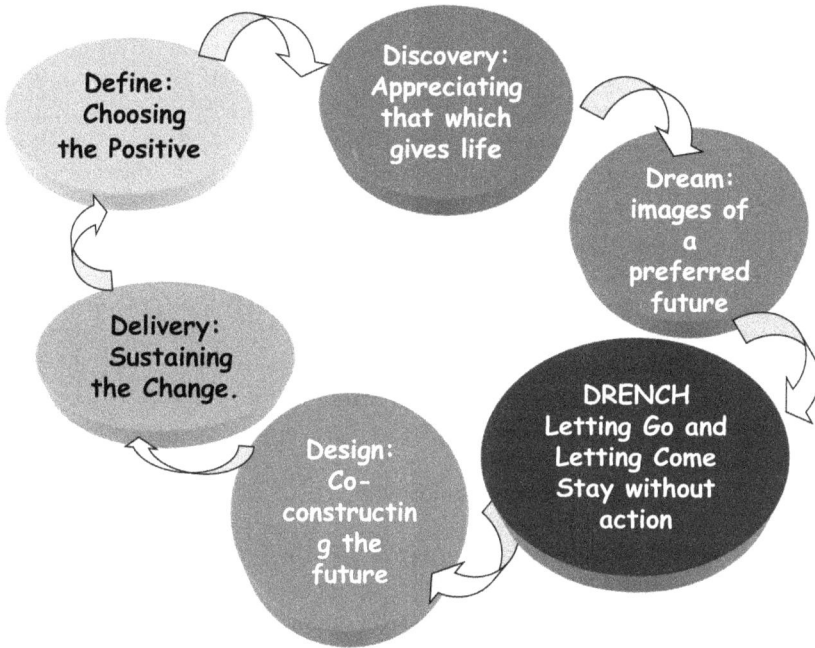

Figure 3.1 6-D Cycle with Drench in between Dream and Design stages of the cycle.

where clarity is important, Drench asks that we remain in a hazy state. It does not mean there is no change going on, just that the change is internal. This is the time where we need to let go of old beliefs (e.g. "This is the only or best way to do things"), Identity (e.g. "We never Fail"), Metaphors and Imagery we hold about the organization (e.g. "This is war- We must defeat our competitors and crush all challenge") and bring in new ways of looking at ourselves and the world. This new view needs to be aligned with our dream, our aspirations. When this alignment is settled, then the "Drenching" is complete, actions become creative, clear and even easy and joyful.

See Figure 3.1 for a diagram of the 6-D as we proposed with the Drench stage.

The Journey of Creation

We studied Indian and western theories and practices that pointed to the need to create and incorporate Drench as the key to make Appreciative Inquiry transformational. Here is a short tour of these studies. More details are available in our ODR article.

Most change efforts in organizations focus on an "object" of t change but ignores the people (subjects) who make that change happen. In this approach, the assumption is that the people who are initiating change have no need to change, they are here to change others, change systems, processes etc.

From a subject-object dualism (Aguiar and Tanelli, 2018) lens, the change agents see "individuals," "people," "organization," and/or "the leadership" as entities that exist separately from them. Appreciative Inquiry through the processes of "Discovery" and "Dream" attempts to break this duality. The power of storytelling in the Discovery phase and the energies unleashed by the Dream phase helps the participants to move from the split of duality to an understanding of the relational nature of the changer and the changed. It is no longer that we as individuals are changing the organization, *but by our changing, the organization changes*. This realization requires some time to sink *or drench* in. This is the key moment when a new consciousness dawns which can lead to transformation.

This experience of "non-duality" at the stages of Discovery and Dream needs to be preserved and amplified. this is a delicate time when something new is emerging. It requires nurture and time to establish itself. Unless we do that, we tend to quickly converge into something actionable within the familiar mechanical mindset. The design stage then becomes the product of known frameworks from the older state of consciousness. The danger of moving into a default future is real, and the process of Ai will not be transformative. The temptation to change the organization without seeing it in a *non- dual* frame needs to be avoided. this can only be achieved by the pause and drencing in the dream.

In their seminal paper, "When is Appreciative Inquiry Transformational," Gervase Bushe and Aniq Kassam (2005) wrote, "Highly consistent differences between the transformational cases and the others led the authors to conclude that two qualities of Appreciative Inquiry that are different from conventional organizational development and change management prescriptions are key to Ai's transformative potential: (a) a focus on changing how people think instead of what people do and (b) a focus on supporting self-organizing change processes that flow from new ideas".

In our experience, we have seen that Drench allows the design and delivery to *emerge* rather than force certain actions from outside like an *action plan*. The decision to act on a dream, to live it in the here and now is not just an act of cognition. It is also not just an act of passion. *It is a movement of our spirit*.

Most modern change theories seem to recognize a phase of inaction, a "neutral zone" that is essential to shift the consciousness of the being that will transform and innovate the ways of doing.

The place of "Presencing" in Theory U (Scharmer, 2007) is somewhat similar to the "Drench" phase, the cusp between letting go of the old and letting come the new. The important aspect of this cusp is the "emergence." This means meditating, waiting, and not forcing the change to happen.

Transformative change is possible only when that happens and the mind doesn't force a certain set of actions that are anchored in the previous state of consciousness.

The concept of "transitions" introduced by William and Susan Bridges (1995) is similar to Drench in many ways. Change is what is 'happening' and transition is what you are 'experiencing'. Transition is the "inner change" that one has to undergo to break through the outer change. Transitions begin by letting go of the inner connections one had to the way things were.

In his book *Managing Transitions*, William Bridges writes, in the "Neutral zone" we go through an in-between time when the old is gone but the new isn't fully operational. It is the very core of the transition process. It is in this flux when we don't feel comfortable yet.

The "Neutral zone" is the space to completely accept the "endings" and retreat from action. This is also the zone to create active imagination and develop "as if" images for future possibilities before embarking into "new beginnings." Drench is like that space of inner transition.

This neutral zone and space for inner transition is called "*bardo*" in Tibetan Buddhism and "*Antara bhava*" in Vedanta. This "yoga of intermediate state" is the gap between two breaths, two thoughts, death of one moment and the birth of the next. Staying in that space allows one to approach change with greater awareness and acceptance.

From the perspective of Yoga, there is a good explanation about Drench and how it works. According to Yoga, all movementin the universe is driven by what is called *prāna* (energy). In the movie Star Wars, it was called "The Force'. It is also known as Chi or Qi in the in Chinese tradition. *Prāna* is the life force, the energy behind all movement of body, systems, wind, planets, emotions, thoughts, a wand that puts desires into action. Like in any movement, transformation in an individual or organization needs the flow of this *prāna* in the direction of that change.

When the organization embarks on transformation, it requires alignment of the *prāna* of the entire system   to move in the direction of the change. It requires a force that will not stop till the transformed state is attained. Transformation requires intense channelling of the *prāna* energy. An example from nature is the energy that bursts forth from the seed for the sapling to emerge.

When we begin a Discovery process, it releases emotions and generates hopeand the possibilities of what can be through story telling.   Emotions are nothing but energy or *Prāna* in motion. When this energy is released, the next step is to channel it in the direction of transformation and the Dream is theprocess that creates this.. When the Dream process is completed, all the energy of the system is focused on the same end point. It is important to note that while the discovery was one of the past and the Dream was one of the future, both were expressed in the present, the here and now. The here and now holds the energy and links the past with the future. Hence, staying in the here and now is critical before stepping into design.

At this juncture, if we jump into Design, the energy doesn't get embodied and amplified. The shadow energies of confusion and fear of change are not addressed and can hijack the dream especially if each person in the system is not aligned and embodied in the new way of being.

Sometimes, you hear people say "All this sounds great BUT...". This BUT is what takes the system back to the old ways of being. The comfortable, default ways of flow of *prāna*... because those are the channels of flow that have been well established and easy. Like a water channel, if a new path is to be created, the groove needs to be deep enough to wean the flow away from the old riverbed into the new channel. Just showing a new path does not entice water to flow in a new direction. Nor does putting up a dam, without a new path. The dam will only submerge all territory – drown the organization in chaos.

We now understand why many organizational transformation initiatives fail, because we don't invest in the process to channel the *prāna* of the organization towards the Dream. This is the process of Drenching. The energy of every stakeholder in the change process must consolidate into a firm belief of the possibility that has emerged. The hope and excitement of the provocative proposition needs to be embedded in the system, this is the energy that keeps the change going, allows the system to overcome obstacles, become an unstoppable force. it is what allows for changes in mindsets and beliefs leading to new and innovative action and behaviour. Imagine the *prāna* to be like the river gushing through the new channel...flowing water, the strong wind blowing are examples of prana moving in a deliberate motion. This is exactly the subtle energy in an organization. Drench creates the unstoppable force.

One of our friends, Nikita Panchal, shared this poem that aptly describes the Drench stage:

"They ask you to feel, not fix.
To listen, not label.
To soften, not strive.
Because in this space —
you're not failing.
You're not behind.
You're becoming.
And though this part of your story may not have milestones or metrics,
it's where the real transformation begins"

What Happens During Drench?

We were discussing about Drench with another Trainer/ consultant of Appreciative Inquiry and she pointed to us that our readers shouldn't think that Drench is a short break from activity before the next one begins. Hence, we want to address what happens during Drench in our experience. Drench begins and ends with honouring the view, i.e. honouring our experience of the Dream in the moment. In order to do that, we need to recall/ relive this experience in our mind, especially the emotional impact of that experience. In other words, during the Drench phase, we relive the new story again and again till it is embodied in our cellular memory. We also reflect on our intellectual doubts about the experience and the fears and anxieties for the future. Hence the mind is not idle during Drench, it is actively focused and uncluttered by other thoughts. Hence, we call the Drench phase as non-action instead of action or inaction since there is no visible external action.

Drench – A New Manifestation

We hope that we have convinced you about the value of Drench as a critical process that enables Ai to be an organizational transformation model.

From 2018, when we started applying Drench in all our Ai projects, we started to unravel how Drench can be embedded more into the process of organizational transformation. The following are the key elements that have emerged for us in addition to the conceptualization of Drench described above:

Bringing the Self in Transformation

Organizational transformation is a step where the organization, and its people let go of the old identity and embrace the new. For some it may happen in a short time span, some need a bit longer. The ability to hold this space, the crucible where transformation is taking place is a skill that a good facilitator needs to build.

Gandhi said *"Be the change that you want to see in the world"* . We have experienced leaders practicing "Be the Change" and seen the positive impact it has on the people and the system as a whole. These leaders understand that transformation is not something you *do to* a system. Transformation happens when we change our being and the system changes along with us. *We are not here to change others or the entity called organization or community. The change is "us", and we have to change.*

This aspect has immense ramifications for the Ai process. Ai processes are mostly at the level of whole system, community, groups etc. rather than focused on the individual (one exception is Appreciative Coaching). Every organizational transformation intervention has to be accompanied with specific sessions around individual change, especially for leaders who need to drive the transformation. One approach is to incorporate coaching as an intervention and/or having focused sessions for self-reflections and inquiry. This is well illustrated in the story of Swasth (Chapter 6).

We offer this step as key to the organization stepping into its destiny. We equally believe that the process is dependent on the facilitator to a large extent. As a facilitator it is important to be drenched in the process of Ai. We have shared the story of how three facilitators (one external and two internal) experienced transformation of the system when we ourselves transformed the way we worked together (see Chapter 7).

Bringing Drench as a Bridge between the Other 5 Stages

While we have articulated Drench as a new stage between Dream and Design, we have realized from our experience that Drench is also a bridge between the other stages. The "micro drenches" between stages gives a pause to reflect, internalize and experience oneself as part of the journey to transformation. The non-dual nature of the experience gets emphasized through this process. We have seen that slowing down works in and for every step of the process. We can take micro steps in Drenching all along the way.

We have an entire chapter dedicated to the ways in which the 6th D and micro drenching have been used in our experience. Surely, there must be many more ways and we encourage you to add to our list in Chapter 10.

One of the stories we have described in Chapter 6 describes how we used mini drenches throughout the entire Ai Summit process and how it led to a real transformation story. This need is felt more in groups that comprise of conceptually sharp people who are also highly impatient for action (the stereotypical MBA types!). They initially view any new process like Ai with scepticism and when they grasp and get convinced by its logic, they want to go all out and get it done. They benefit by holding back and taking a pause before moving to the next stage of the process.

Drenching beyond the Summit

One of the challenges of transformational change is the need for internalizing, abiding and sustaining the insights and learning gathered during the process. When the system gets back to business after an Ai Summit, it is critical that it is not "business as usual". If that happens, the system will slide back to familiar ways and the impact of the insights and learning fade away over a period of time. We must understand that the depth of the insights, the power of the dream and passion for action that is experienced in the Ai Summit is due of the high emotional energy and the innovative thinking unleashed by the process. When we get back to business, the first thing that starts to decline is that emotional energy and in its place three kinds of intellectual processes emerge that create obstacles to the system living the dream and sustaining the transformation:

1. The whole summit process starts to feel like a dream, albeit a powerful one at that. Someone might say "It was fantastic, but I'm not sure whether it was just our emotions running high". We would like to call this as the "Feeling of the impossibility of the process".

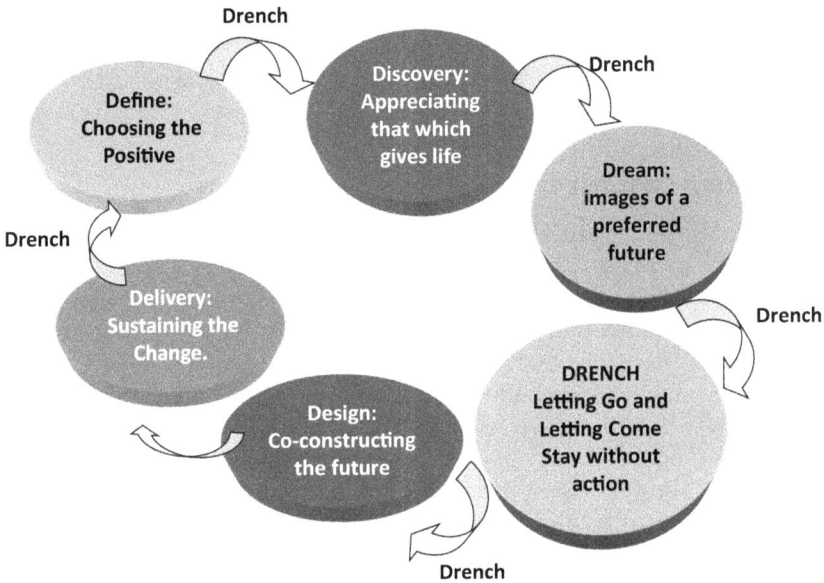

Figure 3.2 Drench Model revisited – Mini Drench after each phase.

2. The dream statement starts to feel idealistic. Considering the circumstances of the business, the challenges of the market and prevailing economic conditions; one might now feel that "our Dream is ideal, unfortunately the world is nothing close to the ideal". We would like to call this as the "Feeling of the impossibility of the outcome".
3. This last one is one of the most difficult ones to deal with. When we get back to business, there could be some experiences that run contrary to the themes that were generated from the discovery stage, the dream statement and/ or the actions agreed during the Design stage. This generates what we call as a "contrarian tendency" or the "Feeling that the opposite happens rather than the ideal".

The Drench process for dealing with the obstacle of feeling the impossibility of the process is to continue telling the stories of the summit, publish some of the stories, and communicate across the organization to those who didn't attend and bringing it as part of meetings, boardroom and coffee machine conversations.

The Drench process for dealing with the obstacle of feeling the impossibility of the outcome is to celebrate small wins, notice and appreciate behaviours and actions that align with the dream, and ensure the dream statement is translated into multiple languages as needed and used in all presentations, websites, offices etc.

The Drench process for dealing with contrarian tendencies is to provide a safe space to express those feelings, engage in difficult conversations to understand and explore how we can shift that perspective and/ or review/ change that specific situation.

Anticipating Obstacles at the Summit

We could also anticipate these obstacles at the Ai Summit itself and design processes to address the same. In one of our Ai Summits, a couple of participants approached us during coffee break and told us that they don't see many people convinced about the work we are doing and they are participating for the sake of it. They were concerned that these very people will sabotage the whole thing when they go back to work.

We decided to address that after the break. We did what is called the "Four Rooms of Change" exercise (Janssen, 1975). The Four Rooms theory believes that people in any system operate out of four rooms of change which are their psychological positions with respect to the change on the anvil. The first room is called the "Room of Contentment". People here believe that everything is good with the organization and we need to maintain it. Any change will negatively impact what is happening well. The second room is called the "Room of Denial". People here believe that all that is happening here is of no consequence and we just go back to business as usual from tomorrow. The third room is called the "Room of Confusion". People here understand the need for change but are confused about the direction to take. The last room is called the "Room of Renewal". Here the people are excited and optimistic about the change that is emerging and are willing to be the change agents.

We named these four rooms and assigned each corner of the conference room to be one of the rooms. We then asked people to reflect on where they were mentally and emotionally with respect to what we are doing and choose any one of the four rooms and physically move and stand there. We also told them that all the rooms are ok and we would like everyone to be authentic about their feelings. We also requested everyone that they will not gossip about who was in which room after the exercise.

It took a while for people to move, they hung out in the middle and started conversations. We asked them to be silent and take their own decisions instead of going by what others do. We also told them that they could go to a corner, reflect if they really feel like that and go somewhere else which seems more right for them. Slowly the four rooms emerged.

We then asked people in the rooms to speak to each other for the next 20 minutes to understand why they were in that room and what the important message they want to give others who were in other rooms is. Then we asked two representatives from each of the rooms to come to the middle and share their messages to the other rooms. This led to some intense and important dialogues around their diverse perspectives and how they need to be listened to and how we should take everyone along for change to be sustainable.

Once these dialogues were completed, we asked them to go back to their seats. Instead of that, everyone moved to the "Room of Renewal' and stood there for a few minutes to symbolically show their commitment for change. This exercise took us two hours behind schedule. It also was the best thing we did and really helped the system to deal with all the obstacles that we named earlier in a proactive manner. Later, during the Design stage, the communication group decided to use this exercise across the organization after they had communicated the Dream and Design to all others who were not present in the Ai Summit.

The above Drench exercise will fit well between Design and Delivery stage of the Ai Summit.

Drench to Address the Organization Shadow

A significant issue that sabotages organizational transformation is the unacknowledged and disowned parts of the organization, also called the organization shadow. In Chapter 2, we have discussed how Appreciative Inquiry can push some of the voices into the organization's shadow when we hold the space only for the "positive". Giving legitimacy to the unspoken, the so called elephant in the room, the defences/ contrarian views that people feel scared to express is an important aspect that Drench can address. Some of the ways we have held space is to welcome diverse views, role model by asking difficult questions and create spaces like "devil's advocate hour" where the Dream/ provocative proposition statement can be challenged.

In one of the Ai summits, we noticed the tension that existed between the senior/ experienced Managers and the young Engineers during the creation of the provocative proposition. We made a process observation about the same. There were some murmurs of denials and some awkward silence. We then did a short fishbowl activity where we asked the young engineers to be in the centre and speak their truth and asked managers to listen and later asked managers to do the same. The young engineers felt that while the provocative proposition sounded very progressive and futuristic, the managers still behaved in a paternalistic and hierarchical way which according to them was antithetical to the dream. The managers experienced being mocked by the young engineers around their lack of knowledge about new technologies and tools and felt insecure at times. The process released a lot of energy trapped in the shadow. There was much more ease and laughter throughout the rest of the process.

Discussion

Drench is the central character of this book and you might wonder why so. Organization Development as a discipline and practice began with the focus on the organization's being and the assumption was that once we strengthen the being of an organization, the effectiveness of doing will be a natural outcome. The advent of change management brought in a new focus on transitional change, taking the organization from point A to B, getting rid of weaknesses, gathering strengths, foraying into new products and services and so on. Change became akin to problem-solving and this led to the deficit orientation.

Appreciative Inquiry came as a breath of fresh air, reclaiming what Organization Development originally started to do which was to strengthen the capacity of organizations to change, to build resilience, agility and vitality in organizations. However, as the practice of Ai unfolded and many new practitioners joined in, Ai started to look like the other end of the pole from deficit oriented change. It became more like saying "till now we looked at what was going wrong and tried to fix it, now let us look at what is good and strengthen it further"

According to us, Appreciative Inquiry is both/ and, not either/or. It is not meant to strengthen the strengths and ignore the weaknesses. It is meant to see the organization appreciatively, discover the energies and possibilities hidden there with all its strengths and weaknesses. Drench helps us to keep this spirit of Ai alive by constantly asking us to look within and see ourselves as part of the system. When we Drench, we see how the energies for transformation are not out there, but firmly within. Like Car Jung said "one who looks outside dreams, one who looks inside, awakens"

References

Aguiar, A. C., Tanelli, M. J. (2018). Dialogic OD and subject-object dualism: A social constructionist perspective on dialogic methods in an organizational context. *Context Journal of Applied Behavioral Science*. 54. 457–476.

Bridges, W., Bridges, S. (1995). *Managing Transitions-Making the Most of Change*, London: Nicholas Brealey.

Bushe, G. R., Kassam, A. (2005). When is appreciative inquiry transformational? A meta-case analysis. *Journal of Applied Behavioral Science*. 41. 161–181.

Janssen, C. (1975). "Four Rooms of Change". Published as PhD Thesis at University of Stockholm, Swweden.

Scharmer, O. (2007). *Theory U- Leading from the future as it emerges*. San Franscisco: Berrett-Koehler.

Section 1 Summary

Bringing the Three Concepts Together

Organizational Transformation

This book is about Organizational Transformation through the process of Appreciative Inquiry and specifically an immersive on Drench. The first three chapters provided our understanding and perspectives around these topics.

Some of the important perspectives on organizational transformation that we have highlighted are:

1. We define Organizational transformation as a portfolio of interdependent change initiatives that lead to changes at three levels – at the level of doing, at the level of learning and at the level of being.
2. Transformation is the shift in the interaction between the system and the people within that system. The common understanding of transformation refers to people or system change. However, in our experience, transformation takes place at the intersection of the people and the system. What transforms is the relationships and the quality of interactions. . Hence transformation is really about the changing nature of conversations, the stories being told about the organisation, and the affective environment that is generated from this contact. From a subject-object view, what transforms is not just the object, not just the subject, but how the subject views and interacts with the object.
3. We reviewed the external and internal triggers for transformation and the linkages between them. In our experience, organizational transformation is about changing the character of how the system responds to triggers. Every system responds to triggers. However, the nature of the response can range from being passive/ reactive to responsive; from being lethargic to agile; from being fragile to resilient and from being problem focussed to possibilities focussed. The maturity, robustness and the wholesome nature of the response is the outcome of organizational transformation.
4. Lastly, we reviewed the planned and emergent models for organizational transformation and how an organic, living systems based approach of Appreciative Inquiry is an attractive choice for organizations today. We believe that organizational transformation is also triggered when individuals in a system, especially those in leadership experience internal transformation.

Appreciative Inquiry

In the second chapter, we introduced Appreciative Inquiry as a philosophy, method and practice. Some of the significant take-aways from that chapter are:

1. Appreciative Inquiry is like describing the experience of eating sugar to someone who has never tasted anything sweet. It is a fundamental experience, difficult to describe and can be understood only when one goes through the experience. We never teach Ai through a lecture, we give them an experience and people get it just like that because appreciation is an inherent part of human nature.

2. David Cooperrider, one of the founders of Ai says that

    "More than a method or technique, the appreciative mode of inquiry is a means of living with, being with and directly participating in the life of a human system in a way that compels one to inquire into the deeper life-generating essentials and potentials of organizational existence"

1. There are many articles written to contrast Ai from problem-solving. We do see the value of problem-solving as a method and hence we don't deprecate it. We tell our clients that even if they want to problem-solve, they could approach problems not from their root cause side, but from the other side – the side of possibilities. The key difference between traditional problem-solving and Ai is in the direction in which one chooses to lookto bring about a change- to the past or to the future. Ai focuses on the future and hence it is generative and energy enhancing. Traditional problem-solving focuses on the past, it is converging and can be energy draining.

2. We have included possible critique of Ai at the end of the chapter. The significant criticism is the temptation to be simplistic and flip the "negative" to the "positive". This approach creates a polarity between what is labelled as positive or negative and when we strive towards one, the other is pushed into the shadow. Cooperrider says "Appreciative Inquiry is valuing the life giving forces in ways that serve our co-constructed future" We appreciate the term "life giving" and that changes the way we look at phenomenon in organizations and people.

   In our own personal lives, the biggest challenge has been to transcend beyond positives and negatives, beyond attractions and repulsions and accept everything that is. We can then make a choice to focus on what life gives as a gift andan opportunity that serves our identity and purpose.

   In the third chapter we dived deep into the Drench process that we have proposed as the 6th D in the different stages of Ai process. We have developed some insights while creating this model. They are as follows:

1. To Drench is to stay with the energy, to *"just be"* and suspend all actions. Drench is counterintuitive. In a world that applauds fast and decisive action, Drench proposes inaction. In a world where clarity is important, Drench asks that we remain in a hazy state. It does not mean there is no change going on, the change is internal.
2. *"We shape the clay into a pot. However, it is not the pot, but the emptiness inside that help us to hold whatever we want in the pot"* says Tao Te Ching. Drench helps to create that "empty space in the system that is necessary to hold anything – be it Define, Discovery, Dream, Design or actions for Delivery.
3. When the organization embarks to transform, it requires alignment of the *prāna* (the life force)of the entire system in the direction of the change. It requires an acceleration and force that will not stop till the transformed state is attained. Transformation requires intense channelling of the *prāna* energy. An example from nature is the energy that bursts forth from the seed for the sapling to emerge.

According to us, Appreciative Inquiry is a both/ and not either/or process. It is not meant to strengthen the strengths and ignore the weaknesses. It is meant to see the organization appreciatively (what gives life, what is there to value) and discover the energies and possibilities hidden there with all its strengths and weaknesses. Drench helps us to keep this spirit of Ai alive by constantly asking us to look within and see ourselves as part of the system. When we Drench, we see how the energies for transformation are not out there, but firmly within. Like Car Jung said "one who looks outside, dreams, one who looks inside, awakens"

Section 2

Drenching Experiences

Chapter 4

Develop Appreciative Eye for Transformation

Key Points

- Defining Appreciative Eye, contrasting with Critical Eye and its importance in organizational transformation
- Experience of a recent organizational transformation assignment.
- Drenching in Ai process as an enabler to activate the appreciative eye.
- Insights and explorations.

"The world we have created is a product of our thinking; it cannot be changed without changing our thinking. If we want to change the world we have to change our thinking…no problem can be solved from the same consciousness that created it. We must learn to see the world anew."

Albert Einstein

Introduction

What do you see when you look at your organization? Do you see a mountain of problems? Or strengths and possibilities? An endless list of things to be fixed that will bring efficiency? Or an endless list of opportunities that can be leveraged?

Surely, if you looked for problems, you would end up feeling frustrated, helpless and end up blaming many people for this. You can also look for strengths and you will feel optimistic, excited and willing to step in and collaborate with others to make those possibilities real.

It all depends on how you look. This chapter focuses on looking through an appreciative eye and the possibilities that this opens up for organizational transformation.

DOI: 10.4324/9781003538059-6

Critical Eye and Appreciative Eye

There are two fundamental lenses through which we approach a situation. These can be called as a critical eye and an appreciative eye. A critical eye is a disciplined approach to understand a situation from a perspective of its benefits and limitations. Its primary objective is to identify solutions to problems and avoid repeating mistakes and their consequences. Critical eye focusses on what is missing in a situation, diagnoses problems through data analysis and reduction of problems into its parts. Critical eye celebrates conceptual and analytical thinking, is evidence based and adapts a logical approach to problem-solving. Developing this critical eye has significantly contributed to human development.

Critical eye recognizes that there is another side for every issue. However, it believes that the other sidehas faulty logic and the other side needs to change it's perspective. A simple example could be a rational view verses an emotional view when taking a decision. Critical eye values rational decision making and does not value decisions based on emotions.

For an "Appreciative eye", there is nothing like an issue or a problem that needs to be solved. Everything is a topic to beaddressed. This removes the value judgement associated with the object of focus. . To compare this with the Critical eye, when you approach decision making through an Appreciative eye, there is neutrality to both, the decisions taken and to whether it was through a rational or an emotional process.

Appreciative eye is focussed on the relational, shared meaning making and the co-creation of reality in any given situation. Appreciative eye is generative and is focused on wonder, curiosity, motivation and the hope that transforms the situation. In other words, an Appreciative eye focuses on the possibilities in any given situation, and how to achieve those rather than how to fix a problem. It is non-linear and brings in all faculties including emotions, aesthetics, creativity and analytical thinking to work with any topic.

Appreciative eye brings commitment and energy to implementation of decisions because of its both/ and approach in contrast to an either/or approach which is the hallmark of a critical eye. Appreciative eye is innovation rather than intervention driven, it is more about *creating* rather than *solving*. It is the ability to see future in the present.

When we have issues at work, we can consider whether the issue is a technical problem to be fixed or an adaptive challenge that require an inquiry. Some of the issues could be both a technical problem and an adaptive challenge. For example, an organization might want to improve productivity. It involves fine-tuning its machines, bring in new technology etc. that maybe technical. This requires critical thinking by some experts in the field. There could also be issues around employee morale, or the trade union accepting new productivity norms, technology etc. They will be classified as adaptive

Table 4.1 Critical eye and appreciative eye – differences

Feature	Critical Eye	Appreciative Eye
Goal	Solve the problem	Identify possibilities for change
Approach	Analytical/ data based only	Both Head and Heart
Process	Converging/ linear	Diverging/ cyclical
Method	One right method	Many paths to change
Mindset	Problem oriented/ reactive	Optimistic/ proactive
Benefits	Best for technical problems	Best for adaptive challenges

challenges and requires an appreciative eye to get curious, be empathetic and listen to multiple perspectives to understand the situation and find different possibilities.

Tojo Thatchenkery (2006) likened this capacity of seeing the future in the present to seeing the towering oak in the acorn. He called it "appreciative intelligence" (Thatchenkery and Metzker, 2006). Michelangelo saw David already existing in the slab of marble and he said "I saw the angel in the rock, so I carved to set it free" (Cooperrider et al., 2013). When we invoke the Appreciative eye, the universe of strengths, values, and life-generating potential can be seen all around us (Table 4.1).

There is also a case to combine both the approaches together for what Grant and Humphries (2006) call as the "productive tension" that develops when critical theory and Ai are combined. They note that "both Appreciative Inquiry and critical theory share a common research objective. Through their commitment to change, researchers in both paradigms seek to encourage and facilitate human flourishing" (p. 407).

Here is a story of an organization where people are amongst the best in the country for their critical approach to problem-solving, and how they developed an appreciative eye. We were involved as consultants to help them transform as an organization to be attractive to a new generation of employees. Drenching in appreciation in order to develop an Appreciative eye enabled them to take the next steps in their transformation process.

The Story

We were invited by a multi-billion dollar engineering group in India to explore the extent to which the core values of their group are still alive and practiced in their units. These units were large individual companies by themselves. The three core values that we were asked to explore were 1) integrity, 2) caring and 3) continuous learning.

This is a 50+ year old group that has grown multi-fold in the past decades. The top leadership of the group wanted the core values that defined the identity of their group to be present and practiced in the units. They feared that individual companies in the organizations would lose these values as they grew in numbers, and a new generation of employees replaced the old guard who were familiar with and entrenched in the core values.

We were asked to work with five of their largest units for this assignment. We started our assignment by meeting with the CEOs, HR Heads and other leaders of these individual units. During these conversations we noticed that the leadership welcomed the initiative and were willing to get personally engaged with the process. We could also notice frustration and irritation among leaders that the new generation of employees in their organizations do not share the same values with them.. Initially, we thought they meant the core values of integrity, caring and continuous learning. Later it was clarified to us that these values were different and on inquiry we were given a new list of values that the leaders believed many of the juniors didn't follow:

1. Company first
2. Loyalty
3. Discipline
4. Learning from seniors.

The leaders of these units wanted us to explore the gap between themselves and their team members around these values. Hence we met with a cross section of employees at the leadership level, middle management level and at the junior level in small groups, workshops and in one-on-one meetings. We facilitated an exploration of the values that the leadership believed were not practiced by the new generation of employees.

These meetings revealed some interesting information.

1. The top/ senior leaders (General Managers and above) consisted of men who have 30+ years of experience. They had joined this organization as engineering trainees from premier institutes and grown with the company and had now become leaders. They had (mostly) never worked anywhere else. There were a few who had joined as laterals but they could be counted on your fingers. The senior leaders constituted 20% of the organization and had complete power to get things done within their domains. Their origins were middle class and mostly from small towns. Over the years they have had a successful career growth and came to experience a good standard of living. Their own children were studying in premier institutes in India or abroad and in their own words "will never join here".
2. The junior employees (Engineers with 0-5 years' experience) formed 65–70% of the organization and they had very little power to influence the system. Over the years, the composition of the Junior Engineers has changed. In the last few years, most of the engineers were recruited from

small town colleges/ institutes. The students from premier institutes do not join traditional engineering companies. They either planned to go abroad for higher studies, or work in Information technology sector, and wished to live and work in the big cities. This group has a 25–30% attrition during their first five years of their tenure in the organization. The new engineers have the same ambition as those who graduate from the premier institutes and a couple of years of work experience compensated for their lack of pedigree.

3. Labour unions are very strong among the workers in the core industries and many organizations face strikes and other forms of worker unrest. Also as technology changed, the need for more educated staff became important. Hence many organizations decided to restrict the recruitment of unionized workers and started recruiting graduate engineers to do their job. These young people came with ideas of designing, planning and managing work and ended up doing the routine activities of the shop floor. Some of them continue because they need the money and do not have a choice of leaving. The ones who are economically well off leave earlier than others. However, some of them work through these jobs and get better opportunities of their liking and stay and grow to become part of the middle management.

4. The middle layer numbers are far and few in-between. They form 10–15% of the organization and most of them are in the system for 15+ years. They felt they had negative power to influence because the seniors and juniors both didn't listen to them! They are the few who didn't leave in the first 5 years and later felt "settled" because of familiarity and also learned how to work in the system. They are also very valuable for the organization since they have grown working from the shop floor level and hence understand the engineering aspects very well.

During our inquiry, we realized that the values listed by the leadership also had opposite values that were important to some of the employees, especially the juniors. The small group discussions we had yielded rich perspectives around these polarities.

The values and the polarities as seen by the employees are given in Table 4.2.

Table 4.2 Competing values

#	Value	Opposite Value
1	Company first	Work- Life Balance
2	Loyalty	Professionalism
3	Discipline	Freedom
4	Learning from seniors	Self-directed learning

Company First and Work-Life Balance

This organization prides itself in contributing to the national economy and a patriotic element is part of the organizational ethos. Hence the expectation is that employees will "sacrifice" their time for the sake of the organization which in turn is serving the nation. This meant that you stayed late, worked on weekends and did everything that needed to be done without complaining since you are contributing to the national wealth. The new generation of employees saw this as a tactic to squeeze more work out of them and avoid paying overtime wages. They see all organizations as profit making engines and they don't want to be exploited to add to the company's coffers. They are also more concerned about maintaining a healthy work-life balance and hence don't believe in sacrificing their mental and physical health for the organization.

When the leaders joined the organization 30+ years ago, India was a struggling economy and dependent on foreign companies for technology and products. Only a few organizations in India had the size, technology and the mettle to compete with the world outside. When this organization won global contracts, it was a matter of pride. The India in 2020's is a very different story. We are the fourth largest economy and there are countless Indian stories of global impact and hence one more global contract is not as energizing as was did thirty years ago.

When the leaders joined the organization as young engineers, there were very few opportunities for life after work. The internet, social media, malls, coffee shops, bars and many other avenues for entertainment and relaxation were not available in the country and the few that were there were beyond their financial reach. Further, the large engineering organizations were based in small towns that didn't have good quality housing, schools and medical facilities. Hence many employees lived alone while their families lived in their home towns. Hence they stayed at work till they were tired, ate at the factory cafeteria, reached home and slept. They expect the same from the juniors not recognising that in today's world, employees lived with their families in the same town and they are spoiled for choices and struggle to find time to engage with all their social needs.

Loyalty, Professionalism, and Integrity

The quintessential "good" employee is one who said yes to whatever his manager asked and worked hard to deliver it without bothering about time and effort that he needs to put in. Loyalty was not just to the organization or the department but to the manager. Supporting your manager in meetings, praising him in public forums, not wanting to change departments, or leave the organization were considered hallmarks of a good employee. Saying no or arguing that something cannot be done in the given time etc. was considered arrogant behaviour and not befitting of a good employee.

Loyal employees joined and retired from the same organization and built strong relationships with their colleagues. Loyalty to a person, organization or any cause is very rarely experienced in today's organizations. Professionals are loyal to their field of work rather than to an entity. Young engineers look what the quality of work they are doing which can enhance their resume and get them better and more lucrative assignments.

Discipline, Freedom, and Integrity

Indian families largely followed a culture of patriarchy where the father or the grandfather's words were considered final and unquestioned. This continues to be so in in many parts of the country. However, some of the metro cities and towns have seen a change and many of the men also don't assert their authority and even if they do so, the other members of the family don't feel as obliged to obey them as they used to be a generation before.

The same model of patriarchy was brought into Indian organizations and the words of the older men in leadership positions were considered an order to be obeyed. When it is not done, it is considered as indiscipline or worse, insubordination. The present leaders have grown up in that milieu and they tend to expect the juniors to do the same.

Autonomy and freedom are two competing values to obedience and discipline. We bring up children to be self-reliant, autonomous and willing to question and not take things lying down. Rebelling against authority comes easily to the younger engineers since they have less fear of consequences as there are plenty of job opportunities available.

Learning from Seniors, Self-directed Learning and Continuous Learning

This is a continuation from the patriarchal society. The belief in these societies is that a senior, experienced and older person has more knowledge than a junior, less experienced and younger person. Information and knowledge were also sources of power and hence whispered only to the most loyal employees. The resultant expectation is also that the junior person will listen, learn and do exactly how it is told by the senior person.

This model worked for many years when the knowledge in a field was reasonably static and changes were linear and hence transferred from generation to generation. This is not so anymore.

The changes in the knowledge systems have become disruptive and no longer linear, information is available with everyone and the advent of generative AI brings in a very different level of knowledge that was never seen before. A young person joining an organization today is not looking up to a person to get the knowledge, but to a system and technology for knowledge gathering and application. Further, the older leaders don't always have knowledge of the latest in the field as taught in the colleges while they do have the wisdom to discern between the important and unimportant knowledge.

Drenching in the Data

Once we completed these meetings and documented them, we drenched ourselves in the data before we made meaning. We experienced that we were not daunted by the strong polarities that existed in the organizations and were excited at the possibility of discovering a new value or set of values that will help one pole to respect the other and see them as both/ and rather than take an either/or position. There was also possibility of helping all employees to develop an "Appreciative eye" for the other.

We were also cognisant that the original project was to strengthen the core values of the organization and these core values were integrity, caring and continuous learning. They didn't come through in these discussions since the system was torn between these poles and this demanded expression. We felt that while the polarized positions will struggle to see the other side appreciatively, all of them can align with the core values. This couldbe the answer to transcending the polarities in the system.

We drenched in all these data, mulled over them and discovered that a large part of how we have documented them indicated the polarities that we ourselves chose, and hence how we saw the other side. This was extremely useful, to recognise and accept our own biases. We realized that we needed to activate our Appreciative eye before we can expect the client to do so. This helped us to take a middle position and see the polarities in a neutral way. We went back to our narrative and edited them to remove any bias that we may have planted into it.

We then shared the outcomes with the leadership teams, HR and L&D partners from these organizations in a one-day workshop. We wanted them to soak into this data, reflect on the same and see their personal location within these poles. There was an initial reaction to the data saying that we need to fix the juniors, they needed to see that it is all for their own good and how some of the positions are non-negotiable etc. Then an older man sitting in the corner of the room stood up and said to everyone "You know when I see what our youngsters are saying, I'm reminded of how I was when I joined this organization. I felt like them too. I'm sure some of you do as well. I wish I was vocal like them and pushed my seniors to appreciate our perspective"

There was silence for a minute or so. The penny dropped and many of them saw themselves in the place of their juniors. The conversations changed. People were sharing stories about their olden days and how they were as

Table 4.3 Value alignment

#	Value	Opposite Value	Possible centre
1	Company first	Work-Life Balance	Caring
2	Loyalty	Professionalism	Integrity
3	Discipline	Freedom	Integrity
4	Learning from seniors	Self-directed learning	Continuous learning

youngsters, how the world was, how the organization was and how things have changed. At the end of the day, one of the HR Heads said in her reflections "I think we have reached a place where we accept that the juniors have different values and it is ok"

The values and the polarities as seen by the employees are given in the table below for ready reference with our interpretation of a possible centre which are the three values given to us at the beginning by the corporate leadership. These are detailed in Table 4.3.

When we analysed company first and work-life balance values, all employees wanted to live both these values at the same time and the polarity is created when they are asked to value the company first by leaders without caring for their work-life balance. This leadership behaviour was perceived as lack of caring. When leaders acted in a caring manner, the juniors would gladly take up some challenges, work overtime etc. in order to fulfil the company's commitments to the nation.

When leaders spoke of loyalty, they meant that juniors make commitments and then disappear. They want the juniors to be loyal to their word. When juniors spoke about professionalism, they meant that they expect leaders to stick to the tasks required, provide adequate resources as needed etc. to do a job and not expect people to deliver miracles. They were also expecting integrity from their leaders, that they walk the talk. When that happens, a professional approach to sticking to commitments will be achieved.

This was similar when we explored discipline and freedom and discovered its link to integrity. Juniors wanted leaders to supervise them for the task and not watch every move they make. Leaders wanted juniors to be more organized and follow the processes and rules at workplace. Both of them were saying that they need to trust the other's integrity to do the right thing even when no one is watching.

All employees believed and practiced the value of continuous learning. They pride in the fact that they have worked on highly complex engineering solutions by learning through their own efforts. Hence all of them seek a culture where continuous learning is encouraged though they differ in the methods. The polarity was created by the uni-directionality of the learning process. When learning happens both from each other and not just from seniors, everyone will embrace and benefit from that process.

These insights that we gathered from drenching in the data helped us to design the Appreciative Inquiry summits.

Appreciative Inquiry Summits

David Cooperrider, one of the founders of Appreciative Inquiry describes the Appreciative Inquiry summit as "a large group planning, designing, or implementation meeting that **brings a whole system of internal and external stakeholder together** in a concentrated way to work on a task of strategic, and especially creative, value."

It is a **whole-system inquiry** where all stakeholders connected with the topic, including employees, customers, and vendors, are invited to participate in co-creating the Dream and the design for living the dream. This approach generates **a comprehensive and inclusive dream and direction for the future.** Appreciative Inquiry summits allow for a more holistic understanding of the organization and its possibilities through **collaboration and shared perspectives.**

We facilitated eight AI summits across the different companies within the organization and each one of them had anywhere between thirty and fifty participants. These participants included members of the top leadership, middle management and junior employees. The summits were 2.5 days in duration and completely residential.

The goals for these summits were two fold and one meshed into the other. The first goal was to create space to explore and imbibe the core values of integrity, caring and continuous learning. This was the objective given to us when we started the project. The second goal related to the seeming polarities that became evident when we started our interactions with the individual organizations. Here the need was to build an Appreciative eye among the employees and celebrate these diverse values and see them as two sides of the same coin.

The meshing of these objectives was based on the insight we gathered during the drenching process. The insight was that when we imbibe and live with integrity, care and continuous learning, we would naturally invoke our appreciative eye and see diversity of values in a different manner. Integrity will help us to respect other's values, caring will open the possibility of wanting to know more and understand the context from where other's come in and continuous learning will help us to see opportunities and possibilities for learning in the diversity of values. Hence, telling stories of integrity, care and continuous learning will naturally bring in the diversities of company first, work-life balance, loyalty, professionalism, discipline, freedom, learning from seniors and self- directed learning. In other words, there was an exciting possibility for the organization to embrace these polarities by aligning them with integrity, caring and continuous learning.

The summits were designed allowing for a good combination of activities, reflections, dialogues and discussions. The design provided opportunities for participants to bring their whole self, using storytelling, theatre and dance, music, collage building, games, dialogues, and presentations. These methods also invoke the free child in them and give expression to their creativity thinking and emotions. The design also provided leaders and juniors to come together in small groups where they could listen to each other and converse in ways that they never did before. The design provided space for appreciation, expressing emotions in a functional way and seeing possibilities together. In short, the design facilitated the invoking and the opening of the appreciative eye in all the participants. We use these words carefully because we believe that all of us have an appreciative eye, it is just that we usually invoke our critical eye ratherthan the appreciative eye.

We had a Drench session where participants were asked to prepare the cover of a book that they will publish three years hence. The book will be a story of their role in building a culture of diversity and inclusion and where the values are lived all the time. The book covers were later displayed and participants were asked to say something about the experience of creating the book cover. A woman leader said

> I used to think that the quote from Gandhi 'be the change that you want to see in the world' didn't apply to me. I can change, but I'm too insignificant to change the world. This is what I thought. Now I **see** that I'm important and I should walk the path and then I can get everyone else to join me.

She invoked her Appreciative eye to see herself, her role and her ability to transform the organization.

We also asked participants to embody the organizational situations through drama and skits. In one of the skits, a group consisting of senior leaders and juniors enacted scenes depicting what happens now in their organization and what they dream to see   post the summit.

In the first scene, the manager tells the employee "We have an urgent request from the client which needs to be delivered tomorrow. Ensure that you finish it before you go home today. I will check it tomorrow". The employee says *"yes sir"* with a troubled face. As he is walking away, the manager again says "No excuses ok? I want to see it on my desk tomorrow morning". The employee walks towards his colleagues and complains about his manager and that he has booked tickets to go for a movie with his wife in the evening. He tells them that this is the third time he had told his wife that he will come home early in the evening and not done so. "She is going to be mad today" he laments. The employee then calls his wife and to say that he is sorry and his wife disconnects the phone in anger.

In the second scene, which is the future scenario, the manager calls the employee and says "The client called and asked for a delivery tomorrow. What do you think we can do?". The employee responds that the work is 70% done and it needs quality control. Hence it can be delivered in two days as earlier scheduled with the client. The manager says "Ok. I understand. I'm trying to see if we can delight the client. Can you stay back for an hour or two and try and complete it?". The employee replies "Sir, I have booked for a movie with my wife today evening". The manager responds "That's important. Can you look at it first thing tomorrow? Give this the highest priority and let us try and deliver it in two days. I will speak to the client and explain the situation". The employee then smiles, calls his wife on the mobile and says "I'm coming as promised... Don't make dinner. We will eat out after the movie".

Interestingly, a senior leader played the role of manager in the first scene and a junior played the role of the employee. In the second (future) scene, they reversed their roles!

We kept a significant time (2 out of the 2.5 days of the summit) for exploration, dialogue, generation of ideas and reflections and developed actions only during the last half-day. Using the 6-D model, we focussed mostly on Discover, Dream and Drench and spent only half-day on Design. Even here, the Design work was more around individual transformations and behavioural changes and less on structural, process level actions.

We ended all the summits with an activity where people wrote appreciations of each other on sheets of paper stuck to their back. This was metaphorical way of communicating how we can turn gossip that people do behind our backs to appreciative gossip. This was a fun as well as a very emotional exercise. In one of the summits, a participant said:

> I'm overwhelmed by the appreciations I got from all of you. I know that each of what you write are true of me. This shows how much strengths you see in me that I don't see in myself. Thank you for showing me a mirror.

He discovered his appreciation for himself through others.

The designs we use for the Ai summits including the exercises, activities, games and other tools are given in a separate chapter.

Outcomes after the Summits

We allowed for a month after the summits for the system to soak into the experience. There were mails from participants and from the organizers as to how they experienced deep openness and a sense of togetherness during the summit and were thankful that it opened new perspectives for them. In other words, they opened their appreciative eye.

While the work was done for one organization with multiple units within, the diversity of learning, impact and subsequent actions ranged from no action to taking up a series of interventions. In some cases, we followed up with a smaller group of cross functional teams to work on specific areas identified during these summits.

We would like to share the story of one of the Units that took up a very exciting process after the summit. The members of this organization who attended the summit saw the power of storytelling and how it impacted them emotionally, how it broke the barriers between senior and junior employees and how it really paved the way for building a more inclusive organization. After the summit, The CEO and the HR Head had a short session with all those who attended the summit and they decided to listen to the stories of around 500 employees from all levels of the organization. For the next three months, the CEO, his leadership team and many managers at senior, middle and junior levels met with most of the employees one-on-one for an average of 30-45 minutes! They also documented all these interviews and the HR Head along with a small team conducted thematic and content analysis of the documentation and arrived at a plethora of findings. This ranged from identifying the core values unique to their Unit, how they practice the core values of the larger organization that they are part of and also the diversity that exist between the leadership, engineers, workers, support staff and even contract labour.

We helped them to create an interview guide, trained some of them on appreciative interviewing, helped them with content and thematic analysis as well as facilitated their second Ai summit. They did most of the work themselves.

These findings were then shared in another Ai summit which we facilitated and the organization continued the process of internalization and institutionalization. One of their senior managers was awarded by the CEO for having conducted the maximum number of appreciative interviews. After taking the award he starting speaking and burst into tears. We all waited for him to compose himself and then he said:

"Initially when HR gave me a list of people to meet, I was reluctant since I had lots of work and this seemed like another thing to do. Hence I went for the first interview wanting to finish it quickly. My first interview was with our security guard who has worked with us for more than 32 years. I just asked him "Tell me how has been your experience of working in this organization?". He started to cry and said "Sir, no one asked me this in 32 years. I feel honoured". He then spoke non-stop for the next 45 minutes and it was like a downpour. I listened to him completely transfixed. From then on, each of my interviews were a privilege for me to sneak into a colleague's life, their families, listen to their stories of struggles, successes and the pride they feel to be associated with us. I don't know if their sharing transformed them, but it definitely has transformed me."

Another Unit specifically worked on the polarities between the values of seniors and juniors through a session where they had some difficult conversations between them. There were a few areas where they could come to agreements on specifics and there were some where they couldn't due to certain policies that cannot be changed by the Unit without approval from their corporate leadership. However, there was appreciation on both sides as to the context and the reasons for their behaviour. The power dynamics reduced and trust in each other improved as they saw each other as people and not as roles.

In one of the difficult conversations around weekend working, one of the junior most employees turned to the CEO and said:

"Sir, I want to be transparent here. I always thought that you saw us as "kaamchors" (Slakers – one who is lazy and escapes from doing work) and hence you asked us to work late or on weekends. Now I see that is not true. You do see us as hard workers. It is just that we are overwhelmed with work, we are short staffed, we don't plan well at times and clients are very demanding. So it is nothing personal. This makes me feel better."

He saw an appreciative eye from the CEO and invoked his own as well.

Insights and Explorations

Appreciative Inquiry is a very easy concept to understand and can seem difficult to implement. The key is the development of an Appreciative eye. Once individuals in a system, especially the leaders develop an Appreciative eye, organizational transformation is a strong possibility.

Leaders have become leaders because of nurturing their Critical eye and successfully solving organization problems. They also believe that if they become appreciative, they will become soft and people will become complacent and even take advantage of them. None of these are true. Being appreciative doesn't at all mean that one is not critical when required. Being appreciative also doesn't mean that people become complacent. Hence these beliefs need to be busted for an Appreciative eye to be invoked. The only way to bust a belief is to see the other side, listen to their stories and understand that when the narrative of their stories change their belief's change and one invokes the Appreciative eye.

Seeing the mighty oak in the acorn, seeing possibilities in the moment require a change in paradigm. This change is best stated by Dewitt Jones (2001) in his video "Celebrate what is right with the world" where he says

"We thought that what we see is what we believe. We actually got that backwards. The way it actually works is what we believe is what we see…".

References

Bushe, G., Kassam, A. (2005). When is appreciative inquiry transformational? A meta-case analysis. *Journal of Applied Behavioral Science*. 41. 161–181. 10.1177/0021886304270337.

Cooperrider, D., Whitney, D. (2005). *Appreciative Inquiry: A Positive Revolution in Change*. New York: Berrett-Koehler.

Cooperrider, D. L, Zandee, D. P., Godwin, L. N., Avital, M., Boland, B. (Eds.) (2013). Organizational generativity: The appreciative inquiry summit and a scholarship of transformation. *Advances in Appreciative Inquiry*. 4. http://esc-web.lib.cbs.dk/login?url=http://www.emeraldinsight.com/books.htm?issn=1475-9152&volume=4

Grant, S., Humphries, M. (2006). Critical evaluation of appreciative inquiry: Bridging an apparent paradox. *Action Research*. 4, 4. 401–418. https://doi.org/10.1177/1476750306070103

Jones, D. (2001). Celebrate What's Right with the World. Star Thrower Distribution Corp., *Streaming Video and Audio*. https://scholarsarchive.byu.edu/streaming/1

Thatchenkery, T, Metzker, C. (2006). *Appreciative Intelligence: Seeing the Mighty Oak in the Acorn*. London: Berrett-Koehler.

Chapter 5

Revere Diversity

Key Points

1. Revere Diversity as an important aspect of organizational transformation
2. Appreciative Inquiry as an important philosophy to drench into DEI work
3. The story of our work with an Indian affiliate of a global animal protection organization.
4. Insights and way ahead

"Our ability to revere unity in diversity will be the beauty and the test of our civilization"

Mahatma Gandhi

Revere Diversity

Diversity, Equity, Inclusion (DEI) as an organizational transformation process gathered momentum in the early part of this century, though it existed in other forms like affirmative action, feminist movements and efforts at racial equity. In India, the DEI initiatives were mostly based on the reservation system for various socially oppressed castes that translated into a certain reservation quota for educational courses and jobs. There were efforts by a few organizations to bring in more diversity at workplace, especially by hiring more women. DEI based organizational culture transformation is a very recent development in India and perhaps in many parts of the world.

We will start by defining the terms diversity, equity and inclusion that we have used in our work and also in this chapter.

Diversity is recognising and embracing the existence of many visible differences (e.g., genders and the gender-fluid; races and ethnicities; nationalities,

DOI: 10.4324/9781003538059-7

religions, caste etc.), and invisible dimensions (e.g., thinking styles; socio-economic class; education backgrounds, value systems; beliefs etc.) among people.

Equity stands for fair treatment, access, opportunity and advancement for all people in an organization. Equity is different from Equality. 'Equality' means that each employee or group of employees is given the same resources or opportunities, irrespective of their privilege. 'Equity', however, recognizes that each employee or specific employee group has different educational, social and economic positions, and allocates the requisite resources and opportunities needed to reach an equal outcome. As Paula Dressel of Race Matters Institute puts it, "The route to achieving equity will not be accomplished through treating everyone equally. It will be achieved by treating everyone justly according to their circumstances".

'Justice' can take 'equity' one step further by developing the social, legal and workplace systems in ways that lead to long-term, sustainable, equitable access and opportunities for the future.

Inclusion is about creating a workplace environment that values and integrates each person's differences in ways that make individuals and groups feel welcome, respected and valued to fully participate. Highly diverse organizations need not be inclusive unless it welcomes equitable participation, and make employees feel like they belong.

According to Ella Washington (2022), there are five stages of maturity in DEI work. The first stage is being aware, then compliant, followed by tactical, integrated and sustainable. The first two stages are reactions to external inputs like a legal issue or following state rules etc., the tactical stage is when the organization starts to see benefits and its internal and external efforts get integrated in the next stage. Ella Washington says that "organisations whose DEI efforts are deeply embedded in their corporate DNA have reached the sustainable stage". Hence embedding DEI (some call it JEDI by including Justice and there are other variations as well) in an organization's culture is seen as a character of mature and humane organizations.

Based on our collective experience, we can see how leading DEI initiatives can be challenging and tends to be more so if the following are not addressed as part of that process:

a. DEI needs to be fully integrated with the core of the organization's culture and values. DEI initiatives fail when they are standalone and not connected to the overall organizational transformation. Nwoga (2023) conducted a meta research on barriers to DEI program implementation and reported that one of the important barriers was the lack of alignment between the organizational culture and the values of DEI.

b. DEI initiatives should provide space for individuals to explore their deeply held beliefs about people who are different from them. At a superficial level, everyone will agree to be diversity sensitive, inclusive etc. However,

when critical incidents happen, people act from their old mindset of patriarchy and privilege. The unconscious biases seen as halo and horn effects
impact actions at the leadership level. When this happens, employees
lose trust in the DEI initiatives.

c. DEI initiatives must address systemic inequities including lack of resources
and support for marginalized people/ groups and not focus only on individual behavioural change.

d. At a behavioural level, DEI initiatives need to address micro-aggressions
faced by marginalized individuals in the system through feedback and
sanctions as required.

Appreciative Inquiry for Diversity Work

When we review the five stages of DEI work as articulated by Ella Washington,
one recognizes that DEI initiatives have their origin in experiences of discrimination from dominant groups. When an organization embarks on a DEI initiative, the trauma of those experiences comes back into the system leading to
emotions of shame, guilt, anger and pain colouring the background. Leaders
then see DEI as a problem to be solved, an issue to be wished away and move
into a reactive and "let's fix it" approach. To acknowledge and own up the
emotions through difficult conversationscan lead tothe discovery that there
are also positive experiences of DEI that can be appreciated, nurtured and
amplified . This requires a high level of integrity, optimism and resilience in
leadership.

Hence an appreciative approach is not the first intervention that comes to
someone's mind in this context. However, it is counter-intuitive to approach
DEI through an Ai process since there is an opportunity to heal the system
before it embarks on a new culture of embracing diversity, equity and
inclusion.

The potential for Appreciative Inquiry to harness positive potential for transformative change is well recognized (Bushe and Kassam, 2005; Cooperrider
and Whitney, 2005). Ai inspires individuals, groups, and institutions to ask
life-affirming questions to lead the change process. Cooperrider and Whitney
(2005) argue that "the questions we ask set the stage for what we find, and
what we discover (the data) becomes the linguistic material, the stories, out
of which the future is conceived and constructed" (p. 51).

Tapia and Polonskaia (2020) explain that, "Storytelling goes to the heart
of trust. Stories move us from intellectually transmitting information to emotionally inspiring transcendent trust. Powerful stories inspire us to connect, to
contribute, and to include". When employees share their lived experiences
authentically, they gain insight into each other's challenges and hopes and
develop empathy and understanding. This shared experience contributes to
healing and releases energies that breathe life to new experiences of diversity, equity and inclusion for the employees in that organization. Sharing and

listening to inspiring stories contributes to self -reflection and ownership in the use of self as an agency to bring change.

Monteros (2024) writes in the ADEI Assessment Report that they decided use Appreciative Inquiry for this assessment because it helps to "Reframe challenges to discover opportunities through creativity, curiosity and innovation, while suspending judgement"

Another important aspect of using Ai for DEI work is the use of Drench for system level and self-level transformation. Drench at the self-level is to stay with hope, anticipation and suspend the voices of cynicism, judgement and fear. At the system level, drench involves seeing the whole, and bring the future aspirations of DEI to the present. Drench at the self and system level help to let go of past experiences, suspend all oppressive voices and allow the new hope to come. It opens the mind, heart and will and connect with "one's inner source in silence" (Otto Schramer (2016)). This "connection with the inner source" at the self and system level are important for designing the DEI roadmap and identifying deliverables

We believe that an Ai based approach to DEI work will help overcome some of the challenges that we mentioned at the beginning of this chapter. We will now focus on the story of an ongoing DEI intervention that we are engaged in with the Indian affiliate of a global animal protection organization.

Our Story

The Beginning

We were approached by the leadership team of the Indian affiliate of a global animal protection organization to help facilitate a process for integrating DEI into their work culture. After consultations with the Operations Head and the Director for India, we agreed on the following objectives for the assignment:

> The primary objective of this engagement is to work with the Indian Affiliate to support in the development of a comprehensive *Diversity, Equity, and Inclusion (DEI) roadmap for the next three (3) years. The activities and tasks include engagement with stakeholders, gather qualitative and quantitative data, analyse this information, and facilitate the creation of a DEI strategy for the next three years.*

The international organization has a DEI vision and strategy and this document was shared with us. It read as follows:

> "We envision a better world for animals and a better world for people. Our DEI initiatives are directed at creating a work environment that is collaborative, energizing and respectful of the full spectrum of human diversities. We recognise the unique talents of all employees and provide them

equitable opportunities to contribute to our vision. Our DEI strategy will have education, engagement and empowerment as the three pillars".

We had intense discussions with the client team to decide on the approach and methodology to be used in this assignment. We are Ai practitioners and we strongly believe that the very fact that the client system is seeking to develop a comprehensive DEI roadmap is an indication that DEI is alive and practised in the organization. The purpose of this project is to amplify, spread and bring more internalization and institutionalization of DEI in the system. Hence we wanted to approach it from the perspective of appreciating what is, envisioning what should be and then creating a path to achieve the same.

While the Director and the Operations Head were aligned with our approach, they wanted us to bring the leadership team onboard before we proceeded with the entire organization. We agreed and conducted two four-hour on-line experiential learning sessions on DEI using Appreciative Inquiry The leadership team experienced Ai and worked with their own diversities in an appreciative way. We also walked them through the process as it will unfold in the larger system. The stories that they shared helped them to come together as a team and appreciate and celebrate their uniqueness and differences. This workshop also helped the leadership align and take collective ownership of the larger process.

From our perspective, this was the first drenching of the leadership team into the transformational DEI journey and the Ai philosophy embedded in the process. We lived the mission and strategy of DEI as stated by the parent organization – we practiced the 3Es of education, engagement and empowerment. We educated the leaders, the stories engaged them with the process and empowered them to be the drivers of this transformation. We decided to replicate this process with every employee and employee group within the organization.

Data Collection and Report

We collected data from a majority (more than 90%) of the 118 employees across the various locations. We visited many of their offices and field sites to meet with employees, either in small groups or one-on-one. Employees from remote locations were interviewed or met in small groups over virtual sessions.

We focussed on the following dimensions and framed questions based on the same:

1. The level of awareness of DEI in the organization including the various dimensions that are visible and those that are not spoken about.
2. Personal and lived experiences where they experienced diversity within the organization.

3. The value of focussing on DEI dimensions as a culture at the Indian affiliate.
4. The current state and the future direction of DEI work within the organization.

Based on the above, the following questions were asked, both in group meetings and one-on-one interviews. These questions were contextualized and language changed based on the group/ person.

1. Tell me a story of a personal experience of diversity in the organization based on the social identities you carry. An experience where you felt that other/ organization recognized and valued your identity and the differences that you bring in to the workplace.
2. Share a story of an experience that showed to you how inclusive your organization is about people who are different from the mainstream.
3. How do you see your opportunities to grow in this organization based on the social identities you bring?
4. What are the aspects of the organization that support DEI culture?
5. What are the DEI challenges in this organization?
6. How do you experience leadership and their approach to DEI?

In addition to the above, we also asked the groups we met to draw a picture of how this organization looks like from a DEI perspective today, how they would like it to be in the future and the steps that they recommend that we take. This brought in a visual and non-verbal expression of how people experience diversity at work and their aspirations for the future. We were unable do this for the groups we met online.

We emphasized to all employees that only themes will be mentioned in our reports, maybe with an occasional quote. However, no names would be identified in the spirit of confidentiality and trust. This was the agreement with all those who spoke with us.

Our approach was to get employees to focus on what works, what can be built upon and the concerns and hopes for the future. The attempt of these interviews was also to help heighten the awareness around diversity among employees. We believe that a certain level of education, engagement and empowerment were achieved through this process.

Personally for us, these interviews were a process of drenching. We soaked in their stories, lived their emotions, shared their hopes and apprehensions and learned from their experiences of being treated for who they are instead of what they do. We discovered their passion and the humane way they treat companion animals, wild life, and animals used for food. We saw how committed they are to bring that humanity when dealing with each other, though they do struggle at times, like we do, to be compassionate, especially with those who think, feel, speak and act different from us. While the task was to collect data and present a report to the organization, the experience of it was transformational for us.

We also discovered new dimensions around DEI that we don't usually explore. We saw how important caste was as a differentiating social identity for many of the staff and how easily they could dialogue around it without any shame or blame. They were completely open about it and saw value in those who come from other castes as well. We struggle to speak about caste in our social gatherings considering it as a taboo and hence caste stays in our shadows.

We discovered how gender roles were important to them while they were open to see the need for more equity and equality. While we speak about equality of genders, we miss the fact that society also needs some gendered roles that ensures a certain sense of balance.

Our way of looking at inclusion was to explore how the organization was inclusive in its culture. However, we discovered that the staff experience a deep sense of inclusion because they belong and are engaged in an important cause that the organization is embarked on. This goes over and above having an inclusive culture in the organization.

We prepared a report for the organization that contained data, stories, dreams and suggested actions that our respondents provided. We also analysed the data and bucketed them to the SOAR model.

SOAR is a strengths-based framework with a whole system approach to strategic planning and leading change (Cole and Stavros, 2019). This framework helps to inquire into strengths, opportunities, aspirations and results that help us to imagine the most preferred future, build a sustainable culture and create innovative strategies and plans for execution.

The SOAR analysis for the DEI space is given below:

The report including the SOAR analysis was discussed at the Appreciative Inquiry Summit where 25 members of the organization drawn from diverse locations joined. We met for three days to drench ourselves in this report, dream together the new possibilities and create a road map for the DEI journey ahead. The description of what is an Ai Summit is given in Chapter 4. In short, an Ai Summit is the coming together of all stakeholders in a system to Discover, Dream, Drench, Design and Deliver the system they aspire for the organization.

Ai Summit: Design Thinking

The design thinking behind the summit included the following considerations:

1. To ensure that DEI principles are followed in selecting the summit attendees. All the senior staff and managers were invited, along with representation from community staff. The aim was to have a fair representation of the entire organization. People were also asked if they would like to volunteer for this work.

Table 5.1 SOAR analysis

Strengths:	Opportunities:
Women in leadership roles	Develop better understanding across regions,
Appreciation for diverse work styles	backgrounds, language and projects
Adequate focus on Gender and Caste intersectionality	Building a vegan organization
Safe space to work	Working beyond typecast gender roles
Flexible work hours	More leadership from field staff
Inclusive work culture	

Aspirations:	Results:
All voices are genuinely heard and acted upon	DEI Training for all
People open up without the fear of being stupid	Hire LGBTQ and physically challenged people
Compassionate and humane culture	Connect reward system to DEI practices of an employee
Expand our circle of compassion	Inclusion dialogues to be initiated
Become a vegan organization	Partnering with stakeholder communities for animal protection
	Engage with tribals in forest areas

2. To ensure that the summit follows the appreciative ethos to celebrate and build on differences. The principles of Appreciative Inquiry were incorporated as our focus for building the culture and climate in the training room. Some of the principles of Appreciative Inquiry we used were:
3. To ensure that the workshop flows in a continuum from the data collection approach, the 6-D model of Appreciative Inquiry (Ramamoorthy and Joshi, 2019) was used as the basic model for the exploration. The model uses stories, dreams and other non-linear approaches to developing the vision and roadmap for DEI implementation. Please see below the customized 6-D model for the DEI intervention.
4. To ensure that the Summit workshop processes are inclusive, we provided spaces for expression through breakout sessions and used both English and Hindi as workshop languages.

Ai Summit: Design Flow

A brief outline of the flow of the summit is given below so that the readers can get a picture of the process followed. The first day began with the MD setting the context and welcoming all the participants. We invited participants to set an intent, a high-dream that represents their desired outcome of the workshop.

Some of the high dreams that participants shared were:

- I can speak my truth without fear of consequences.
- We don't compromise work- this will affect team dynamics.
- We don't just talk – we also "DO".
- I can share all my experiences in the organization openly.
- This is a dynamic roadmap that will serve us for many years.
- We have a clear north star at the end of 3 days, that we are all aligned to.

Following this we sensitised the group to understand DEI, not as an abstract concept, but as specific and clear practices that one sees on a day-to-day basis in our lives and organizations in particular. The group was shown a video that highlighted the microaggressions and diversity related issues that can happen in the workspace.

The group then explored their own experiences of diversity, power, privilege and rank. We used a World Café design for this and asked questions to elicit stories about their experiences in life, people who influenced them, their inspirations, judgements about others and how free or conscious they are about their social identities. This led to some intense discussions and powerful insights for some of the participants. Similar to the leadership team, the larger group of participants engaged with each other and felt empowered to take leadership of the DEI process.

After engagement and empowerment, it was time for education. This was a presentation of the data collection report and an activity to debrief the

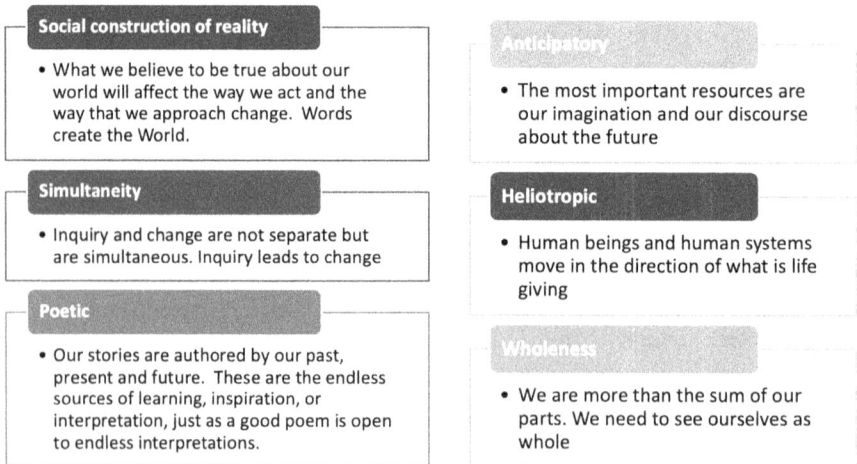

Social construction of reality

- What we believe to be true about our world will affect the way we act and the way that we approach change. Words create the World.

Anticipatory

- The most important resources are our imagination and our discourse about the future

Simultaneity

- Inquiry and change are not separate but are simultaneous. Inquiry leads to change

Heliotropic

- Human beings and human systems move in the direction of what is life giving

Poetic

- Our stories are authored by our past, present and future. These are the endless sources of learning, inspiration, or interpretation, just as a good poem is open to endless interpretations.

Wholeness

- We are more than the sum of our parts. We need to see ourselves as whole

Figure 5.1 AI Principles reframed for DEI.

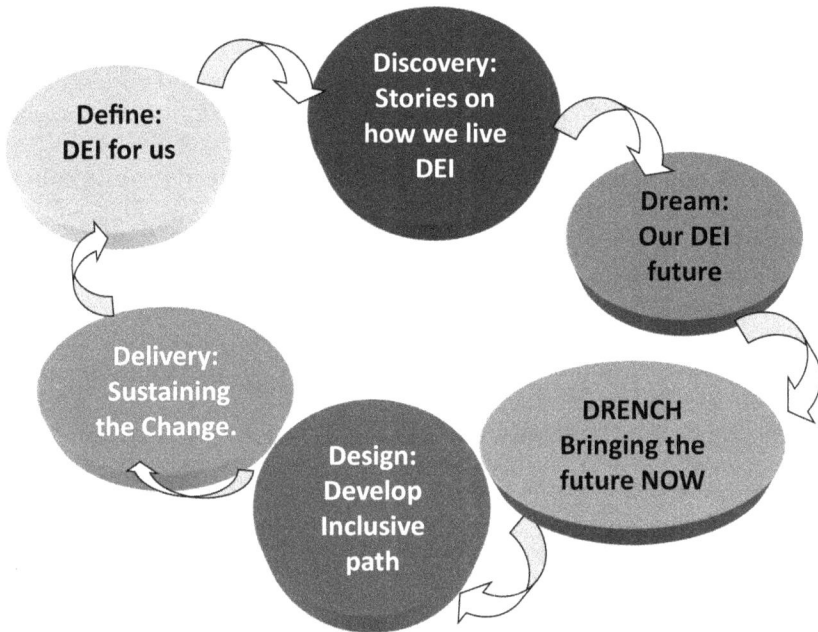

Figure 5.2 6-D Model for DEI intervention.

experience of listening to the presentation. We asked them to reflect on *"What are you celebrating?"* and *"What biases are you becoming aware of in yourself?"*

Participants worked in groups of four and this led to some deep insights and reflections about themselves. There was a lot of alignment with the elements with the report, and some questions. They expressed how they were feeling. There was a desire to move into action and address some of the issues being raised.

The day ended with a game. This was received with relief as it had been an emotionally intense day and this allowed for physical movement and moving stuck energies.

This game is a simulation which brings out the issues of structural basis of power, privilege, rank, disability and discrimination. The game brought out how diversity plays out on a day-to-day basis and brought awareness among participants on what they need to do to build a collaborative and inclusive environment.

The second day began with a check-in and some energizers. We asked the following questions for a milling around.

- *What do I appreciate in you?*
- *What is different about you that I am curious about?*

This was followed by a story telling session on when participants experienced the organization at its best. We broke the participants into small groups and asked them to identify the themes that emerged from the stories that they heard. The groups further organized the themes into the following buckets:

1. **We are Trailblazers** – We show the qualities of fearlessness, courage, authenticity, dynamic, action oriented, passion, hard -working and learn from failure.
2. **We never Settle** – We show perseverance, determination, resilience, adaptability, motivated, tenacity and are ambitious.
3. **We have Leadership** and presence
4. **We collaborate and share** – We support, we are vulnerable, we are honest, trusting, empathetic and compassionate
5. **We are Learning oriented** – We have curiosity, scientific approach, knowledge and expertise, and risk taking
6. **We take Pride** of that fact that we are Value driven, joyful, inclusive, diverse, impact focused, and quality oriented and responsible.

These were presented in a fun way through a combination of song, dance and a regular presentation.

The discovery of their strengths as an organization brought in fresh energy and vitality to now work on their DEI dream. In order to create the dream, we asked to create a collage from used magazines that represented their dream for how DEI would be lived in our organization.

The collage emerged as people pasted pictures from the magazines, added to other's pictures and built a pattern of pictures.

The collage was then analyzed and reviewed by small groups to identify key words that describe their dream of a DEI organization. These key words/phrases emerged: Build, Value, Connected, Freedom, All Voices, Together, Opportunity, and Belong. This led to the provocative proposition that stated:

> "We are one though many, together though different
> We celebrate our differences and connectedness"

This was left here and the group agreed to include many other voices that are not in the room and then create a collective dream statement on DEI for the organization.

Having completed the identification of the strengths of the organization and envisioned the diverse, Inclusive and equitable organization, the workshop process now shifted to get participants to soak into this whole process. We call this Drench. This is important to change the discovery and dream processes from just being cognitive and intellectual and make it a living, experiential reality.

In order for participants to drench into their DEI dream, we asked them to write the cover of a book that they will write sharing with the world the story of their DEI journey and their own contributions towards the process. The books were written as if they were writing it after three years where the Indian affiliate has lived its DEI journey and how they played an individual role in the same.

The third day began with an exercise to have a conversation with someone else who is different from oneself, especially with someone where one finds it difficult to accept the diversity in the other person. The experience was very helpful and some participants shared that though they had thought the conversation would be difficult, it was relatively easy. This exercise was done to get participants learn ways to manage differences.

After this exercise, we moved into the Book gallery and launch of the books. Each participant spoke about their book and the essential message that wass being conveyed. The participants then formed small groups to identify some of the specific behaviours that were highlighted in their books that can become the set of norms for behaviour in the organization. This formed the "Champions Pledge" and the participants presented the same to the Board members later in the day.

The participants were then formed into different groups. The groups worked on the DEI roadmap for the Indian affiliate. One group worked on top three DEI priorities and arrived at specific action plans. Another group worked on fine-tuning the Champions Pledge. A third group worked on a presentation that was to be made to the board members visiting from their International office.

Once this was done, we closed the workshop with an interesting exercise called "Appreciation behind the back". The idea behind the exercise is to change the behaviour in the organization from gossiping behind someone's back to actually appreciating them. This is also a fun closure exercise. The output document is something participants can savour for a long time.

Postscript

The leadership of the India Affiliate met to review the next steps of the process. It was decided to constitute a DEI council (called the Panchayat) with diverse members who will then work on communicating the outcomes from the Ai Summit, draft the charter, align with the international model and build education, engagement and empowerment in the system around DEI. The journey continues....

One of the fallouts of this intervention was the realization that the system needs to strengthen their leadership and managerial acumen in order to inspire and execute the cultural transformation required in the organization to fully integrate and sustain DEI in their ethos. We started this process of capability building and strengthening managerial competencies with a view to focus on awareness, education and empowerment of leaders in the system. This will also help in shaping their DEI dream of "Each one of us, for all of us"

Insights

Integrating Ai as the DEI intervention gave many benefits. It gave employees an insight into their colleagues' journey of living the value of DEI and their own experiences in the organization. Small steps towards changing the culture began with these interventions. The conversations during the survey and the subsequent summit gave everyone an opportunity to participate and become aware of DEI work in their own culture. This work also fostered education, engagement and empowerment of the staff as steps to institutionalize DEI as a way of life in the culture of the organization.

The organization moved from the stages of awareness, compliance and tactics to the stage of integration through the DEI intervention project. Complete integration and developing a sustainable roadmap for organizational transformation are the next steps in the process. The formation of the DEI council and the panchayat will be a major step in this regard.

Personally for us this assignment is challenging and enlightening. It is challenging to work with diversity especially around power, rank and privilege when one is aware of the same within and how it plays out in our role as consultants. We need to acknowledge and own our privilege, and yet not allow that to influence and impact the system. We have to hold the space for people to feel safe, empowered and be brave to act with agency. It is also important for us to be neutral when we hear stories and experiences that doesn't fit our worldview, and have the openness to appreciate that there is different way of thinking. Difference just means difference, it doesn't mean it is wrong.

One of the challenges with our approach is the tension between the desire for action and the need to Drench into the process. We suspended action on day 2 of the summit and asked people to stay with the Dream and their role in shaping the same. This was our hope and commitment to stay in rhythm within and bring readiness to change rather than jumping to action. We believe that this is an important aspect that we wish our colleagues in the field of Ai based DEI and other organizational transformation work will adopt and help systems and people to soak in; to internalize, let go of the past, suspend action and let come in the future.

It is also important to note that we as consultants should be careful not to impose our "modern" values on to people who hold "traditional" views (for example around caste, class, gender roles etc.). Valuing diversity and being inclusive also means listening and respecting all views and seeing opportunities to build bridges rather than highlight schisms.

Way Ahead

We asked the Director and one other leader about the impact of the Appreciative Inquiry work just before we sent this chapter to the publishers. The Director said

> "The workshop has helped us think beyond our ideas of what DEI is and should be and it's been eye opening to seethe diversity in our needs and expectations. We are currently doing further exercises with each of our staff and gathering all feedback from our staff on what they think we should be prioritising. Once this data gathering is done, we will form the council and start our work".

The other leader added "I think the workshop served as a powerful catalyst, igniting essential dialogues, driving meaningful conversations and empowering us to cultivate a truly inclusive space. For the first time, we came together and made each other responsible for making this space inclusive and equitable."

The experience of working with Appreciative Inquiry for DEI based organizational transformation has convinced us that this approach is philosophically appropriate. Drenching in the Ai process from start till end helps in personal and systemic healing, engage people at an emotional level and empower them to take ownership and integrate DEI as part of their culture, both in work and life.

Some specific innovations are required to inquire into highly sensitive topics like caste, untouchability, sexual orientation etc. that are in the unconscious of both self and the system as far as the Indian context is concerned.

The process of capability building of leaders and managers is an important step for the way ahead. Many of the Managers have been brought up in a cultural context very different from this organization and they need to unlearn and let go some of their old worldviews before they can be ready to walk the talk.

We hope to see the fruit of this intervention within the next one year in terms of specific DEI based interventions at a systemic and individual levels.

References

Cole, M., Stavros, J. (2019). *SOAR: A Framework to Build Positive Psychological Capacity in Strategic Thinking, Planning, and Leading*. New York: Springer. 10.1007/978-3-030-20583-6_23.

Molefi, N. (2017). *A Journey of Diversity and Inclusion in South Africa: Guidelines for Dealing with Inclusivity*. Johannesburg, South Africa: K.R. Publishing.

Monteros, P. (2024). *ADEI Assessment Report*, Ohio Net. https://archive.org/details/journeyofdiversi0000mole?>

Nwoga, A. (2023). Breaking the invisible wall: Barriers to DEI program implementation. *Journal of Business and Management* . 11, 4. 10.4236/ojbm.2023.114100

Ramamoorthy, S., Joshi, W. (2019). A crucial stage in the practice of appreciative inquiry. *Organization Development Review*. 51, 3. 50–55.

Scharmer, C. O. (2016). *Theory U: Leading from the Future as It Emerges*. New York: Berrett-Koehler.

Tapia, A. T., Polonskaia, A. (2020). *The 5 Disciplines of Inclusive Leaders: Unleashing the Power of All of Us*. Oakland: Berret-Kohler.

Washington, E. (2022). The five stages of DEI maturity. *Harvard Business Review*. https://hbr.org/2022/11/the-five-stages-of-dei-maturity

Chapter 6

Embrace the Dream

Key Points

1. Dream as a provocative proposition and its link to vision.
2. The power of imagination and bringing dream to a clear vision
3. Stories from three experiences of transforming dreams to a living reality.
4. Drenching as a process to bring readiness and preparedness to live the dream.
5. Insights and explorations.

"The future belong to those who believe in the beauty of their dreams"
Eleanor Roosevelt

Introduction

We were conducting a training on Appreciative Inquiry for a group of consultants and trainers. We took them through an experience of the 6-D process including creating a dream for their consulting/ training practice. The process was exhilarating for the participants. They let their imaginations loose, passionately sought their desires and amplified their strengths that they had discovered from the previous session. People presented their dream statements and images in the form of a provocative proposition (explained later) and we celebrated each other. During the end of day checkout, one of the participants shared that she is depressed because her dreams are big and audacious, and she doesn't believe that it will ever happen. The class was ending and some people left and some of us stayed back to talk with this participant who was in tears.

During the dialogue, she shared that she has no clue how to live her dream and that non-clarity puts her off and she takes the position that it is just a

DOI: 10.4324/9781003538059-8

dream and not possible to realize. Someone noticed that in her dream statement, she had written "I'm a passionate, authentic trainer who accesses both her knowledge and ignorance...". This person showed this to her and said "Do you know you are living your dream now? You are authentically sharing your passion and sharing your ignorance of how to get there". That statement helped her to see that the dream is not something that might happen someday, it is bringing the future into the present and living the dream every moment. In order to do that, we need to first transform the dream to a vision with clear focus and direction. This will give us the strength and conviction to start living the elements of the dream in the here and now.

Transforming the Dream into a Vision

In appreciative inquiry, the discovery phase enables an organization to locate the energy for transformation. The collective stories generated from the discovery phase infuse belief, passion and energy to propel the organization towards its dream. The stories bring knowledge of where we are and gives reason to envision the future. The dream process unfolds in Ai as the amplification of the present, stated in bold terms and imagining "when we are this way all the time, every time, what will our world be?"

Dream in Ai parlance is called a provocative proposition. A provocative proposition is a statement made of the future in present tense seeing the possibilities existing in the seeds of today. The provocative proposition changes the understanding of how we see the 'now' and with that new vision and knowledge we can see possibilities emerge that did not exist before. It gives hope where sometimes none existed before.

Dreams are largely un-manifest and contain energies, hopes and desires about a future without a clear path for realization. Dreams are an inside-out process of envisioning based on the present whereas the vision is mostly an outside-in process based on opportunities that are manifest, concrete and with a clear road map. Dreams open up possibilities without getting bogged down by constraints. Further, dreams are an amplification of existing strengths as identified from the discovery phase and hence more credible. The energy unleashed by imagination and passion is very contagious and helps to cascade the dream across the organization.

In the movie "Inception" the protagonist, Dom Cobb plants a dream in someone's unconscious mind so that they start believing it as their own dream. He says in the movie "How powerful, it is to plant an idea in someone else's mind, as if it's their own"

How powerful it is for a collective to implant their minds with a single dream? For organizational transformation, a shared dream planted in the collective psyche of an organization is a powerful force. The collective dream is planted when people listen to their own stories of the past, identify the themes that led to peak experiences in their organization and imagine how the world will be when those themes are lived in every moment.

However, there is a catch here. Like any contagious emotion, desire and aspiration, dreams struggle to sustain over a period of time. The energy and passion that helped to co-create the dream starts to fade after a while and reason steps in to show constraints, roadblocks and questions the readiness and preparedness of the system to live the dream. People can easily lose steam, and cynicism can set in, especially if the organization has an experience that is contrary to the stories told in the appreciative inquiry. Dreams can also lose their fizz if unaccompanied by a clear vision, strategies, values and actions required to bring the dream to the present. Hence the planted dreams need to be watered, fertilized and nurtured in a safe environment so that they develop the clarity of form, shape and dimensions of a vision.

The discovery phase brings in the knowledge and the reason for change but it is not enough to make that leap of faith. The left brain, the reasoning brain is a formidable executor, and it requires things in black and white. The provocative proposition is a powerful imagination of the future and it includes both words and images of the future. The provocative proposition is a product of passion and intuition and the thinking brain part of us doesn't get to work unless there is a clear image of and direction to the desired future.

This is where Drench comes in. It holds the power of the dream, internalizes it and empowers the individual and the system to be ready and prepared. There is a crucial transition between planting the dream, and transitioning to a tangible vision giving direction for the organization transformation process. While Drench is a process that pervades all the other 5-Ds of Appreciative Inquiry (See Chapter 1 on Drench), it is a clear and vital step that follows the articulation of the provocative proposition, bringing that dream in the here and now reality of the system. It is the process of making a rational and well thought through choice to live the dream while nurturing the imagination, passion and desire that came alive from the dreaming process. It is like embarking on a life together with your partner and face the realities of the world while nurturing the romance, love and the dream that brought us together.

The physicist David Bohm (1983) postulated two different frameworks for understanding reality. He called it the explicate order and the implicate order. The explicate order is the manifested/ unfolded and normal day to day understanding of reality. Underlying that explicate order is an enfolded reality called the implicate order. The explicate order is based on the implicate order and together they form a whole. He used the analogy of the hologram where each part contains the information of the whole image. In appreciative inquiry, the vision forms the explicate order that create a consensus reality on the direction that the system wants to move towards and is based on the dreams which form the implicate order underlying the vision. Dreams are based on imagination and provide the energy for the vision to be accomplished. Unfolding the vision from the enfolded dreams require a pause, a time to soak in to the dreams and allow it to sink in at a deeper level. This is the process of Drench.

Success in Organizational Transformation

Organizational transformation is a much written about and even maligned in management literature. John Kotter (1995) wrote an article in the Harvard Business Review in 1995 stating that very few transformation efforts become successful, because of what he called as critical errors. At the end of the article, Kotter wrote "In reality, even successful change efforts are messy and full of surprises.....just as a simple vision is needed to guide people through a major change, *so a vision of the change process can reduce the error rate*" (italics are the authors). The process of pausing to create a *vision of the change process* is what we call drench.

In May, 2023, a second article on organizational transformation was published by the *Harvard Business Review* called "6 key Levers of a successful organisational transformation" (White et al., 2023). The authors of this article write

> "In 1995, John Kotter found that 70% of the organization transformations fail, and nearly three decades later, not much has changed. Our own research, in which we spoke to more than 900 C-suite managers and more than 1,100 employees who had gone through a corporate transformation, showed similar results: *67% of leaders told us they had experienced at least one underperforming transformation in the last five years*"

From an Appreciative Inquiry perspective, we would like to explore some of the organizational transformations which might form the 33% of the ones that were successful. We were engaged in some of them and we tell those stories in this chapter.

The authors identified six key factors that contributed to a successful organizational transformation. They were:

1. Leadership's own willingness to change.
2. A shared vision of success.
3. A culture of trust and psychological safety.
4. A process that balances exploration and execution.
5. A recognition that technology carries its own emotional journey.
6. A shared sense of ownership over the outcome.

The authors further pointed out that "Our research also found that a key difference in successful transformations was that leaders embraced their employees' emotional journey"

In this chapter we will share stories that focus on each of these factors and how the process of Drench played a significant role in nurturing the key factors for a successful organization transformation.

How do we embed the above factors in our organization transformation project? We believe this can be done when we Drench in these factors as we transition from the Dream to a vision of the change process.

Story 1: Swasth

We were introduced to a young pair of co-founders during a workshop and they invited us for a meeting to discuss about their organization. We discovered before the meeting that they were both Engineers and were ex-consultants with a large international consulting firm in India. They left their careers to set up a not-for-profit organization to offer affordable and ethical health services in the slums of Mumbai. When we met them, they had opened fourteen clinics in the city.

We met in an office which had a few chairs, one table and piled up with cartons of medicines which were waiting to be transported to the clinics. There were five people in the room and when we entered, one or two of them had to step out to provide space for us to sit. In this physical mess of a place, we found the co-founders and the others in the room highly energized, with a certain sense of purpose, determination and above all smiling and welcoming us.

We got talking and they had a long list of issues like any other start-up, issues around operations, administration, and staffing, locating venues to start the clinics, and so on. They were both highly process focussed and they discovered to their angst that they sometimes struggled to deal with people issues. However, they were clear that they will deal with those issues in due course and do not need our help, though suggestions were welcome. One of us also have a public health and medical background and could offer some ideas to deal with them. Then they came to the crux of the meeting. They said "We set up this organisation to be different from all the health organisations that we consulted with when we were in the consulting field. We want to build an organisation that is grounded on the ethos of our country and it grows beyond us as founders. How can you help us build such an organisation?". I remember saying at that time "you want a healthy organisation working for public health". They nodded and said "yes and beyond that!"

We gave them a brief background about us and the work we do using Appreciative Inquiry. The philosophy of Ai excited them and they were ready to start the work. We facilitated a process, using Ai to discover their core values as an organization through the stories of when they experienced living their mission. We met all the employees in the clinics, the administrative staff and the founders in groups and asked them to share a peak experience of working here. This was followed by a Vision/ values workshop facilitated by one of us. The process generated a list of values and they started the process of communicating these values to all their employee and also generated a list of practices for these values. One such value was "happiness". While this value was logically derived from the stories, there was a feeling that "happiness" is a temporary state of being while the organization was focused on sustained wellbeing of the underprivileged in our cities.

My colleague was coaching one of the founders and he spoke about his need to go deeper into the meaning of their work. During one of the coaching conversations, he took the offer to meditate on the deeper meaning. He meditated on this for about 30 minutes while the coach held silence. At the end of that period, he said that the word "Joy" emerged in his mind continuously. He experienced his whole body soaked with that joy and he could envision how his employees and the patients who come to his clinics will be when they experience joy.

This led not only to a word change, but a transformation of the whole vision of change. A new spirit emerged with the word "joy" and this resulted in changing the mission, vision and the branding of the organization where experiencing joy in the whole process of health engagement became the focus of what the medical centre stood for. The vision statement was rewritten as "Health and Joy for All" articulating the link between health and joy. This vision brought the energy in the organization to experience joy when health service is provided.

Today Joy as a value is not only part of their culture, but also an element in assessment of employee and clinic performance, community engagement and all other processes of operations. The founders also drenched themselves in Ai and applied the process for all engagements at the clinics, and with community members, and so on. Joy is a keystone for their work and Appreciative Inquiry is their way of being.

When we examine the Swasth story with the six elements of a successful transformation, we can identify where the drenching for transformation took place. The first one was leadership's own willingness to drench in the change process. Their insistence to go beyond being a low-cost, ethical health provider and discover joy in health is an example for that. The drench happened through the meditation within that coaching process. This was the tipping point.

Secondly, the transformation process was strengthened by focusing both on execution of processes and also exploration at self and system level on how they internalize the value of Joy. A balance between both helped them to engage both at the being and doing levels. You can read more about Swasth on their website www.swasth.org

Sundeep Kapila, one of the founders says, My journey with Joy has been best captured in the words of Rabindranath Tagore, a Nobel Laureate, – "I slept and dreamt that Life was Joy. I awoke and saw that Life was Service. I acted and behold, Service was Joy"

Story 2: Keystone Foundation

Keystone Foundation is a story of diversity. The Western Ghats of Southern India is perhaps one of the most biodiverse region in the world. The diversity of the tribes who live there, their language, customs and worldview are as much as the biodiversity of nature. Added to that is the diversity of the three friends from north, east and south who came to a southern corner of India to set up Keystone foundation. Keystone works to empower indigenous people and local communities by building socio-ecological resilience through green growth and sustainable development. They work on issues of natural resources and rural development, and addressing the challenges of conservation, livelihoods, and enterprise development, through appropriate knowledge and action.

Keystone has succeeded over the last three decades to work with diverse communities and create an "Us and Us" feeling, a feeling of inclusion, a respectful embrace of cultures and people. They have also brought in sustainable livelihood for tribal artisans and other occupations.

This is the story of Keystone that began with an Appreciative Inquiry summit bringing people from the communities and the staff together. A group of around a hundred people assembled in a large open conference hall atop a hill in a small town called Kotagiri in the western ghats of south India. These were no ordinary folks. They were tribals from the forest, honey gatherers, artisans, village elders, women and children from the nearby villages along with staff and leaders from Keystone foundation. The diversity in the hall was a visual delight with all the colourful dresses that both the men and women and an auditory delight with all the sounds of different languages spoken, songs sung in beautiful melodies and playing musical instruments of all shapes and sizes. Celebrations were in the air. It was more of a "mela" (a village fair) than a conference to discuss the future of these tribal villages!

Keystone foundation has been engaged with these tribals for a few decades and helping them to maintain the biodiversity of the region, research on all the varieties of plants and animals, food products and so on. Keystone felt that the time has now come to organize these groups, get their produce to the world and create sustainable livelihood.

The process of discovery and sharing stories from the community was an eye opener for us. They experience joy in small things, celebrate every moment in life and seem to take struggles and problems in their stride.

In the Ai summit, the whole community recounted stories of the past, right from Keystone formation till date. These stories ranged from individual triumphs to specific program impacts to transformation of relationship between the organization and the community. Singing and dancing interspersed the stories, which was very much part of their local culture.

If the discovery phase was an eye opener, the dream phase was a riot! We asked them to create a collage using pictures cut from old magazines, depicting how they would like to see the future of their communities. Everyone wanted to put their picture and the collage went on increasing in size till it filled the entire large hall! The folks enjoyed doing this and had a lot of fun, laughter and energy. The collage looked haphazard to begin with and slowly it took a form and a pattern emerged. The group developed a provocative proposition based on the collage of dreams that each one has for their collective future.

From our perspective as consultants, the whole process of coming together for a day was as important as the output generated from the workshop. The whole day was a Drench. It was drenching for the community to sit together with Keystone members, share their thoughts, sing, eat and dance together. It was drenching for the staff to experience oneness with the community, listening to them, following their path rather than telling them what to do...and more importantly, sharing in their dream. The boundaries were broken that day, a real sense of togetherness was established and a shared dream emerged.

This dream aligned with the visions of Last Forest and Aadhimalai collectives, organizations created for bringing tribal produce to the world in a sustainable, ecological, ethical way following principles of fair trade. One can see the impact of that work today in the growth and spread of these institutions.

A shared vision of success and ownership and a culture of trust were the factors that contributed to the success of the transformation process. Keystone foundation had built that trust over many years and the Ai summit cemented that further by creating a shared vision and ownership for success.

The expression of trust and partnership that we experienced in that summit inspired us and opened our eyes to the possibility of contributing to the process. We decided to forgo our fees and instead took some shares in Last Forest. This was our small gesture of continuous engagement with them.

Five years later, the success of the organization is not the funding and the recognition it has received, nor the learning and expertise people have gathered, but the depth of engagement with the communities and seeing them grow.

This story of organization and community transformation follows many of the key factors for success. Some of them that we could see were:

1. Leadership's own willingness to change- The founders of Keystone approached their mission by partnering with the community and not telling them what is to be done. They didn't push any new technology or modern practices and change the traditional way of work. They changed their way of working by learning from the community.
2. A shared vision of success- We saw this in action during the summit. Neither the founders offered their vision as final nor did the community members look up to them to set the vision. There was a sense of equality and togetherness in the process.

3. A culture of trust and psychological safety- We believe the above two contributed to building a culture of trust and psychological safety between the
organization and the communities.
4. A shared sense of ownership over the outcome – The power of shared
ownership was such that we also wanted to be a part of it! Living the
dream together, transitioning the dream into reality through relationships,
roles, systems, structures and processes could happen due to this sense
of shared ownership. The two institutions – Last Forest and Aadhimalai
Collectives were strengthened due this process.

You can read more about Keystone foundation at www.keystone-foundat
ion.org

3. Story of a Large Pharma

In the two earlier stories, staying with the dream and transforming the dream
into a clear vision were achieved through the process of Drench. This is a very
different story. Here, the team that we were working with were excited by the
prospect of their dream and were jumping into execution. Their dream was
also stated in terms of a concrete vision and the steps of design and delivery
were also developed with clear action plans. We were holding them back and
asking them to suspend action, much to their disappointment.

The client was a large pharma company with an R&D, global delivery and
sales organizations. They had a problem. The time taken from R&D to manu-
facture a drug (Time to Market) was way too high compared to competition.
This was hurting them. They instituted an internal study and identified lack of
collaboration between the various departments engaged in the process as one
of the major issues that contributed to the time delay.

Their Global HR Head invited us to help in building a culture of collaboration and break the silo working between the departments. We met with
all the heads of departments to understand their perspectives on this issue
through one-on-one meetings. While they agreed with the issue of lack of
collaboration, they blamed the others for not being collaborative. All of them
equally felt the pain of not delivering and wanted to find a way out of the
situation.

We invited them to a two-day workshop on Appreciative Inquiry at an off-
site location. We began by asking them to share stories of a time when they
did collaborate and achieved results that they thought were difficult. There
were about thirty top managers from R&D, Product Development, Supply
Chain, Manufacturing, Marketing and Sales present and they all said "we
don't have such a story". The room was tense and we were stumped for a
second. They said that they were ready to talk about stories when it didn't
work. We both felt that the group needed an opportunity to vent their feelings

and said "let's do that then". There were many outpourings of stories happening where people shared how things didn't happen. Initially there were arguments and we then set some norms for the process. Slowly there was listening, acknowledging, understanding and one person from a sub-group raised his hand and asked us "Can we now go back to your original question of sharing stories when we did collaborate"?

We checked with the group and many said yes. We didn't want to quickly jump from the catharsis of telling all their woes to stories of success. So we gave them a Drench time. We asked them to reflect on the last one hour and identify themes that led to those situations, their role in the story and their learning from the same. People were busy writing things on the note pad and once they completed, we gave them a tea break.

On resumption, we asked them to form groups of four and walk around the gardens and share the stories of collaboration and come back after an hour. When they returned to the conference rooms, everyone had a broad smile, some were seen patting others on the back and there was positive energy all around. One of them shared "We thought we never collaborated, but when we started sharing stories of collaboration, more and more stories came up". Another person added "We always cribbed when we didn't collaborate and we never celebrated when we did".

Hence we arranged for another mini Drench, a time for celebrating and soaking in the fact that they do collaborate and they do deliver at times. We then had the lunch break and the HR Head arranged for a cake as part of the celebrations.

The group derived the themes from the stories of collaboration and we asked the dream question "Imagine we live these themes of collaboration in every task we do with each other, every time. Then how will we be as an organization?". The group was highly energized by now and got into the task very quickly. There were many people with management education who were used to visioning and strategizing in the group. They contributed to building a very powerful vision statement and -the Design, a set of strategies to achieve the same. At the end of the day, the sub-groups presented their dream/ vision statements to each other. We told them to take a break and allow the information to sink in and meet early in the morning next day and continue the work. This was another way to slow down the group and drench them in their dreams/ vision.

The groups were ready to get into action the next day. There was high anticipation and impatience to go ahead and come out with a roadmap. We were wondering how to rein them and get them to recognize that if they moved too quickly to action, there is a possibility that the passion and hope that this process generated could be lost. It is important to go slow to go fast here. We were also told by the HR Head that their owner and Managing Director was coming in the afternoon to understand what the group was doing.

We asked the group to prepare a short session to take the Managing Director through the process they went through and the outcomes that have been arrived at. Here we said to them "Put yourself in the MD's shoes and see what will generate the same feeling of hope and anticipation in him and he will start to believe that a transformational change is just round the corner". This put the group into a pause, and the room fell silent for a long time. It dawned on them that they need to dream and generate innovative and diverse actions that change the way people work together. "This cannot be just a transition, it needs to be a transformation", one of them said.

The group spent two hours in going back to their experiences, revisiting their dream/ vision statements and drenched themselves in the underlying value of collaboration in creating a common presentation to the managing director. They realized that they were actually living their dream in the moment as they worked together to make that presentation. The group went on to Deliver on their actions and succeeded in bringing the time to market from 3.5 years to 2.4 years which was an organizational transformation.

When we analyse this transformation, we realize the importance of balancing exploration with execution. This is especially important for organizations that value execution more than exploration. The breaks, holding back and the preparation for making that presentation to their MD, all helped to drench and explore into their vision for collaboration. The experience of working together to prepare the presentation helped to experience collaboration in action in a safer environment and internalize the value within. This was a significant reason for the success of their transformation.

Our Insights

The link between the powers of the Dream to vision in action is the Drench. We would like to offer an Indic perspective on Drench with the concept of "prāna". A close translation of that word in English will be life energy or life force. The movie Star Wars called it the 'Force'. It is also known as Chi or Qi in Tao and Zen Buddhist philosophies.

According to Indic schools of philosophy, all movement in the universe is driven by prāna. Hence, any organization transformation requires alignment, acceleration and channelling of the prāna of the entire system in the direction of the transformation. In case the prāna stops or changes its direction, the transformation process will lose its momentum.

The story telling process in the Discovery phase of Ai releases intense prānic energies in the form of joy, pride and hope. Emotions are energies in motion. These energies were previously obscured by the disappointments, failures and the perceived obstacles in the system.

These energies of joy, pride, hope etc. are channelled in the direction of the future during the Dream phase of appreciative inquiry. At the end of the Dream phase, one can sense palpable energy, life force ready for action. At this stage, the energies need to be contained, aligned, embodied and internalized within each person so that they don't get released in a fragmented or misdirected way. There is also the other prānic energy that is equally strong and gets suppressed in this process of excitement…the energy of doubt, confusion, the fear of leaving the old ways…the energy of "But".

This "But" is what takes the system back to the old ways of being. The comfortable, default ways of flow of prāna…because those are the channels of flow that have been well established and easy. Like a water channel, if a new path is to be created, the groove needs to be deep enough to wean the flow away from the old riverbed to the new channel. Just showing a new path does not entice water to flow in a new direction. Nor does putting up a dam, without a new path. The dam will only submerge all territory – drown the organization in chaos.

In Conclusion

We are revisiting the six key factors that contribute to a successful organizational transformation as described by White et.al in their *HBR* article (Table 6.1). We are now analysing the same from the perspective of drenching based on the experiences given in the stories above.

Table 6.1 Drench factors for successful organizational transformation

Factors	Drench perspective
1 **Leadership's own willingness to change**	Willingness has two dimensions – preparedness and readiness. Preparedness is an understanding that the system and they themselves are prepared for the positive and negative fallouts from the transformation process. Readiness is an emotional state when one feels ready to let go of the past and open hands to welcome the future. Both these require one to reflect, contemplate, clarify, express feelings and soak into the dream completely.
2 **A shared vision of success**	Shared vision suggests that everyone engaged with the process are on the same page with respect to future. This is tricky since each word in the dream/ vision/ provocative proposition statement will lend itself to different interpretations. Hence spending time on generating a common understanding of the words through dialogue is very important. Using multiple ways of expressing the vision like skits, drawings, poem etc. will also add to the richness of understanding.
3 **A culture of trust and psychological safety**	The process of dreaming should lead to building trust and creating a safe space for people to express themselves completely. Breaking barriers of hierarchy, power, privilege etc. is important not just for the current process but for sustaining the execution of the vision. Drench focuses on trust and safety by focussing on the readiness of the system to embrace the future.

Table 6.1 (Continued)

Factors	Drench perspective
4 A process that balances exploration and execution	There is a general tendency to act immediately once there is a clear future direction. The excitement of the dream can also goad the system to go for it immediately. In case there is a setback from the first set of actions, the system will hesitate to go further, the culture of trust gets eroded and the psychological safety is reduced. Hence the need to go slow to go fast. Spending time on strategic drivers, choices, possible scenarios of success/ conflicts etc. help the system and leadership to deal with initial setbacks in a mature way and explore alternate approaches to living the dream.
5 A recognition that technology carries its own emotional journey	Technology is a means to achieve vision and not an end in itself. These days everyone is going head over heels about Artificial intelligence without exploring the possible stresses and emotional fallouts when it is implemented in a system. Good leadership recognizes that every technology transformation will require emotional management. Like we said in the section on leadership's willingness to change, preparedness and readiness assessment before technology implementation is a drenching process for the system.
6 A shared sense of ownership over the outcome	The strength of the chain is equal to the weakest link in the chain. Lack of a shared sense of ownership is sometimes the weakest link that snaps in the course of the transformation journey. Once it snaps, it requires enormous efforts to rebuild the same. There is a leadership fallacy that when people are excited about the future, they have a sense of shared ownership for the same. Oftentimes, people are excited about the possibilities of the future vision and they are banking on the leadership team to deliver the same! Hence developing a distributed responsibility and accountability matrix for the execution is an important step. This can be done only when the vision is really understood in the same manner and there is a culture of trust and psychological safety. Both these require reflection, dialogue and review which presupposes the drenching process.

There is one reason why transformational initiatives succeed, beyond the reasons stated at the beginning of this chapter. They succeed when we channel the prāna of the organization towards the Dream -the process of Drenching. When we Drench, the prāna of every stakeholder consolidates and converges into a firm belief of the possibility of living the dream. This consolidated prāna gets embedded and become part of the core being, bringing energy to change, overcome obstacles and become an unstoppable force. Imagine the prāna to be like the river gushing through the new channel. Drench by pausing, by internalizing, by removing the doubts and even by staying with the confusion can create that unstoppable force for transformation.

References

Bohm, D. (1983). *Wholeness and the Implicate Order*. London: Routledge.

Kotter, J. (1995) Leading change – Why transformation efforts fail. *Harvard Business Review*. 73, 2. 59–65.

White, A., Wheelock, M., Canwell, A., Smets, M. (2023). 6 key levers of a successful organisational transformation. *Harvard Business Review*. / www.harvardbusiness. org/wp-content/uploads/2023/05/2023_05_6-key-levers-of-a-successful-organiz ational-transformation.pdf

Chapter 7

Nurture Use of "Us"[1]

"Never doubt that a small group of thoughtful, committed people can change the world. Indeed, it is the only thing that ever has."

Margaret Mead

Introduction

This is a very different kind of chapter. This is a story written by three of us, two internal consultants and one external consultant working for bringing a culture of collaboration between two departments in a large online retail organization. This is not a story of what we did to facilitate transformation. This is a story how we were, how we shifted the view and that helped the client do the same. This is a story of the "Use of Us" as a collaborative unit that lived all that we wanted to see in the client system and how our living those values helped to move the client system in the same direction.

Use of Us

Before delving into the story of this work, let's explore the perspectives on internal and external consultants in the field of organization development (OD).

DOI: 10.4324/9781003538059-9

OD is a multifaceted field that encompasses various roles, with internal and external consultants being two key players. Both roles have their advantages and challenges, impacting the effectiveness of OD initiatives.

Internal consultants are employees who are integral to the organization. They are hired for their skills in OD and their cultural fit within the organization. They possess a deep understanding of the organization, both from a business and human processes perspective. One of the challenges for internal consultants is navigating between two identities: one as a team member and another as a change agent. This duality can generate anxiety for both the consultants and their internal clients, potentially leading to resistance. Internal consultants have existing relationships with stakeholders, which can work both ways – clients may trust them or question their neutrality. Additionally, internal consultants may fear that powerful clients could influence their career advancement within the organization, making them cautious and hesitant to deliver bad news. Lastly, Internal consultants have to keep managing changing priorities of the organization. Nancy Zentis (2018) calls the above challenges as organizational, interpersonal and intrapersonal challenges.

A research into the efficacy of internal OD consultants, conducted by Kenton and Moody of Roffey Park institute (2003) points to two significant opportunities and two significant drawbacks of internal consultants. The two significant drawbacks are a) struggle for role clarity and b) internal clients expecting instant solutions to problems they define. Among the two significant opportunities, the report highlight the need for establishing a "shadow" consulting relationship between the external and the internal consultant and developing a process consulting approach with the clients.

External consultants can theoretically bring unbiased perspectives to an assignment, although they may have initial biases, as I did in this assignment. They are hired for their experience and expertise in OD consulting. This can work in two ways: they may be respected and their diagnosis valued, or they may be seen as experts with clients expecting solutions to their problems, which is not their role. Building relationships with clients based on short interactions and understanding the cultural nuances of the organization can be time-consuming, and the project may not allow such flexibility. This can be an Achilles' heel in any project, and this is where internal consultants can support external consultants.

Internal consultants bring inside knowledge, client acceptance, and cultural understanding, while external consultants offer specialized expertise, experience, and objectivity. Internal consultants can communicate changing situations in client teams (e.g., significant exits or entries) to external consultants, who can, in turn, train internal consultants on OD knowledge and skills. Combining these strengths can create powerful synergy, highlighting the need for collaboration.

Collaboration can lead to a more comprehensive approach to projects by considering the realities of the client system, improving change management (i.e., tracking progress), and better navigating the change process and internal capability building. However, collaboration between internal and external consultants doesn't happen overnight. Clarity of roles and responsibilities, clear and open communication, and shared goals are helpful first steps in the process. The most crucial aspect is building mutual respect and trust, which forms the foundation for all collaboration and the basis of the OD assignment I embarked upon.

A distinct character of OD is the "Use of Self". Use of Self (also called by NTL Institute as "Self as an instrument of change"). As an OD Practitioner, we recognize that we are an instrument in our work and we can directly impact and affect the systems and dynamics that we work with and are ourselves affected by the same. Mee Yan Cheung-Judge (2020) did research on Use of Self with David Jamieson and published a global Use of Self Research Report. In this report, Mee Yan defined Use of Self as "To be 'aware of' and 'use' our own emotional, perceptual and cognitive processes to create the impact that is needed in the system and bring our whole selves to the work we do."

In this assignment, we expanded the concept of Use of Self as "Use of 'Us'" since it represented three additional dimensions beyond Use of Self. These are:

1. Our individual awareness of how we are impacting each other in our consulting group and use the emotional and perceptual processes to do what is needed for us to work together. Further, to recognize that how we work together as a consulting group creates a transference on the system we work with. In other words, "Use of 'Us'" is to be aware that how we work together is mirrored by the system.
2. The second dimension is to be aware of how our view of the system as a group of consultants is unconsciously influencing the way the system operates. Shifting our view of the system facilitates the system to transform. Rosenthal (1968) used the term Pygmalion effect to hypothesize that expectation engender self-fulfilling prophecies by inducing corresponding performance. Similarly, our belief that the client system can collaborate, sets up the expectations on the client system. This in turn induces a corresponding performance from the client system.
3. Lastly, we expand the definition of "Us" to include the group of internal consultants, external consultants and the entire client system. We focus on the relationship within "Us" over and above the issue and the task.

To summarize, Use of "Us" is the recognition that we as consultants significantly impact the client system through process of mirroring, relating and transference.

The Story of Use of Us: Sankar, External Consultant's View

Two members of the Learning and Development team from a large organization reached out to discuss the possibility of engaging me as a consultant to facilitate collaboration between their operations and technology teams.

In my previous assignments, I have faced challenges in getting teams to acknowledge their lack of collaboration. People rarely admit to not being team players, as it is considered socially unacceptable in organizations. Instead, they tend to blame others for the lack of collaboration. When collecting data for diagnosis, responses from the two teams often skew towards blaming each other. Despite my initial biases, I saw this assignment as an opportunity for a shift in my view and decided to take it up.

I learned that the members of the Learning and Development team would be part of the assignment team and work as internal consultants. This opened up an interesting possibility: to facilitate collaboration between the client systems, we need to collaborate as well. My hypothesis is that unless internal and external consultants collaborate, we won't achieve the project goal of collaboration between operations and technology. This possibility excited me to dive into the project.

The initial meetings with the client confirmed my hypothesis that each group blamed the other for not being collaborative. However, there was a twist. While the operations group blamed technology for not collaborating, the technology group blamed the lack of adherence to systems and processes as the main reason for the lack of collaboration. The top management representatives, including the COO, CTO, and CHRO, all agreed that the lack of cooperation was impacting business and needed to be addressed. Interestingly, the current CHRO and COO were previously heads of technology and operations, and they believed they collaborated well; the problem lay with the new incumbents.

At the start of the project, new players entered the scene, and suddenly I found myself working with eight people instead of the two L&D Managers I initially expected. The team now included the heads of operations and technology, their chiefs of staff, their HR heads, and the two L&D Heads. Each person had a different understanding of the situation and varied ideas on how to proceed with the project. I also realized that they had personal agendas that were not explicitly stated. However, one thing united them: high levels of anxiety. They were all aware that the project had top management visibility and needed to show success. They had also invested in an external consultant and were uncertain if he could ensure the project's success.

I could foresee the pressure, stress, and anxiety affecting the system, potentially causing a lack of collaboration between the sub-systems. Therefore, the first step, even before diagnosis, was to reduce anxiety levels and help people see the silver lining. This involved immersing them in an appreciative process, allowing the system to recognize that collaboration, which they believed was lacking, had been experienced before and was desired more frequently. Just as we crave sweets because we have tasted sweetness before and want more, the craving for collaboration stems from its presence, not its absence. I needed to believe this myself, and if I could get the group to embrace this thought, the project would be successful.

One of the first OD interventions I conducted was an education session for the internal team of eight on Appreciative Inquiry. The two L&D Managers had some exposure to Appreciative Inquiry whereas the others were new to the paradigm. This brief teaching session helped the internal team to gain a new perspective and vision for the project. They started seeing this as an opportunity to be harnessed rather than a problem to be solved. Emotions of anticipation, hope and a bit of excitement helped to reduce the levels of stress and anxiety.

In addition to the above, I approached the internal team as a client system and decided to regard my work with them as a Process consultant (Schein, 1999). Schein defined three types of consulting roles in his path breaking book, Process Consultation. They can also be seen as three levels of consulting. The first level being a Pair-of hands consultant: where the client scopes the problem and the solution, and the consultant's skills are used to solve it. The next level is that of an Expert Consultant where the consultant's currency is their expertise, and where the problem is defined and the solution offered by the consultant. At the next level is a Process Consultant who works in collaboration with the client and plays the role of a helper while the client owns both the problem and the solutions. By adopting the role of a process consultant with the internal team, our relationship changed. Their dependency on me as an expert reduced and they took on the role of process consulting with their internal client system.

The rest of the story will be how drenching in Appreciative Inquiry and in the process consulting role, we built the collaboration between the internal team and me. This in turn impacted the opportunity identified in the project i.e. strengthening the collaboration between the operations and technology departments. This story will be told from my perspective as an external consultant as well as from the perspectives of the internal team. We approach this from diverse perspectives which adds to the richness of how this collaboration worked.

The Story of the Use of Us: Srividya, Internal Consultant 1

It was the start of a new week, and a sense of anticipation hung in the air. I had been summoned to a meeting unlike any other in my three years with the organization. Leaders from the two largest functions, rarely seen together were in the room. My usual partner-in-crime, a fellow internal OD consultant, was by my side, providing a sense of camaraderie and shared purpose.

What unfolded over the next thirty minutes was both exhilarating and daunting. The leaders had reached out to us, the internal OD team, to address a pressing business challenge: post-pandemic, collaboration and empathy between the two functions had faltered, affecting business outcomes. The stakes were high. This was a first-of-its-kind project, with visibility at the CXO level and a real opportunity to shift business metrics. For the first time, our OD expertise would be tested in a live, high-impact setting.

Yet, the butterflies in my stomach were real. We had never attempted an intervention on this scale. The success of our efforts would depend not only on our own skills, but also on our ability to collaborate with a seasoned external OD consultant, someone whose credibility and approach would need to resonate with our leaders. Would the business leaders remain committed amid their daily pressures? Did we, as a collective, have the patience and resilience for a true OD journey?

With a leap of faith, we trusted the process and took our first steps.

Our initial conversations between myself, my peer, and the external consultant set the tone for the project. Together, we crafted a blueprint: clarifying roles, establishing governance, and defining clear channels of communication. This was not just about project management; it was about creating a partnership where our internal knowledge of the organization's culture and the external consultant's fresh perspective could blend seamlessly.

We decided to phase the project, aligning with the classic OD Action Learning model:

1. Diagnosis and Playback.
2. Co-creation and Solution Design.
3. Implementation & Sustaining Change.

As the time approached to share our diagnostic insights, one function leader requested a private preview. My initial reaction was concern. Would this compromise the authenticity of our findings? Here, the external consultant's experience was invaluable. He reassured us that such requests are common and can actually foster greater leader engagement. Trusting his guidance, we held individual debriefs. To my surprise, the leaders were open, self-aware, and ready to act.

This moment underscored the value of our partnership: the internal consultants brought sensitivity to organizational dynamics, while the external consultant provided perspective and reassurance grounded in experience.

The next phase was nothing short of transformative. Over two days, we convened 50+ leaders from both functions for a co-creation workshop, the first such gathering since the pandemic. The energy was palpable: new connections were made, challenges were debated, and, most importantly, four pillars of focus were identified.

Here, the external consultant played a pivotal role in facilitating dialogue and ensuring that every voice was heard. The internal consultants, meanwhile, ensured that the process resonated with the organization's unique culture and history. Together, we fostered a sense of joint ownership and accountability for the solutions.

One working group, focused on People and Culture, initially included only senior leaders and HR. In hindsight, we realized that broader inclusion of a larger leadership cohort could have driven deeper ownership,a lesson in the importance of distributed leadership in culture change.

Post-workshop, the initial momentum waned. Despite our best efforts to sustain engagement through virtual meetings and structured blueprints, the core groups struggled to prioritize the project amid business pressures and the resurgence of the pandemic. As internal consultants, we felt disappointment and frustration.

Yet, our partnership with the external consultant provided a crucial anchor. Together, we stayed connected, reflected on possible re-entry points, and remained attuned to the organization's pulse. This period of waiting was a lesson in humility and patience, a reminder that organizational change is not linear, and that timing is everything.

When the business cycle allowed us to reconnect with leaders, we discovered something remarkable. Despite the apparent pause, collaboration and empathy between the two functions had improved, yielding tangible business results. The intervention, it turned out, had begun the moment we entered the system. The conversations, coaching, and connections initiated during diagnosis had already started to shift mindsets and behaviours.

This was my "aha!" moment: Appreciative Inquiry and OD interventions create ripples that extend far beyond formal meetings and workshops. The partnership between internal and external consultants is not just about executing a plan-it's about holding space for possibility, nurturing relationships, and trusting in the power of dialogue.

The Story of the Use of Us: Nidhi, Internal Consultant 2

Nidhi shares her experience using fairy tale as a metaphor. She describes the story of a horticultural garden called Orivia.

Orivia is a garden known for its order and smooth running. Two important groups kept the garden alive and well: the Gardeners and the Carriers. The Gardeners grew the crops that fed the people, while the Carriers transported those crops to the villages and towns. For many years, these two groups worked side by side in harmony. The Gardeners would harvest, and the Carriers would deliver – everything flowed smoothly. The Gardeners were headed by Horty, a respected, friendly and feeling person and the Carriers were led by Techy, a highly erudite and thinking type person.

One day Horty noticed delays in the deliveries. The wagons would wait long hours before loading, and sometimes harvests rotted before they reached the people. She felt worried and decided to speak with Techy.

Horty shared what the Gardeners were experiencing and Techy replied: "We try to reach you to plan deliveries, but sometimes you don't answer. You say the harvest will be ready at a certain time, but it isn't. Our wagons stand still, and the people waiting get impatient."

Horty replied, "We want to help and do our part, but the fields have been unpredictable. Some tools are broken, and the weather keeps changing. Our leaders change often, and sometimes it feels like no one notices the hard work we do until there's a problem."

Horty and Techy called a meeting with people from both groups, along with advisors. Everyone came – some hopeful, some tired, some defensive. Everyone spoke and shared stories of frustrations and small victories. While both groups cared deeply for their work, they didn't bother that much for the other. After many hours, everyone promised they would care for Orivia's success and not for gardeners and carriers.

Something didn't sit well with Horty. She went to Techy after the meeting and told him that. Techy agreed and said "I don't sense it either". Soon, their gut feel came true. Everyday pressures, urgent problems and progress slowed. There were some small improvements, they largely went unnoticed.

Horty and Techy were sad at the turn of events. Horty cried and said "what to do now?". Techy remembered that he knew someone from another place called Oddy who is wise in these matters. They decide to invite him to their garden.

Oddy heard Horty and Techy and asked "do you both work well together?". "Yes, we do" both of them together. Oddy continued "do the gardeners and carriers see that? experience that?". There was some moments of silence and Horty said haltingly "I... I don't think so".

The penny dropped for both of them. Unless people see that we care for each other and for other's work, how do we expect others to do so? Oddy knew what they were thinking and added "People mirror you both, whether you like it or not".

Horty and Techy started walking in the garden together, talking to individual gardeners and carriers, finding out how things are going, appreciating success, and giving directions and so on. They heard their concerns, reminded them about caring for Orivia.

Days went by and the gardens looked more inviting. Gardeners sang songs when they harvested and Carriers engaged in chorus to take the fresh flowers and fruits to the market. However, one false step by either of the groups meant small fights and return to blame games.

Horty called Oddy again for advice. This time Techy was not available. Oddy asked Horty "Do you believe that Techy and his Carriers can really improve?". Horty blurted "Of course…". And added "you know something, I have never believed that".

Oddy went to meet Techy and asked him the same question. He replied "I know Horty doesn't really believe in us. Gardeners think they are superior and everything happens because of them. We are just labourers".

Oddy called a meeting of both of them and said "this is the elephant in the room. We don't believe in the other". Horty and Techy nodded. Oddy said to them "When we believe in the other person, the other person starts to imbibe that belief and voila, they perform beyond our expectations". Techy replied "I have heard this before, they call it Pygmalion effect, right?". "Bingo" Said Oddy "you knew this and never practiced it".

A remarkable change came over both Horty and Techy. They started spending more time with each other's functions. Horty was busy loading and unloading with the Carriers and Techy could be seen removing weeds from the garden. They realized that not only they believed in each other, they believed in Orivia!

One day after a bumper harvest, all the produce reached markets on time and there was a big celebration in Orivia. A bigger meeting was called, with more people involved. This time Oddy, Horty and Techy together facilitated the meeting. The groups were huddled for a long time and at the end one gardener and one carrier stood up holding hands and asked everyone to take a pledge. There was a roar among the people as they took this pledge:

"We, Gardeners and Carriers decide that from today we will learn each other's work, work for other's success and celebrate success through gardener songs and carrier chorus". Following this there were another full hour of singing and chorus.

Some eons later, Horty, Techy and Oddy met and decided to tell their story to all other gardens to be like Orivia. Our story is simple they said in a sing song chorus way "Our story is about mirroring, believing and celebrating".

Oddy added "It is not just once. We need to be drenched in these three processes all the time…when we do that miraculous transformations happen".

Orivia had another miracle that didn't go unnoticed. Gardeners no longer called themselves as such and neither did the Carriers. They now called themselves "the Orivians".

Orivians learned another important truth: transformation happens not when people are told what to do, but when they are truly listened to, seen, and invited to build something better together.

Insights and Conclusions

As the reader, one could see the diversity that we are as people and how we see situations so differently and express them in very diverse manner. However, one can also see how we drenched in collaboration and mirrored to the client the values of appreciation, trust and teamwork.

Srividya speaks about appreciating herself to pull off this complex assignment, appreciating her "partners in crime" as she calls Nidhi and me, the external consultant. This is how the drench began, starting with appreciating self and others. In the fairy tale metaphor, the relationship between the two protagonists began with transaction, and trust developed later as they started to believe in each other. Trust begins with appreciation and transforms relationships.

Trust is another important value that we drenched ourselves in. Srividya says " To my surprise, the leaders were open, self-aware, and ready to act. This moment underscored the value of our partnership". In the fairy tale, Oddy said to Horty and Techy "When we believe in the other person, the other person starts to imbibe that belief and voila, they perform beyond our expectations". Trust is an act and is based on how much we value, appreciate and believe in the other person. Trust requires us to drench deep into our beliefs about people whom we claim to have relationships with.

Lastly, teamwork between the consultants and their belief in the ability of the clients to work together in the same way has an immense impact on the transformation process. Like in the fairy tale, it says "Orivia had another miracle that didn't go unnoticed. Gardeners no longer called themselves as such and neither did the Carriers. They now called themselves "the Orivians". Real transformation could happen in our project only when the two groups were able to transcend their identities as departments and experience the emergent reality that they were one system.

Post Script

Many a times I have been stumped by the question that many clients ask "Have you worked for similar businesses or similar issues for other organizations?". I'm not very sure whether my prior experience works in their favour or otherwise. In this project, my prior experience was a barrier to how much I believed this client can transform the ways of collaboration. I had to unlearn a lot and I am thankful to the two internal consultants who gave me the new experience of collaboration to drench myself in.

I hope clients ask me these questions instead. a) "Do you practice what you are going to help us transform into?" and b) "Do you believe that we have it in ourselves to transform?". When I take up an assignment, I have to really explore deeply within myself to answer these questions authentically. If my answers to either of these questions is "no", I know I will fail the client. I have to feel "Us" with the client system for me to be effective as a consultant. I doesn't mean I own their problems, or offer them solutions. It means I care for them, I empathize with them and I have a relationship with them. In my paradigm, relationship with the client is what leads to transformation whether in a coaching or in an OD assignment. It transcends issues and the task.

Similarly, I need to examine how I will work with my internal consultant partner/s. In a recent experience, I decided not to take up a project because the CHRO I was dealing with didn't inspire trust that we would work collaboratively.

I need drench myself into "Use of Self" when I facilitate a client to transform and I need to similarly drench into "Use of 'Us'" when I work with client's team. These are pre-requisites in our work.

Note

1   This chapter is written by the first author in collaboration with Srividya Natarajan and Nidhi Malhotra.

References

Cheung-Judge, M. Y., Jameison, D. (2020) *Global Use of Self Research Report*. Retrieved on July 1, 2025, from www.proquest.com/openview/1574cc89ea864 33581729dfb667a9adf/1?pq-origsite=gscholar&cbl=36482

Kenton, B., Moody, D. (2003). *Role of Internal Consultant*. Roffey Park Institute. (www.roffeypark.com)

NTL Institute of Applied Behavioral Science. *Change Begins with You*. www.ntl.org

Rosenthal, R., Jacobson, L. (1968). Pygmalion in the classroom. *The Urban Review*. 3, 1. 16–20.

Schein, Edgar H. (1999). *Process Consultation Revisited*. Cambridge: Addison Wesley

Zentis, N. (2018). *Consulting on the Inside, Role of Internal Consultant*. Institute of OD. (www.instituteod.com)

Chapter 8

Pause within

Co-creating the Research Vision

Lalitha Iyer

Key Points

- Entry into a large system.
- Experience of reiterative work.
- Drenching in AI process.
- The story of the AI summit.
- Reflections.

"Human freedom involves our capacity to pause between the stimulus and response and, in that pause, to choose the one response toward which we wish to throw our weight. The capacity to create ourselves, based upon this freedom, is inseparable from consciousness or self-awareness".

Rollo May

The story is a part of an initiative to transform higher education in a state in South India. Appreciative conversations helped set the stage for projects and initiatives in the different universities in the State. As the processes flowed into universities, the appreciative approach opened up dialogue and unleashed the power to collaborate for enhancing research. This experience is captured here and it describes in detail the use of the AI approach in one specific University. An AI summit set in this large institution helped bring together academics across science disciplines to foster joint research and hence build a culture of collaboration between Students, Academia and Administration.

Institutional cultures are socially constructed and they reflect what people value, how they define their environment, and how they construct that environment in terms of what it could become. Institutional culture is expressed through intangibles that bind the community together such as the physical environment, shared symbols, artefacts, organizational stories, role models, practices, rituals and ceremonies. It is a challenge to convey and foster these

DOI: 10.4324/9781003538059-10

"binding forces". Schein (1985) states that the role of leadership is to be that binding force. He stated "the only thing of real importance that leaders do, is to create and manage culture". This is especially important for quasi government institutions like Universities in India where there is a very pervasive worldview that is based on scarcity and competition for resources which createsa culture of limitations, control and bureaucracy. Hence a collaborative culture can be achieved only when this socially constructed reality is changed. This paper is titled "Pause Within" to indicate the process of ending the current social construction of reality to embrace a new way of being and doing. This was achieved through the Ai Summit.

"Pause within" as a concept refers to the cessation or ending of something internally, whether it's a feeling, a thought, a process, or even a state of being. It implies a stopping or discontinuing from within oneself or in a group or community. Pause within is an active drenching process with a conscious effort of letting go rather than just a passive fading away. This process helps in freeing the system from the pervasive world views that bind the system to create and foster new ones.

Context

It was a season of churn in the higher education system in this state in South India. The political leadership was upgrading the quality of higher education by inviting nationally renowned institutions and universities (both privately-owned and government run) to open their portals in the state. Simultaneously there was pressure on the older universities to step up to meet student expectations and match the performance of the newcomers.

I was invited to facilitate a dialogue among the Vice Chancellors (VCs or university heads), the administration (since most universities were government owned and run) and academics. The external consultants shared their broad overview of the strategic pathways for transforming higher education. The objective of this workshop with educationists (like Vice Chancellors) and administrators (like the senior bureaucrats) and political leaders was to build a broad agreement around the strategy and develop ideas to prioritize and to trigger action on the ground.

The facilitation team (of which I was a part) relied very much on Appreciative Inquiry methods (like appreciative interviewing) to tease out ideas that could be tried. The venerable professors (mostly men) were at first surprised and soon relaxed to enjoy their interactions. The conversations were direct and honest and some new avenues of collaboration were thrown open. The workshop led to the leaders of universities in the state picking up projects they would like to do around the new strategy.

The projects were about improving academic quality, infrastructure, affirmative action for inclusion of students from marginalized communities, improving employability, social awareness, gender balance in recruitment and promotions and so on. The details differed across institutions, given the specific issues in each one.

Pathbreakers

The Administration found an interesting way to support the VCs to start off the new initiatives. A batch of interns were enrolled and one or two of them assigned to each university VC to function as project managers. They would work closely within the university to start off one or more projects as pathbreakers.

This young group was a great contrast to the group of academicians. Many came with impressive international exposure and backgrounds in education policy research. They were keen to demonstrate what they could accomplish in a brief internship of around 6 months. Working with this batch as part of their orientation, I used the appreciative approach and indicated how they could take it into their work

As a complete outsider to the academic world, I thus relied purely on collaborative approaches based on Appreciative Inquiry in both parts of my engagement. In my mind, my assignment was complete with the orientation for this batch, and I had no expectations of doing more work with the system.

Invitation

I was therefore quite surprised when, a few months later, one of the interns from the Government department called me to check if I could facilitate a dialogue within the university she was assigned to work with. The Vice chancellor was keen to bring together the thought leaders and research-oriented Professors across disciplines to identify how they improve research quality. He felt that the AI approach could work better to open up conversations.

It seemed a big ask given the dynamics of the situation. Though there were many ifs and buts about the dates, I could not say no to this opportunity to see how the ideas floated on a lofty plane could be "earthed" in the rough and tumble of a large staid university. I was also persuaded by the idealistic and enthusiastic young intern and could not bring myself to say no to her. When I look back today, I am still amazed that it all happened and that there was a "happy ending" to it.

The University

The University was established in 1954, and the campus is spread over 1000 Acres. It had 5 constituent colleges, accommodating 54 departments and offering 72 programmes. The administrative system was (is) complex. The authorities were often caught between several pressures, responding to expectations from the State Government (administrative) and the State

Council of Higher Education (academic) besides national bodies like the University Grants Commission (quality). Internally there were many academic departments. The priority was the academic calendar with the syllabi to be updated, classes conducted, and learning assessed. The university was home to many reputed academicians of international standing. Yet their brilliance was often pushed into the background. Many of them were keen to further their research interests and foster a culture of innovation and creativity. In the bustle of university routines this desire was often relegated to the back burner. The Vice Chancellor was himself an internationally acclaimed scholar. He nourished dreams of housing cutting edge research in the university and one of the projects he proposed was around the theme of improving Research in the university. He knew that there were colleagues who shared his passion and set about planning on using the opportunity.

Drench

The Vice Chancellor and the intern were alive to the challenges within their system. They were aware of the prevailing culture. It was one of upholding the system over the individual, expecting the student and the teacher to fit themselves into the prevailing hierarchies. A class system prevailed and ranking and grading were core elements to select, assess and reward both teachers and students. This went so far that there was a classification of disciplines as more important and less important. The pressure was to demonstrate the importance of the subject through the metric of employability and the top placement pay package.

Yet they were determined to make a gentle shift. They were hopeful that the moment was opportune for pushing the boundary. They could recollect AI based conversations they had been part of and the flow which it generated. These were experiences which gave them a glimmer of hope. I see this as an example of a process of drench. It took the system a while to trust this approach and take it into the very heart of the university. When the intern got in touch with me, they had decided that they needed a dose of what I had offered!

The time gap gave me a drench experience as well. In my work over the year, I had worked closely with the system at different levels. I had been part of various conversations and facilitated two events using an appreciative lens. I had directly experienced the culture of the entire edifice, and I could identify some strong elements.

A Metaphor for the System

Just as the system took in what I had shown as a possibility, I developed a deeper empathy for the system as well. It seemed to resemble a medieval fortress with several layers of defence. The high outer wall with strong ramparts seemed to be the government administration, which owned the system and funded its growth and expansion. It was the custodian of the physical assets and held a mandate for inclusion, innovation and talent creation. The next wall was the equally powerful Higher Education Society, comprising academic administrators with the mandate to continuously upgrade the content and quality of education in this system. They held the responsibility for knowledge management. Within this fortress with two external walls were the universities – 16 of them each within their own smaller compound walls. They were immediately concerned with assessing what the teacher is teaching, and the student is learning. They certified to the outer world the accomplishment of the student with the degree, marksheet and rank. Within the university were the colleges themselves, offering learning opportunities to students. The students were captives in the classrooms and laboratories in the ivory tower of the college. They were eager to fly out into the "real" world through campus placements, or to the next admission into another more prestigious ivory tower.

The guardians of each level of fortification were often clueless about the whole picture. They were programmed to strictly guard their turf. Those on the external ramparts were clear about the standards they should uphold and the property they should safeguard. Similarly, the inner walls gave individual students entry or denied it based on their assessment of merit or social category. The guardians knew the "rules" and did their best to uphold them. Any exception was a nuisance, to be kept out.

As this imagery grew on me, it seemed to come straight out of a Saga like The Lord of the Rings with the Students being the ones holding the one ring to bind them all!!! I could well imagine how being part of a system without a clue of the whole picture could make a person defensive and anxious. I dreamed of the new culture in the university and that brought in a new metaphor of an open field in the place of the fortress. The field was open to new possibilities, a field of experimentation, low levels of control and no ivory towers.

As I reflected more deeply, I realized that the OCTAPACE model for organizational ethos (Pareek and Purohit, 2010) could be the path towards creating that open field culture. The name OCTAPACE is an acronym that stands for the values of Openness, Confrontation, Trust, Authenticity, Pro-action, Autonomy, Collaboration and Experimentation. When an institution like the University can begin to live these values, the shift in the culture towards the Open field will begin.

Any effort to move in these directions will mean a shift towards a more vibrant academic community. It was my wish and dream to take this shift into the teaching institutions. I also realized that in order to bring that shift, the system needs to pause within and stay with the dream culture and the OCTAPCE values before the institutionalization of the change is possible. It is similar to how the shift in the metaphor from the fortress to the field happened within me after my "pause within". This pause within enabled me to absorb, assimilate and develop clarity in my own self about the system I was engaging with.

Clarifying the Purpose

Once I was called in by the university, I had several conversations to understand expectations and clarify what to expect. The Dean (R&D), a gentle soft-spoken physicist, heading a specialized research lab, was coordinating the arrangements for the workshop. He seemed worried about the disappointment I may suffer and the potential damage that it may cause with the bureaucracy and administration. He relaxed, with some reassurance from me and the intern. Based on the discussions, we agreed upon the formal objectives. We shared them with the Vice Chancellor who was open to the proposed objectives and the methodology. He was at that time looking for ways to bring people together in an institution where knowledge, resources and even students were viewed in silos. The theme proposed was to build a "vibrant R&D culture" in the university. The appreciative approach was accepted, because some of the senior academicians had seen it in practice earlier. The overarching theme emerged from this discussion –"Towards Vibrant R&D Culture".

We agreed that our intervention will have the following objectives:

- Discover core strengths through sharing achievements and the "inside stories" behind ostensible impediments.
- Identify the life-giving forces and process values required to nurture ideas for innovation and track impact of such change.
- Envision together the desired transformation in the research culture to enable this university to emerge as one of the top 10 universities for research in India.
- Prioritize Entry Point Projects and create a roadmap for holistic resolution of existing issues and ensuring sustainability of the solutions.

Once the idea was agreed upon, the outcomes expected were that the group will

- Gain a better understanding of the strengths of the University.
- Imagine the contours of what research leadership will look like.
- Develop a road map to move towards this dream.
- Identify Entry Point Projects to initiate actions and introduce functional practices to set this change in motion.

There were around 60 participants and they were Research Leaders, Researchers and Research Administrators. With the enthusiastic support of the intern and two or three research students, all arrangements were completed in time.

Plan for the Workshop

I worked with the Intern and consulted the Dean and finalized the plan for the workshop, including the schedule and flow. This is given in Table 8.1. We knew amongst us that the design is eminently changeable though the start and end times are fixed.

The workshop began informally. Participants were invited to move around, greeting friends and getting to know strangers. The norms for participation in the workshop were introduced and the approach of Appreciative Inquiry and the principles were presented briefly. An attempt was made to stay with what is working, and this helped the participants very much.

The next step was to relive moments of success, and the appreciative interview was used for this activity. Participants were invited to choose a partner who was a relative stranger and share a recent experience of contributing effectively to research and questions were provided to help the process. The interview guide used is given in Table 8.2.

Participants worked in pairs and listened to each other using the above Appreciative Interviewing format.

As they shared recent positive experiences, they could identify the commitment of their colleagues to ensure high quality research despite the constraints of time, money and other resources. For example, research scholars shared instances where their Ph.D. guides and other professors helped them untangle the red tape around fellowships and research funding. Professors and academics shared their stories of support from the registrar team. The administrative office team spoke about their efforts to guide scholars and professors to fulfil the requirements and formalities. These examples of collaboration

Table 8.1 Window pane for the AI summit

	10.00-11.30	12.-1.30	2.30 – 4.00	4.30-6.00
Day I	Discovery		Diagnosis and Drench	
	Research leadership		The Research Triangle	
	Introductions		Role mirroring	Questions for
	Appreciative interviews and		using TO	reflection
	summary		techniques	
Day II	Dream		Design	
	Choosing Priorities			
	Mind mapping and converging		Action	Valediction
	and identifying priorities		planning –	
			individual and	
			theme wise	

Table 8.2 Appreciative interview guide

Appreciative Interview Guide
Exploration about "My demonstrated Research Leadership"
Take about 15 minutes for each person
Share the story of an experience where you were able to effectively contribute to the
success of a research project. Share the details with your partners.
When did it happen? Where did it happen? Who were impacted? Why are these
high-points or peak experiences significant for you?
What did you value most about your own contribution?
What stimulated you and brought alive these qualities in you?
To conclude express to each other how you feel after the sharing
and the listening.
Make sure you encourage each other to talk by asking the indicated questions.
Listen carefully with an open mind, without cutting in even when you disagree.

Table 8.3 Themes for group discussions

Themes for group discussions
What they learnt from the appreciative interviewing on ideal researchers
What they learnt from the appreciative interviewing on ideal research guides
What they learnt from the appreciative interviewing on ideal research
  administrators
What three qualities do you wish for to become an ideal research leader?
What are the most important values you see research leaders upholding?
What stimulates and energizes research leadership qualities?

were sufficient to demonstrate that collaboration is possible, and it set the positive tone.

Exploring the Best of "What Is"

To gather insights from the stories shared about Research Leadership, participants were asked to form 6 groups (with the earlier pairs breaking up to join different groups) and discuss the experiences shared. Care was taken to go beyond the logical-rational frame and the hierarchy of teacher-student during the workshop. Visual depictions, physical movement, informal seating, acting and cross functional non-hierarchical group formations were deliberately used to break entrenched barriers and go beyond verbal expressions. The guidelines for the discussions are given in Table 8.3.

The groups summarized the points that came up on charts which were then displayed. We could see the poetic principle at work – members began drawing images on the graffiti space and their charts. (see Figure 8.1).

They recognized their shared interest in advancing knowledge and it's sharing as a life-giving force. The core values they seemed to be in touch with were integrity, collaboration and new knowledge creation.

Metaphors!
Toward Ph D- at a snail's pace!
Blocks- Knowledge, Background,
Values
(as depicted by a research scholar)

Metaphors!
Researcher – like a bull running blindly
round the ring - guides show the exit

Figure 8.1 Metaphors.

Metaphors!
The lotus of knowledge from the brackish water of ignorance

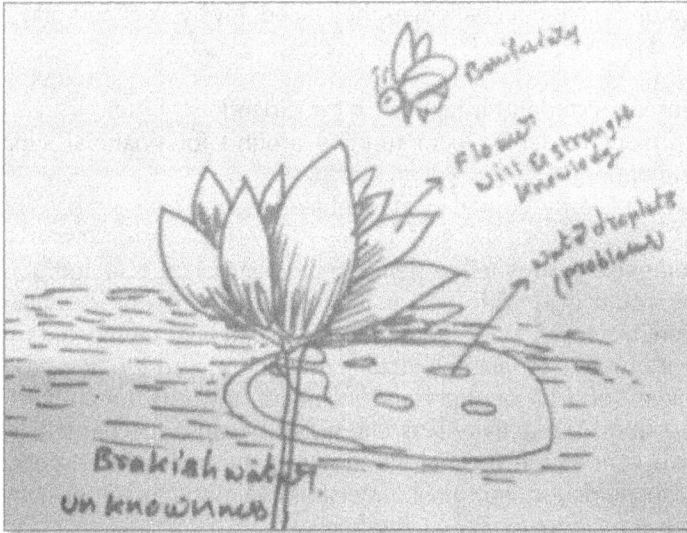

Figure 8.1 (Continued)

Drenching: "The Research Triangle"

The process of discovery continued and the group was ready to dive deeper. Their conversations during the phase of generating themes from their stories and drawing the pictures metaphorically depicting their present state led them to a deeper exploration. During conversations, it was clear that there were several images about the "other" that were floating in the room. It was not possible for the group to truly appreciate the other sides to the R&D story. To go beyond this barrier, a mirroring activity was used to explore the "research triangle" that exists in the system. The "research triangle" is meta-phorically experienced as the victim-oppressor-rescuer framework. Typically the Researchers saw themselves as victims, with the Administrators being Oppressors and the Research Guides needing to take up the role of rescuing the Researchers from the Administrator's oppression. However these roles kept shifting when administrators were confronted with campus unrest or student protests and the guides were themselves victims of red tape or apathy, forced to work with students they were not happy with. This was the discovery that emerged from the mirroring activity.

The group was again subdivided into three equal segments and each segment was requested to assume one of the roles – researcher – research guide-administrators. The feelings generated in working together were discussed in each group. The animated sharing and the relief of talking openly about issues proved cathartic.

To process the feelings generated, the subgroups were invited to present role plays of the typical challenges they faced. Lively skits and plays brought out every day tussles.

- The research student struggling for his stipend.
- The project leader & team running around for financial sanction for equipment.
- The administrator bullied by student leaders.

The audience was invited to step into the play (as "spectactors") and enact how they could deal with the situation differently. Many innovative "solutions" were depicted. With the notion of spectacting, members of the audience went on stage to take the victims role and played it differently. This led to the release of a lot of anger and frustration towards the authority figures and the system. The activity was energising because the participants could safely give vent to the frustrations they face periodically. Discussions and role-playing helped in improved understanding of the three perspectives and generated some empathy for each other.

The participants, many of them senior academics with very dignified personas, engaged in this activity with enthusiasm, giving safe expression to the challenges they saw in each role. For example, when the theme depicted was the delay in a scholar's fellowship, those playing the role of guides used their links with the administration to sort out the issues. When the issue depicted was a problem with the writing /rewriting of a thesis and the guide was too busy, fellow students stepped in to help.

In enacting such possibilities, the group was able to empathize with the others and accept more deeply the need for supporting the other roles. This method took the group away from blaming individuals and towards cooperative ways to resolve issues and bottlenecks.

The groups ideated on the ideal persona of a Research Scholar, Guide and Administrator in order to break out of the Research Triangle. They also explored what they called "soft factors" that will be enablers for building a new culture of Research in the University. The ideas presented were summarized in Tables 8.4 and 8.5.

A mood-check to wrap up the day indicated that the Drench into that Research Triangle and working through the ideal roles and factors helped people to see hope for transforming the culture and develop a new social construction of reality. The participants were relaxed and thoughtful, though

Table 8.4 The ideal persona

Research Scholar	Research Guide	Research Administrator
Has basic knowledge Chooses topic that has use and social relevance	Prepares students and equips them Personally involves in research Expertise and exposure	Offers awards and encouragement Is well informed about trends in research

Table 8.5 The ideal factors

Stimuli and energizers	Values	Leadership
Efficient automated routine. Academic Freedom Gap funding for ongoing work Improved travel support	Shared knowledge within res earch community without "Pride or Prejudice" Committed to truth and social concern	Regular monitoring & reviews Open minded, encouraging new ideas Concern for current and future relevance Not egoistic

there were a few sceptics. However, they uniformly saw the value of the dialogue that helped them to see each other as people and not merely see each other as instruments for a task.

Drench Again

When the first day ended the group was able to reach a level of openness and trust where people freely shared their stories and discovered similarities and strengths. The churn was visible when they returned the next day. Overnight, they were able to drench themselves into the situation, identifying how they were building or eroding the culture of constructive collaboration for research. There was an opportunity to absorb the feelings around collaboration and move beyond anger and frustration. This overnight drench in the current reality and the feelings generated became the base for building ideas for the future and contributed to a cheerful, brisk mood for day 2.

Dream

After an initial check-in, the group quickly moved to building a dream for Research in the University. We asked them the following question to reflect:

Imagine that you are in this university in 2020 and that you have FULLY attained these ideal qualities. What changes are most visible in this university in 2020? What has changed between 2020 and 2016?

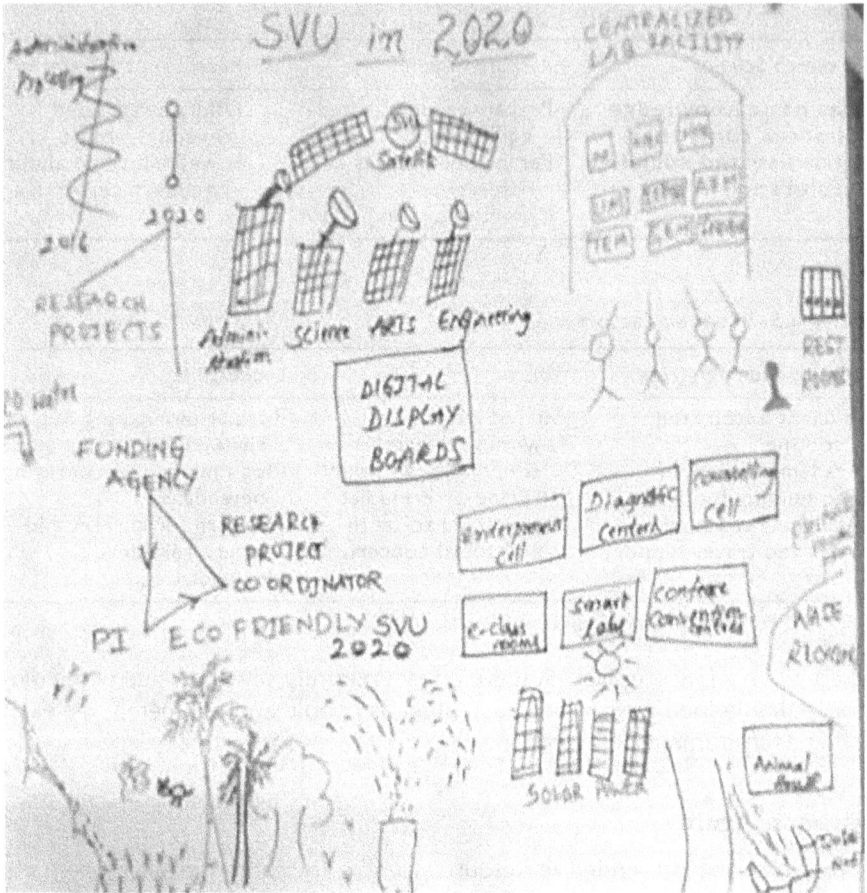

Figure 8.2 A vision of technology – smart university in five years.

The participants worked in new groups to depict their dreams as pictures. Again, the visual presentation took the academics away from their intellectual selves for a while and they gave their imagination wings (see Figure 8.2).

Some themes which recurred in the images were:

- Improved ranking in India based on R & D.
- IT enabled and tech savvy campus.
- Research scholars enjoy freedom, efficient lab facilities, funding, and industry collaboration.
- Improved physical facilities in campus.
- National and international collaborations.
- Green and sustainability initiatives.

Based on this activity members were invited to contribute ideas, phrases and words to develop the mission statement for the new University organization of 2020. This process was quite intense and helped the group to really drench in their dream and reconstruct their mental model of reality. The mission statement that came up after the 90-minute discussion was as follows.

The University R &D Mission is to build teaching expertise and research culture for innovative and effective research with transparent, friendly, and accountable processes and be in the top ten universities in India by 2020.

Designing the Future

To identify priorities, the participants were asked to imagine that they had a magic wand and note down the one (most important) thing they will change to realize the mission for research.

They were then invited to move around and find five six others who have similar chits and share ideas around the theme. This was an adaptation of mind mapping to fit into the Ai flow.

The broad themes that came up were as follows:

Digital Upgrade: Improved IT infrastructure and usage was much emphasized. Urgent steps include establishing servers of the university, issuing ID cards, installing CCTVs, smart labs, rooms, online lessons, assignments & assessments, e-library, e-notice boards and e-governance.

Infrastructure Development: The University needs the funds to improve student facilities like toilets, waiting halls, counselling cell for research students, learning facilities like labs, steady reliable power supply, solar power, drinking water (RO) and student stipends.

Advanced Research Facility: This facility should be headed by the Dean (R&D) and take care of research Projects and Doctoral Research with adequate staffing (five to ten teachers and equal number of support staff). It will work on four broad aspects:

Academic relations: Visits to acclaimed research facilities, studying their best practices and adapting them, establishing collaborations and MOUs, student and faculty exchanges.

Industry /user relations: Collaborative research, innovation and incubation centres, guidance on patent filing and IPR.

Support for researchers: good quality space and facilities, power supply, solar backup, well maintained instruments and labs, pre-publication and editing support, encouragement to register for and complete doctoral work.

Improved research quality: Well aligned direction policies and rules, ethics, protocols and supervision for animal/human trials in labs, interdisciplinary work, grant Ph.D. in few broad areas and stipend support to students.

Work culture: Commitment to hard work, Motivation and positive attitude, Collaborative culture. Disciplined personal conduct and Yoga for Physical and emotional wellbeing.

Towards Delivery

Based on the clusters which were emerging (see above), the group identified five broad themes to create a radar chart and indicate how the group rates the status and the gap between ideal and status. The rating was completed through a show of hands and a weighted average calculated for the five aspects that were seen to be most important. As academics and researchers, they were able to quickly adopt this rough and ready rating approach! The ratings highlighted the need for mindset change and more openness above all else and the need for greater collaboration between the three groups viz. Researchers, Guides and Administrators were seen as important areas for work.

Based on the discussion they prepared presentations to be made to the Vice Chancellor.

Action Planning

After the lunch break participants completed their personal action plans and programme feedback. Volunteers were invited for the proposed advisory group and many signed up. Many specific actions were identified by the group and the ideas that emerged were practical. Priorities identified were

1. Setting up of core group to take the mission forward.
2. Sharing the mission widely within the campus.
3. Participatory approach to address the behavioural aspects identified.
4. Working with volunteers to improve many aspects in each department.
5. Practicing open-mindedness and collaboration in each setting they are part of.
6. Plan for improving IT and Physical facilities.
7. Project management support for this initiative.
8. Collaborations among departments.
9. Involving students and encouragement for student efforts.

Valediction

The Vice Chancellor, Rector and Deans (Development, Foreign Relations and Alumni) joined the group by 4.30 pm and shared their perspectives on the importance of improving the R & D culture in the university. Participants described their deliberations over the two days. The leadership then studied the chart work by participants and had informal discussions on the emerging ideas for the future. The programme concluded on a positive note.

Some Reflections on Appreciative Inquiry Practice

This opportunity to revisit this experience allows me to see my practice more dispassionately. I notice that in the methodology I have experimented with tools and methods which are not "classic Ai".

For example, the device of mirroring is not usually adopted. With hindsight I realize that it was an effective technique to release angst about authority figures and peers and moving on towards a positive mind set. This I view as coming from my roots in T-Group practice. It also helped the group to build systematic view of how the various elements should fit in smoothly to create impact.

Another device I used was spectacting, taken from the practice of Theatre of the Oppressed (Boal, 1979). This was based on my understanding of the dynamic of a "drama triangle" at play (also called Winner's triangle (Choy, 1990)). Forward movement is blocked by the drama of control and power play in the system in which each group, while feeling powerless internally, postures as powerful outside. Bringing in the spectator allowed the demonstration of a shift in the power dynamic towards more empowering and assertive behaviours in the system.

Another method I used which I would not think of in an Ai workshop was the ranking for action priorities and the display of their ranking summary as Radar Chart. This was prompted by the fact that the group was from hard core science research. While they were ready to dive into the Ai experience, they would, I thought, quickly revert back to their "scientific" selves. The emotional impact of the Ai experience was evident in the way the rankings showed up. They identified that openness was the key area for improvement and message reached them in a quantified way!!! I did not have to preach or explain the need for basic listening and mutual trust. It was "proved" to them in a language they were used to.

For me as an Appreciative Inquiry practitioner, the "Drench" opportunity I had to experience the entire landscape of the Higher education system was crucial in enabling me to work with relational empathy towards this system. Relational empathy to quote Maureen O'Hara (1997) is "a more multi-levelled or holistic way as a way of being in, belonging to and knowing the relational contexts in which human beings find ourselves situated." I now think that drench is as important for the facilitators as it is for the participants. In my practice of Appreciative Inquiry it has helped me when I slow down and observe the system I am working with, its quirks and its contours.

I see the need for the Drench experience for the participants as well. This happens when they can move out of their comfort zone and appreciate what is working well for them. The Appreciative approach incorporating the time to absorb the individual interpersonal and systemic processes they are grappling with becomes the foundation for change. The work can flow beyond the euphoria of positive affirmations when there is sufficient time and opportunity to embrace the whole system.

Longer Term Change

Today, this university is well ranked nationally and in Asia and its cross disciplinary research centre is the first to come up in the state and has been functioning for the last three years. The credit goes to a host of factors including funding and policy initiatives. Yet it is good to see that the collaborative space created then has been sustained over the years.

In a recent conversation with the then Dean (R&D) he recalled how things came together after the program. The university has seen many changes in the last few years, and the Appreciative Inquiry based workshop was very useful in his view.

Acknowledgements

Thankyou Sankar and Wasundhara for inviting me to contribute to this volume, offering feedback on my first draft and helping me see the project from an objective lens.

References

Boal, A. (1979). *Theatre of the Oppressed*. London: Pluto Press.
Choy, A. (1990). The Winner's Triangle. *Transactional Analysis Journal*. 20, 1. 40–46. doi:10.1177/036215379002000105
O'Hara, M. (1997). Relational empathy: Beyond modernist ego-centricism to post-modern holistic contextualism" in Bohart, A. C. and Greenberg, L. S. (Eds.), *Empathy Reconsidered: New Directions in Psychotherapy*. Washington, D.C.: American Psychological Association. 295–319. https://doi.org/10.1037/10226-013
Pareek, U., Purohit, S. (2010). *Training Instruments in HR and OD*, 3rd edition. Uttar Pradesh, India: Tata McGraw Hill. 564–567, 759–763.
Schein, E. (1985). *Organization Culture and Leadership*. San Francisco: Jossey-Bass.

Chapter 9

Honour the View

Key Points

1. The context of public health in the city of Mumbai and introduction to the city.
2. Social construction of new reality.
3. RCT research details.
4. Learning and insights.
5. Postscript.

Introduction

> *"You came to us like teenage dreamers with stars in your eyes.*
> *We were the old cynics with all our past baggage of bitter experiences.*
> *You came and we softened, the human face appeared*
> *behind the uniforms.*
> *Now even we dream a bit, smile a bit and it will spread.*
> *Today we honour the view you put back in our eyes"*
> *Written by the Medical Officer of a*
> *Maternity Home after an Ai workshop (Dec 2006)*

This is a story about an intervention made by the Authors in a public health system. It was designed as a comparative trial to test the efficacy of Appreciative Inquiry as a behavioural change model. The story takes place over the years 2004–2008.

The Society for Nutrition, Education and Health Action (SNEHA) is a non-governmental organization founded in 1999 by a group of doctors and social workers to create better outreach in terms of health, education and nutrition for women and children in urban slums. The core mission is to value every

DOI: 10.4324/9781003538059-11

mother and child in Mumbai. In the year 2004, SNEHA collaborated with the city corporation (the Municipal Corporation of Greater Mumbai, responsible for public health and facilities), an Indian private entity (the Social Initiatives Group of ICICI Bank, India), and an academic research group (the UCL Centre for International Health and Development, UK) to launch the ambitious City Initiative for Newborn Health (CINH).

Health Care in Mumbai

The neonatal stage (the first four weeks of life) is the most vulnerable stage for human survival. The neonatal mortality rate (NMR), defined as the death of a live born infant within 28 completed days of birth per 1000 (live and still) births. It is regarded as a very sensitive index of the health of a country. The NMR for Mumbai was estimated to be 24. These figures are worse for the poor, whether they live in urban or rural areas (National Neonatology Forum, 2004).

The Municipal Corporation of Greater Mumbai (MCGM) is the government body primarily responsible for healthcare in the city *(henceforth referred to as the public health system)*. This is provided at a greatly subsidized cost and is often completely free especially for basic health care. It is mainly used by the poor and socio-economically deprived sections of the society. It has an impressive infrastructure, with three tertiary care hospitals (providing super-specialty care with modern ICU's), 14 General Hospitals, 26 Maternity homes (providing routine maternity, antenatal and postnatal services) and 167 Health Posts (which are community outreach centres).

City Initiative for Newborn Health (CINH)

The goal of CINH was to increase the survival of new-borns by lowering the Neonatal Mortality Rate (NMR) in the urban poor. CINH was conceived as a two-pronged strategy to work with the Maternity homes which delivered the care. The first was improving the technical quality of care, which included improvement in infrastructure and systems, and creating medical and administrative protocols. The second dimension was to change the motivation, attitudes and behaviours of the caregivers. We were associated with the latter, "softer" component of helping to bring about change in attitudes and behaviours of health care providers.

The intervention held the firm belief that without the "softer" dimension being addressed, (the adaptive challenge) the more technical interventions would not be sustainable; indeed, many such previous attempts to improve the quality of service have failed because they did not focus on this dimension. Both the above approaches were undertaken from a research perspective as the project was designed to create a sustainable and replicable model for urban health. This made the intervention design more challenging. This article will focus on the experience with the 'behaviour change' aspect of the intervention, which used Appreciative Inquiry as the change method.

Social Construction of the Health Care System

The public health system in Mumbai is a reasonably efficient system, serving the millions of urban poor and sending most of them home healed or cured and in good health. This is not its image, however. It is often perceived as "unfriendly", and the staff is seen as being rude and insensitive. It is seen as a last resort, even by the poor and is plagued by news reports of its inefficiency and poor performance. It is not surprising, that even for those who work within this system it is a world where the social construction of reality is one of despondency and dissatisfaction. The stories repeatedly told are ones where things go wrong and where the system has been seen responsible for the final unhappy outcome. This has led to a defensive culture and a reluctance to be accountable or accept responsibility for anyone or anything. This belief is reinforced as these stories are repeated in the communities that the public health system serves.

The Change Model

The brief for this project was to change the perceived unfriendly behaviour and insensitive attitude of the health care providers. We considered many change models, most of which took a "problem-solving" approach. This is a paradigm that is very well understood by the health care sector. In the initial few workshops, we met with limited success. While problems were identified, they were all "out there", with the system or the client system, or someone else. The exercises always ended by holding someone else responsible for the problems as well as the desired change. This amplified the feeling of helplessness and hopelessness for change for the better. It was an energy draining exercise for the participants as well as the facilitators.

We believed (from our own experience) that despite all the stories, the system did function rather well, but the positive experiences are not the stories that did not become part of the folklore of the system. When we sought to hear these stories, we heard innumerable stories of commitment, courage and caring. We found ourselves and the participants energized and hopeful. We had found the energy for change, the life-giving forces of the system. In this context, Appreciative Inquiry seemed suited as the model for bringing about change.

Appreciative Inquiry

Appreciative Inquiry (Ai) was developed by David Cooperrider and Suresh Srivastava at Case Western Reserve University, USA, in the 1980's. (Cooperrider & Srivastva, 1987) It was primarily conceived as a method for systemic intervention and transformation. It is now used in large corporations, educational institutions, social and community organizations as a paradigm for change management.

It is a philosophy to change the way a system functions, based on appreciation of what "works" as against "what's wrong". The fundamental philosophy of Ai is to shift the focus from a *problem-oriented* approach to a *possibility oriented* one. It looks at the existing strengths of an organization or community to focus on strengths as a basis for creating a co-constructed desired future. It is also highly participatory and democratic, both of which encourage ownership and sustainability.

The first few pilot workshops with this methodology taught us a lot. The participants rediscovered the value of their work, and their pride in themselves as people practicing a noble profession. The participants were happy to take ownership of their success, and the energy levels were high. There was a shift in the perception of the reality of the workplace, the perceived lack of hope and a commitment to change. This initial experience with the groups led to using Ai as the primary driver for change.

In this project, Ai has been used in many ways. It was used as a method for organizational change, a philosophy which underlies all the initiatives undertaken, as a training method and data collection tool.

The Background Research

The team first set about understanding the issues regarding the perceived "unfriendliness" of the hospital staff. The understanding of the importance of this came from several data sources.

1. The outcome of a study conducted on the population accessing a Maternity Home. This showed that "unfriendly staff" (including rude and abusive behaviour) was one of the reasons that people did not prefer using the facilities offered at the Maternity Home. (CINH report, 2004).
2. Formative research that included interviews with all categories of health care staff across different Maternity Homes. This showed that leadership, poor communication especially by the supervisory staff and a work culture that was unappreciative and did not encourage risk taking affected the attitude and behaviour of the health care staff. (Kanbur, Kerketta, 2006). There was further work done to define the criteria which would be used to assess impact. 116 items were identified which were then tested for validity. After a factor analysis five themes were finalized for the study.

The Research Hypothesis

There was some debate on how to approach the change in behaviour. There seemed to be a need to focus on the provider-client interaction, as improving this was the objective of the intervention. However, the consultants felt that the focus needed to be internal and that unless interaction improved *amongst the staff*, it would not change with the clients. Conducting training in service orientation or inter-personal communication might have a temporary effect but would not change attitudes and long-term behaviour.

Evaluation was a strong component of the CINH project and to test the assumption stated above, a randomized trial was designed. Of all the 26 Maternity Homes, nine were randomly assigned to the intervention group, and nine to the control group.

The research hypothesis we were testing was as follows:

"Appreciative Inquiry will lead to a change in the social construction of reality among health care staff of Maternity Homes resulting in change of attitudes and behaviours. This change in how they see themselves and their role as care givers will be reflected in a change in perception of the facility by the women accessing the services".

Social construction of reality is the staff's worldview of themselves and their patients, in the context of being at service for pregnant woman accessing their services. The hypothesis pointed to the possibility that once they see their role as care givers and see the women as clients, their attitudes and behaviours towards service will change.

The Research Design

The study was designed as a case-control, before-after study:

To test the first part of the hypothesis [*Appreciative Inquiry will lead to change in the social construction of reality among the health care staff of Maternity Home]* the staff of all eighteen maternity homes was asked to fill in inventories before and three months after the Ai intervention.

Qualitative data were also collected through interviews and focus group discussions held after one year. The study in the Maternity Homes was designed to assess changes in the following attitudes and behaviours resulting from the change in the social construction of reality:

1. Respect.
2. Concern and encouragement.
3. Communication with others.
4. Attitude to work.
5. Supportive supervision.

To test the second part of the hypothesis *(this will be reflected in a change in perception of the facility by the women accessing the services)* patient exit interviews were conducted in all eighteen Maternity Homes before the intervention, and at an interval of three months and one year after the intervention. Some of the changes to be measured were:

1. Attentiveness of doctor.
2. Attentiveness of other staff.
3. Overall patient satisfaction.
4. Overall attitude of the doctor.
5. Overall attitude of other staff.

The Intervention Design

The Entry (The First Drench)

The first step was to get the buy in of the staff, which was the subject of the intervention. The initial dialogue and discussions had been held with the administrative head of the public health system. The Maternity Home staff had not been a party to the decision, and we expected that there would be some resistance to the initiative. To reduce this and to build a partnership, it was proposed that the heads of the intervention group of Maternity Homes should experience AI as a prelude to the larger process

The Medical Officers (MOs) and the Head Nurses of the nine Maternity Homes were invited for a meeting. They underwent a short version of the 4D process in two hours. The focus of the inquiry was "planned change". The result was a better understanding of when planned change in an organization succeeds. Participants from the initial pilot AI workshops were also present and shared their positive experience and the impact on the facilities. By the end of this meeting, we had the support we were seeking.

The trial of the design was explained to the heads of the Maternity Homes which were in the control group as we needed the data from this group for the trial.

The Design of the Intervention

The initial 4D cycle was designed as a summit for each Maternity Homes which would include as many of the staff of the facility as possible. A brief outline of the sessions is given in Table 9.1.

We aimed to achieve ninety percent staff in attendance at each facility. An Ai summit is a design where the Ai process is conducted in a single schedule and includes all stakeholders Since Ai is an inclusive process, all categories of staff i.e., the doctor-in-charge, nurses, housekeeping and cleaning ladies, ward attendants and peons and male helpers, laboratory technicians and counsellors comprising approximately thirty participants were all invited to participate in the summit.

The Ai Summit Experience

The Ai summits were a path breaking experience for the participants. Public institutions in India have a very high power distance between the Leadership

Table 9.1 Design of interventions

Session	Activity
Session 1: **Discovery**	Many icebreakers were used to get the group to talk to each other. Sharing stories of excellence and peak experience at the workplace and listing wishes for the hospital.
Session 2: **Drenching in Discovery**[a]	Retelling of stories in other groups and drawing the themes for what makes the experience of working in the health care sector meaningful, and for quality care.
Session 3: Dream	Dreaming of a facility that gave the best care to its patients. This was written as a newspaper report about the Maternity Home after five years. This was interspersed with games.
Session 4: **Drench in Dream**[a]	Participants were asked to do a mock-interview for a newspaper reporter on what has changed for them, the maternity home and the patients. This was a fun activity and helped the group to live the dream in an as if way.
Session 5: **Design**	Creating a rough roadmap for achieving their dreams. Here the focus was on what was possible to achieve at the facility level. This usually emphasized the need to change the behavior of the staff towards each other and towards the patients.
Follow Up (Drench)[a]	The monthly follow up meetings were held for a year in each Maternity home.

Note:
[a] We didn't call it Drench in those days and when we look back at the design, we realize that the seeds of Drench were present then, though we didn't have a language for it.

and the staff. Some of the staff had not sat down with their leaders for a discussion for the last 15 years. The experience of sitting together on the floor, at the same level as their seniors and speaking about their lives and their work was very moving, for them and for us. This simple act had a huge impact on the staff. For the cleaning staff, it was often the highlight of their service. The appreciation by the doctor who listened to their stories and their struggles was more effective than any motivational speech, or even the rest of the AI process.

After completion of the first two summits, it was obvious that the cleaning staff learnt more from communication and team building games than exercises which required them to think. The communication games were moved to the first day, to allow the group to get used to the new process.

The Interview protocol:

- Think awhile about the qualities you possess. Can you tell me what you are proud of about yourself?
- What do you like most about your work (at the hospital)?

- Tell us a story about a time when you felt very proud about something you achieved at work. What qualities of yours helped? Who all contributed to this achievement?
- What are the three wishes you have for this hospital?

The exercise was done in small groups. The start of the interviews was often awkward. The Indian culture is one of reticence, and speaking of one's qualities is seen as boastful. The tendency is to downplay one's own contributions and importance. It has taken persuasion and skill by the facilitators to allow the discovery phase to flow.

Some of the recurring themes were sincerity, understanding, risk taking, commitment and punctuality. These were quite contrary to the perceived image of the system and the people who worked there. This was the first step towards a change in opinion and perception of themselves as a group. Some of the best stories were shared in the larger group. This session was always energizing.

In the Dream phase, a personal dream was followed by a vision for the hospital in the next 5 years.

The summit closed with a broad plan for the design. This was a crucial part of the intervention design. We had piloted Ai in 2001 in similar settings on a smaller scale. The experience then was that even though the immediate impact was impressive, the energy dropped after three months. The change in momentum could not be sustained. We realized that this new culture of self-driven and self-sustaining change was very fragile and it was easy to be drawn back into the routine of daily issues, and familiar ways of dealing with them. This included blaming the system and a sense of helplessness and lack of power to make any changes.

At the summit, we completed the following steps for the design:

1. Participatory Rapid Appraisal (PRA) (Chambers, 1992) techniques like Transect walk were used to understand staff and patient perspectives and to identify the requirements to offer better services.
2. A Venn diagram was used to look at the various interpersonal issues.
3. Action groups were formed in each facility to address the different action points. This was the key to a sustained change, and this led to the 'Drenching', though it was not called that in those days. However, experience and intuition both led to the addition of this phase.

Each participant was presented with a certificate of participation and appreciation at the end of the summit, which was signed by a team member and the doctor heading the facility. This has remained as a memento of the summit and was appreciated by all. To this day of writing, staff from these hospitals remember these summits with fondness and are proud of what they achieved after the intervention.

Immediate Impact

Analysis of immediate post training feedback forms showed that 99% respondents rated the content of the program excellent and 82% found it was useful to them.

The primary learning from the AI summits was as follows:

1. 'A change in the way we see ourselves would definitely change one's attitudes and behaviour.'
   Participants stated that they learnt a lot about *work related behaviour*, how to enjoy work, how to work with motivation, work with unity and behave well with patients.
   Social construction of reality changes when many people learn to look at things differently. It is possible to work together by forgetting differences of opinion, with unity, honesty, love and affection within the available staff and resources.
2. 'If there is a will there is a way'
   A positive approach towards work and inspiring the staff with little outside help, learning newer ways of working, accepting problems as challenges and solving them.
3. 'Communication with each other and with patients.

Follow Up

We were mindful that the design phase needed special attention. While we had not yet created the 'Drench' phase, this was what was intuitively woven into the design.

We has learned from the pilot phase, that there could be a tendency to transfer the onus of the design on to the central administration. This was due to their past lived experience that they did not have much agency to bring about change. At the same time, we had also seen that there was much possible within their range of agency, once they were able to think creatively and out of the box. Games and activities that seeded this thinking and ability were deliberately woven into the intervention.

Drenching was achieved by a monthly follow up for a year to ensure that the "Destiny/ Delivery" became a reality. This was of key importance as the project progressed.

People forget, and this served as a reminder to their commitments and each meeting was like a renewal. The meetings were also a means of reflecting on the group dynamics. The group was given the observations after each meeting, which the group reflected on. All interventions and observations were made using the "appreciative format". The focus was always on possibilities and not on "what did not happen' or "what went wrong". The meeting format included discussions on happenings in the Maternity home, feedback about group processes and dynamics and end reflections about "What went well, what they would like to see better next time and how could that happen?"

These were also significant interventions for change within the facilities, which driven by these groups. When people heard about actions by other units, there was an urge to act in their own units. The social construction of reality that changed tentatively during the workshop started firming up with the experience of these meetings.

The follow up meetings were not very regular at many places, and required a constant follow up, with changes in time/date due to unexpected reasons like, emergencies, sudden meetings that required the presence of the doctor, or just a low staff attendance on some days! The consultants suspected that this reflected resistance to change. Initially there seemed to be a fear that the meetings would demand accountability and would be used to take people to task for not keeping commitments. This caused poor attendance, and they were seen as a compulsion. Everyone felt guilty, those who were responsible for arranging the meetings (because of poor attendance and late coming), and those who did not come (as they had to hear about it later), and those who did attend, as they felt responsible for not keeping commitments. It was threatening to undo all that we wanted to change- the culture of blame.

The strategy was changed, and it was clearly stated that meetings were to be a learning ground. It was a place to resolve interpersonal issues where people could look at themselves as a group and how they functioned, in the "Here and Now". We did not take up any task related agenda, unless the entire group wanted to talk about it. Giving feedback on observations of group dynamics helped build the groups.

Our role modelling to constantly look for what is changing and the possibilities thereof helped. From being seen as "evaluation sessions", these came to be seen as "valuation" sessions and the groups to start looking forward to these meetings. This was yet another new social construction of reality!

The leadership played an important role in sustaining the follow up meetings. In those maternity homes where the leadership saw the value of the work and the meetings, the intervention has been much more successful.

Drenching achieved a change in how the staff perceived itself, the agency possible within the system and by reconnecting with the sense of purpose and joy the work gave them.

The following processes were noted over the period of one year that the follow up meetings were held:

1. Initial "high" following the first summit followed by some resistance and conflicts.
2. Resolution of conflicts and Acceptance and slowly building trust.
3. Re-energizing for action.

Outcomes from the Research Study

We had randomly assigned nine maternity homes each as an intervention group that went through the Ai process and a control group that had no intervention. In the facility survey and the facility observations, respondents from each maternity home were studied in two groups:

1. Doctors and nurses.
2. Support and administration staff.

The total sample size from each category was as shown in Table 9.2.

The sample size varied slightly between the intervention and control groups and between the two time periods owing to variation in the availability and attendance of staff. The figures in Table 9.2 are the average for each group across the two time periods.

Survey Instruments

Three instruments were designed for the maternity home staff, the observers, and the patients respectively along the following themes. Behaviour patterns were categorized across these themes through extensive formative research at the outset of the project (see section on hypothesis). These themes were:

• Respect
• Concern and encouragement
• Communication with others
• Attitude to work
• Supportive supervision

Questionnaires for facility staff were designed keeping in mind the socio-demographic characteristics of the respondents. Emphasis was placed on psychometric robustness, internal validity, and consistency. This is true even of the translated versions of the instrument. Owing to the lower levels of literacy among staff, the scale and format were kept simple and easy to understand

Table 9.2 Sampling

Group	Doctors and Nurses	Other staff	Observation of Sr. staff	Observation of Jr. staff	Patient Exit interview	Total
Intervention	90	130	36	35	77	368
Control	82	125	30	33	77	347

across all levels of respondents. The scale was designed as a straight-line continuum from 0 ("Disagree") to 10 ("Agree").

The observation tool used by the Ai team scored participants across the same themes of appreciative and non-appreciative behaviour as the facility questionnaires, to make the findings comparable.

The patient exit interviews used a more conventional format of multiple-choice questions to assess patient experiences across the responses of "Never", "Sometimes, "Frequently", and "Always".

Findings and Results

Data was coded and analysed using a Statistical analysis software. Data from the three instruments was analysed and compared across the time periods using one-way ANOVA method.

Maternity home staff: For doctors and nurses, there was no significant difference in the groups along any dimension. For the junior level staff, there was a significant improvement within the intervention group with regard to *attitude to work and the workplace*.

Patient exit interviews: The intervention group showed significant improvement along the following dimensions:

- Attentiveness to patient needs by the doctor
- Attentiveness to patient needs by other staff
- Doctor's ability to clarify patient's doubts
- Overall attitude of the doctor
- Overall attitude of other staff

Discussion on Results

The patient exit interview results showed a clear division between the intervention and control groups. There is a marked improvement in the intervention group, while the control group shows no change.

While 89% of patients were satisfied with the treatment they received before the Ai intervention, this number rose to 96% after the intervention, which was statistically significant. This persisted even after one year (when a last survey was conducted). There was no change in the status of the control group.

Attentiveness of maternity home staff as experienced by the patients showed a 28% improvement after the Ai intervention, while the control group showed no change.

The treatment of Staff with each other showed a 20% improvement after the Ai intervention, while the control group showed no change.

These were some of the significant improvements that were reported from the qualitative study conducted using focus groups:

- Work adjustments between staff members reportedly became better.
- People appreciated each other more.
- Listening to each other has improved.
- More immediate actions were taken when problems were reported.
- Better rapport between staff of the various maternity homes and an appreciation of the larger picture. Listening and learning from stories of other Maternity Homes led to amplification of the change momentum.

Interviews with some of the Doctors, nurses and other maternity home staff after the Ai intervention also provided anecdotal evidence of a positive impact.

At the facility end, the staff has repeatedly reported improved *communication* within their facilities and with their patients. They felt Ai has helped them resolve internal conflicts amicably. It has *motivated* and given them a *shared understanding* and *learning* of the limitations of their workplace as well as the potential for change amid a constrained environment.

A number of maternity homes have discussed an increase in *respect* and *empathy* between staff across levels, and of the importance of role models for junior staff. A sense of *ownership* around facilities as well as an ownership of challenges and problems has been a recurring theme.

Introspection, before affecting change in others and in the system, has been flagged as an outcome that has helped staff shift focus from blaming others for their problems.

The following quotes exemplify some of the above themes and learnings:

"Earlier, I felt change in the system was impossible, but now I see it as a possibility. I can think in terms of a vision for my maternity home. I know that if I take charge of the problem, I can make change happen in spite of limitations. It's up to me to make the change."

"My seniors never listened to me or my problems. After the training, I feel heard. They are sensitive and understanding in a way they have never been before."

"We are all human beings first. If we recognize that we need to respect ourselves and each other, we'll be able to do the same for our patients."

"Ai has completely changed my attitude towards my work and my co-workers. I feel motivated to perform better."

"I would encourage my own family members and relatives to use maternity home facilities. This is not something I would have said before I experienced AI."

Three staff members were identified as future facilitators for one of the Maternity Homes. They underwent training on communication and conflict resolution and had the backing of the Chief Medical Officer.

The Facility staff at many of the Maternity Homes stated that they have come closer and feel united in their mission of serving the community. There have been many examples of times when they have stood by each other and dealt with difficult situations. This they say would not have happened prior to the intervention.

Learning and Insights

The experimental study while limited in some aspects of its design and implementation provided conclusive evidence of the impact of the Ai intervention in Maternity Homes. This is best displayed in the results of the patient survey. There was substantial qualitative data and evidence to support these results. Together, the case for the need and success of an Ai intervention in this setting is strong. Further, since quantitative studies on Ai are rare, this study builds on the existing body of knowledge.

The best Drench strategy that worked well was the monthly meeting that brought together a cross section of the staff of all the Maternity Homes who participated inthe study. They shared success stories and learned from each other. This was more effective than an outsider like the facilitator sharing the same. When a Nurse heard how communication improved in another place, she tried the same technique in her workplace and reported back. Every success, however small was celebrated in these meetings. These meetings also persuaded the few who were not convinced about this work to give it another chance.

What worked also was the "never say die" attitude of the Facilitation team, and the belief in people and the process. The Maternity Home staff saw it as a role model, and they began to question their own lack of belief in themselves and their ability to bring about change. Like Gandhi said, "Be the change that you want to see in the World", the Facilitation team believed that system has the ability to change and grow, and we saw that happen (Wasundhara et al., 2006).

The project was a life changing experience for all of us, personally and professionally. Some of the many lessons and insights are given below:

• Appreciative Inquiry philosophy and the methodology have universality in its application.
• Appreciative Inquiry method needs to be adapted into the client system based on the uniqueness of the situation- from time, language, pacing, interspersing this with other methods etc.
• The important factor that contributes to change in any system is whether we as Change Agents/ Facilitators/ Consultants believe that the system can change. We need to be drenched in the appreciative process for us to facilitate the same for others.

- There is a need to build attitudinal change component into any largescale systemic change efforts. Without this, such efforts go futile.
- Change need not be momentous. A small shift in the social construction of reality will result in a new behaviour and new language in conversations, seeing themselves in a different place…all that constitutes significant change.
- Drenching, Follow-up sessions and constant valuation of impact are prerequisites for sustainability.
- Another important factor that significantly impacted the results was the quality of leadership. Leadership that saw meaning and value in the work, facilitated huge changes and those who did not, ensured that nothing much happened.
- Finally, enjoy the journey. This is the most important lesson of all. We enjoyed every moment of this process and we are as excited about this as we were when we started.

From an Ai perspective, the most important learning from the project is the need to Drench groups in their social construction of reality. How groups see themselves in the context of their roles and the service they offer to the world determines their identity. When we allow them to reflect, explore and challenge this, we have the possibility of them seeing themselves and their world anew.

Postscript

One of the significant outcomes of this project was the establishment of 15 clinics for Antenatal, Postnatal, and Neonatal care at the government urban primary health centres. Because of this project, the staff of the centres were less resistant to starting these clinics – a true achievement in a highly bureaucratic system! Due to the dedication and motivation of community organizations and concerned citizens, space was found, resources collected, over 200 volunteers mobilized, and four Community Resource Centres were setup to disseminate maternal, neonatal health information to their communities. The final culmination of the Ai project was the formation of a multi-sector consortium consisting of members of the municipality, state government, corporate sector, NGOs, community, and public and private healthcare systems to develop a body that will guide, monitor, and advise the work done on maternal and neonatal health at the Ward level.

Today, SNEHA (the NGO who led this project) is working with many other municipal corporations in cities across the state of Maharashtra, replicating some of the models that we created way back in 2006.

The neonatal mortality rate in the city of Mumbai in 2006 was 22 deaths for every 1000 births and in 2023 it was 11 deaths for every 1000 births.

This means that the city of Mumbai has already achieved the UN sustainable development goal of less than 12 deaths per 1000 much before 2030. We don't take full credit for this achievement, though the energy unleashed by the Appreciative Inquiry process in the City for Neonatal Health (CINH) project contributed to the same. SNEHA, the NGO, continues to work on this project that has been extended to 10 more cities in the state of Maharashtra.

References

Chambers, R. (1992). *Rural Appraisal: Rapid, Relaxed, and Participatory*. Paper 311. Sussex: Institute of Development Studies Discussion.

CINH project report SNEHA. (n.d.). *Mumbai 2004: A study of the Utilisation of Maternity Services at Urban Health Center*. Unpublished: Dharavi.

City Initiative for Neonatal Health. (2004). CINH protocol SNEHA. Mumbai. www.snehamumbai.org

Cooperrider, D. L., Srivastva, S. (1987). "Appreciative inquiry in organizational life" in Woodman, R. W. and Pasmore, W. A. (Eds.). Research in Organizational Change and Development. Stamford, CT: JAI Press. 1. 129–169.

National Neonatology Forum (2004). Homr page. https://nnfi.org/

Wasundhara, K. J., Manju, K., Jaya, N. (2006). *Exploring the Factors which Impact the Attitudes of Health Care Workers Towards their Work*. India: International Conference on Urban Health Initiatives.

Section 2 Summary

How Drench Leads Organizational Transformation

Key Points

1. Towards a new model of Drench.
2. Insights and conclusions.

Towards a New Model of Drench

When we started constructing the book chapters, we intuitively arranged them in an order based on the recall we had, amount of information available and ease of writing. Once we completed these chapters and read through them, a significant pattern emerged about how the Drench process itself unfolds in an organizational transformation process. A picture of the same is given below:

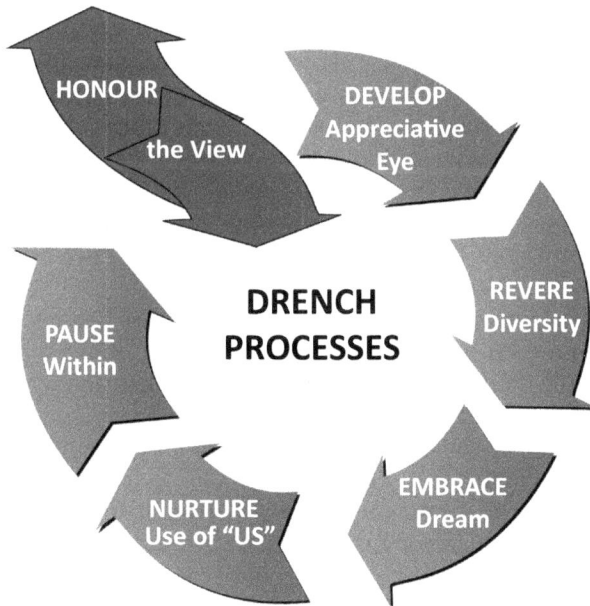

Figure 12.2 Drench processes.

Honour the View is the first process in the Drench Cycle. It begins the inquiry into the possibilities of organizational transformation. It is akin to seeing the mighty oak in an acorn. This is extremely important at the Define stage of Appreciative Inquiry. You will read in the chapter on Drench methods how reframing the problem into a possibility is one of the most important steps to begin the inquiry. **Honour the view** is also the end process of the Drench cycle where a new way of being and doing is honoured as a way of bringing the future into the present. This also leads to new possibilities and a new inquiry begins with the definition of the topic of inquiry.

All the stories that we shared in chapters 4 to 9 have this Drench process built in. Honouring the view in the beginning of the cycle starts with an aspiration and ends with a determination to be the transformation.

Develop appreciative eye is the both the process and the outcome of the Discovery stage of Appreciative Inquiry. Telling and listening to stories about when the system and the people were at their best changes the usual ways of deficit thinking and problem-solving orientation. People learn to appreciate who they are and the system they belong to. Chapter 4 outlines the processes for developing an appreciative eye in a highly critical thinking oriented organization.

Revere Diversity is accepting and valuing the gifts of diversity. Welcoming all voices, differing stories, perspectives and values is the next step in the drenching process. We have shared the story of an organization in Chapter 5 where revering diversity itself was the process of organizational transformation. Revering diversity is an important drench process before the Dream stage of Ai since allows for multiple dreams, desires and aspirations to have a shared space within the system.

The two processes of developing an appreciative eye and revering diversity are the important shifts that organizations make irrespective of the content of the Discovery stage of Appreciative Inquiry.

Embrace the Dream is a process to internalize and become one with the shared Dream for transformation. The additional 'D' of Drench that we proposed to the 5-D model is to pause, reflect, internalize and thereby embrace the dream and become one with it. This is highlighted in Chapter 6 with three stories of staying with the dream and drench in it thoroughly and hold back the impatience to act on that dream.

Nurture use of "Us" – This is another crucial step in the transformation process. The important realization that we are the instruments of change and each one of us individually and us collectively have to transform to bring the future dream to the present. Chapter 7 brings a unique story of how Consultants Use of "Us" became a catalyst for the transformation of the system. This is also akin to discovering the personal, interpersonal and systemic resources for transformation as part of the Design stage of Ai.

Pause Within is another key Drench process where one stops before taking the leap of faith. he stories given in Chapters 8 bring out how one develops the faith through others work, hearing their stories, confronting them and having difficult conversations. Pause within happens when we take a deep breath, take it all in and act with clarity, commitment and collaboration with others.

Honour the view also means to honour everything, to embrace it all, without dismissing anything. Focus on what gives life and energy so we can reframe it into possibility. We make a choice to focus on the possibility, without negating the problems. This is the central message of Chapter 9.

Insights and Conclusions

We developed some insights while creating this model. They are as follows:

1. Drench has various nuances when we dive deeper. It is a series of mental transformations related to self, others and the system. Mostly we understand action as a combination of three factors – knowledge, skill and conviction/ confidence to act. Drench model brings in belief as the fourth factor and it is not just belief in self. It is also belief in others and the system or community.
2. When a system is engaged in an Ai based organizational transformation, a good practice will be to do a dipstick to check whether these Drench processes have been internalized. If one uses a three dimensional view, the Drench process model given above, sits underneath the 6-D Ai stages model. We could move superficially from one stage to another without diving deeper into the Drench processes. However, that will result in the failure of organizational transformation process or at best it will be unsustainable. Hence Drench becomes key to organizational transformation.
3. Lastly, you might wonder why honour the view has two arrows, one pointing within and outside. At one level this is to depict the two views that are important for organizational transformation – the view of the system and the internal view, the view within the self.

At a deeper level, it is to depict what Carl Jung said "One who looks outside, dreams, one who looks inside, awakens" For any transformation to happen, both these views are important – look outside to dream audaciously and to see inside and discover that all that one dreams is already within.

Stay Drenched

Chapter 10

Drench Methods
Interventions for Deepening the
Process for Transformation

Key Points

1. The value of structuring a Drench process.
2. Drenching methods for the stages of define, discovery, dream, design and destiny in appreciative inquiry.
3. Stories from our experiences of using these methods.
4. Contributions from our colleagues.
5. Insights and explorations.

The Value of Structuring Drench Process

Drench is both a stage in the 6-D model as well as a process to be followed at all other five stages of Appreciative Inquiry (please read Chapter 3 on Drench). In this chapter we will offer some of the intervention methods we have used in our work.

The intervention methods that we offer here are what we learned from our experiences, borrowed from fellow colleagues or from our reading. We express our gratitude to those from whom we have learned some of these methods. Some of the activities offered here are borrowed from the Indic tradition of Yoga and Vedanta. We are offering all these interventions in the spirit of sharing and with joy..

Appreciative Inquiry as a process, unlike problem-solving approaches, is based on generativity, imagination and locating the energy for change. The success of an Appreciative Inquiry summit is measured as much by the energy and passion generated in the system to explore new possibilities by transcending the current problems as by the action plans arrived to solve those problems. In Ai, it is well understood that the quality of solutions and its sustainability will be enhanced when we operate from a possibility rather than a

DOI: 10.4324/9781003538059-13

problem orientation. "Going slow to go fast" is a good expression of what we try to do in these interventions.

However, the general culture in organizations is biased towards action and the groups that one works with are focused on problem-solving. At the end of every stage of the Ai process, the members are ready to take the outputs and move over to the next stage of the process. Here we need interventions to deliberately pause them, reflect on what they just did, share their feelings, insights, and consolidate their understanding before they move to the next phase. There are times when groups do come back to what they just did before the break since they have some new insights. This is the drenching in between the stages of Ai process.

The most basic of all drench methods is to ask people to take a break, maybe sit alone or take a short stroll and allow the mind to reflect, introspect and explore the discussions that just happened. This is used when we have less time for a deeper drench. This works well in some groups. In some groups, the lack of a structured intervention leads participants to engage with their phones and laptops! Hence some structuring is useful.

The basic structure of these interventions can be classified as shown in Table 10.1.

Table 10.1 Drench methods at a glance

Stage of 6-D cycle	Types of Interventions
Define	**Pivoting** – changing the direction or focus of inquiry to address a new aspect around the topic. **Re-framing** – changing the way one perceives a situation from a problem to a possibility **Virtuous cycle** – It is a positive feedback loop where one desirable occurrence leads to another.
Discovery	**Retelling stories** – Asking the listener to retell the story that he heard in the first person. Deepens the impact of the stories and builds empathy. **Expressing themes** using song/ dance – Bringing the whole self to the room and not just the cognitive self. This also helps in opening the creative channels. **Still images** – similar to the above, unleashes group creativity and brings in a lot of fun as well.
Dream	**Nature Imagery** – Allowing one to move into a different context, one that is close to nature. This could be done through guided imagery or self-directed visualization. **Vision Board/ Collage building** – Group activity to build a collage using pictures, drawings, painting etc. that articulates the dream in a visual way. **Theatre** – Group activity to depict the dream using forms of theatre, street play, drama etc.

Table 10.1 (Continued)

Stage of 6-D cycle	Types of Interventions
Drench	**Live event** – Ask participants to create a live event in the new organization (say a meeting) and ask people to look, dress, have conversations, use new language and demeanour based on the dream and be aware of how one is feeling the new world. **Meditation and Journaling** – Use any mindfulness meditation method and focus on the dream images. Then reflect and journal the experience of meditating on the dream/ share it with a partner. **Embodying** – Embody the archetypes like those of emperor, magician, warrior, joker and lover to experience the new you in the dream world. **Book writing exercise** – asking people to write the cover of the book they will write five years into the future describing their experiences of organization living its dream and the role played by them in that process.
Design	**SOAR activity*** – Strengths, opportunities, aspirations and results can be used to enable the group to visualize the capabilities, opportunities they have to realize the dream, their own personal aspirations around the dream and the results/ milestones they would like to see achieved to live the dream *(*based on Stavros and Cole's (2013) work)* **Our top five** – This is an activity that helps to identify the top five strategic drivers needed to achieve the dream. This helps to ground the dream. **Value clarification and exploration** – This helps to identify, understand and explore the values that we need to practice in order to live the dream.
Destiny	**Virtuous cycle exercise** – identify actions that will be successful and will lead to success of a subsequent action and onwards. This is a way of building on success. **Personal change** – participants identify one personal change that they would like to bring in themselves so that they can live the dream. **Appreciative Eye** – Help participants to appreciate each other in a creative way and help to build a culture of catching people doing things right. This could be achieved through publishing the stories from the Discovery phase to keep the entire organization drenched in the new reality and develop an Appreciative Eye to discover more. **Coaching** those who provide leadership for the dream organization. Preparing them to identify personal and systemic transformations needed to live the dream helps them to keep drenching in the dream and thereby keeping it vibrant and vital.

We will now explain in detail a few of the intervention methods mentioned above.

Drenching During Define Stage

In our experience, most clients approach us with a problem to be solved and at times with both the problem and the solution and us as consultants are supposed to make it happen! We know that the presenting agenda of the client is mostly different from their real agenda. From an OD perspective, all client statements are symptoms and we should help them to find the underlying cause and address them rather than the symptoms.

We respond to the client by articulating the social construction and anticipatory principles of appreciative inquiry. According to the social construction principle, realities are created in the moment and there are multiple realities. We ask the client if it is acceptable for them to speak to a larger number of people to see whether this is a shared reality. If the client agrees, we do a short inquiry with some of the stakeholders.

The anticipatory principle states that the very fact that the client is bringing this issue indicates there is hope for its resolution. We want to tap into this hope. Hope gives energy to imagine a future where this problem doesn't exist. We ask the client to imagine "how will your organization be when this problem doesn't exist?". This shifts the focus from the past (problem) to the future (possibilities). This is important from a transformation paradigm as well. When we address and solve problems, we help them to transition into a better organization. When we bring the future possibilities to the here and now, we help them transform as an organization.

There are clients who are so caught up with the problem that they just can't see anything beyond. In this situation drenching them in social construction and anticipation may not work. Their angst with the problem, impatience to find a way forward and fear of negative consequences if the issue is not resolved block them from seeing possibilities and going beyond the presenting agenda. We allow them to express all the problems, get them to state their emotions connected with the problems and slowly take them through a process of imagining the future by asking a series of questions "what will change when we solve this problem?", "What will that change contribute to?", "And then...?".

Another important method at the define level is re-framing. This is a powerful method that helps the client to see the problem as a "topic for inquiry" and as an exploration rather than analysis. A simple method of re-framing that we find useful is to flip the statement. For example, the client says "we have an attrition problem. We lose 25% of our staff every year". We ask the flip question "do we know why 75% of our staff stay with us?". The answers to the question about why people leave will be very different from why people stay. The organization wants more people to stay and it will be more helpful to find answers for why people stay. This is based on the principle that what we focus on will become our reality.

Similar to re-framing is pivoting. Here a related question that deals with a new aspect of the topic is asked to the client to widen the horizon of understanding. In the same example around attrition, a pivot question could be around "Do we have people who have returned or have expressed wanting to return? Do we know why some people want to come back?".

The above methods are used by most Ai practitioners and all of us have found them helpful to shift the client's frame from problem to possibilities. However, they may not help in changing the client's attitude towards the problem itself and better to transcend the problem into new possibilities. This is due to a phenomenon called vicious cycle.

When clients seek help from consultants, they are sometimes in a vicious cycle. A vicious cycle is a self-reinforcing negative feedback loop where an initial problem has worsened the situation, leading to further and more difficult problems. Hence the clients say "we have this problem and this has led to multiple other problems impacting the whole business". Hence it is not one problem for which we need to find possibilities or reframe, but a host of negative outcomes that create further problems. We have a definition issue here and a *Drench process becomes essential to change the vicious cycle to a virtuous cycle.*

A virtuous cycle is a positive feedback loop where one good thing leads to another, creating a self-reinforcing chain of positive outcomes and continuous improvement. A virtuous cycle is a situation where positive actions or events consistently lead to further positive results, creating a snowball effect. This is the opposite of a vicious cycle and the drench process helps the client to see the possibility of shifting from the vicious to the virtuous cycle.

We had a client who kept harping on a problem that he believed was the root cause for everything else happening in the organization. This was an oil and gas company and the problem was around safety. The company recently had some safety incidents and while they have tightened the implementation of the safety rules, the client was unhappy with the lack of safety attitude among employees. He had invited us to help in building a more positive attitude to safety. We tried applying all the methods that we have mentioned above with limited success. We had the intuition that the client had positive experiences that transcended this stated problem. However, there is a disappointment that the problem is not disappearing and seem to repeat despite strict implementation of rules.

We used the exercise of "Then what?" – This is opposite of the "5 whys". Here we ask to expand the possibility... "What will happen if we have a success? If that success happens and what will then happen...". We asked the Client "what will happen when we have zero safety incidents for a month? Then what will happen?". The Client was taken aback with the question. He didn't even consider that possibility. He replied "That will be great. When that happens, people will see the value of following safety rules". We continued "Then what?". He continued "People will support and educate each other about safety rules". "Then what?". He smiled and said "Maybe then, we don't have to be the only one to own safety in the company, all the employees will". We then said, "Maybe this is what you really want. You want safety to be owned by all employees and not just by the Safety department". He agreed and we took this as the definition for the Appreciative Inquiry.

Drenching During Discovery Stage

One of the most powerful drench processes that have experienced is retelling stories. We conduct the initial story telling process in pairs and once the pairs return to the conference room, we ask three or four pairs to form a small group of six or eight participants. We then request the pairs to retell their stories to the others in the group. We add a twist in this exercise. We ask one member of the pair to share the story of their partner as if it is their own story. They have to do it in the first person. We also tell them that it is okay if they miss some details as long as they can share what really impacted them when they listened to the story. Once the person finishes telling the story, his partner will then share the experience and emotions of listening to his own story from another person. People feel understood and experience empathy from others. This is an intense and moving experience for the group, for the person who shares the story and the person whose story is shared.

We also follow it up by taking up one story from each sub-group to share in the plenary, very much in the same way as it was done in the small groups. A community gets built in the process. Participants tell us after the experience that it opened their eyes about their colleagues, started seeing them in a positive light and understood how privileged they are to work with them.

In one of the Ai summits, we had over 40 participants and we had the story retelling sessions in groups of 8. When we finished that process and wanted to group to draw out the themes of discovery, they refused and wanted to hear more stories! We had to do multiple groups' sessions for over two hours so that people could hear most of the stories in the community. The energy that this process unleashed was visible in the quality of the dream that they co-created.

Drenching During Dream Stage

The Dream in Ai is stated in the form of a provocative proposition (PP). A provocative proposition is a statement of the future stated in the present tense as if it is operating and practiced to the maximum. It is the statement of bringing the future to the present. It is an amplification of the current strengths as discovered in the earlier stage that is the desired future and dared to dream of. It changes the understanding of how we see the 'now' and with that new vision and knowledge we can see possibilities emerge that did not exist before. It gives hope where sometimes none existed before.

The provocative proposition is created from words that emerged from the stories and knowledge of what is true for the people who write it. It is endorsed by reason. But reason alone is not enough to make change. The left brain, the reasoning brain is a formidable executor, but it does not have the power to create. In our experience, while the group may be on a total high with the energy unleashed during the discovery and dream process, we have all seen it become depressingly back to status quo in a few days. The brakes that reasoning applies come right back on. This is because reasoning kicks in. and it raises all the reasons why the provocative proposition is not possible other than what is the default already in place which is everyone's comfort zone.

Hence, we allow the group to drench in the power of imagination, the power of creation. The provocative proposition is powerful and energetic when the group drenches itself both in the power of imagination and reasoning. We use 7-step process that we call "double loop" which is described below:

1. We start by asking the genie/ miracle question. (E.g. imagine you have the Alladin's lab and you rub it and the Genie appears. The Genie offers you three wishes for you having freed it from the lamp. What will be the wishes you will ask the Genie to grant?) This is to prime people to dream. We have seen this again and again, that many people find it hard to dream of what may be possible if the current limitations did not exist. And they especially cannot dream of something for themselves. That is too "selfish". They ask for something for the family, the organization…we encourage them to dream about what they really desire.
2. Then participants are asked to share their wishes (by choice) in small groups. Articulating them aloud is an act of courage and intention.
3. Then we select a fewer number of themes (5–8) from the many that may have emerged from the stories. As always, those with the most energy and emotional connect are chosen. There are many ways to do this, and they are all available on the generous resources shared online by the community of Appreciative Practitioners.
4. After selecting the themes with the most energy, we ask the participants to create a collage using pictures, or a drawing to depict the desired future which is an amplification of these themes. This is done by taking them through a guided visualization process (more drenching) before they get to the creation phase.
5. Next, the group soaks in this collage image in silence. These are just pictures. Few words. (This may take some monitoring as the habit of using words is strong!)

6. We do a second level of abstraction here. We ask the participants to draw out words that the images evoke in them. Feelings, action words, processes, values, outcomes…
7. The provocative proposition is created by using a mix of both sets of words. This is perhaps the most challenging aspect of this process. The Provocative proposition is a statement of intent, it is a commitment. It is also written in the present tense, like it is already a reality. This is an unfamiliar way of thinking. It is like an affirmation.

In one of the workshops, a participant came to us after this activity and asked us whether she can do this for herself to look at her future. We told her that she is most welcome to do so. She stayed back after the sessions in the evening and prepared a collage for herself based on her three personal wishes from the genie. We met her next morning before the session and she showed us the collage. It had pictures of women smartly dressed, looking like executives etc. and pictures of babies, children and women with children. We asked her what does this mean to her and she answered "I'm going to adopt a child". She was a single woman in senior leadership and she was considering adoption but was not sure about how she will manage post that with her career and so on. She told us that she spent three hours at night in her room doing this exercise reflecting on it and she is now determined to fulfil her dream. A year later, she informed us that she is adopting a baby girl and she would like us to be the godparents. We visited her and the baby and we continue our relationship with her and her teenage girl.

Drenching in Drench

This is one of the most important steps. We have written about the concept of Drench in Chapter 3. We have also given numerous examples of Drench and why it is important for transformational change to happen. We will cover one of our favourite Drench interventions after the Dream stage. This is called the "Book Cover Exercise"

The key to transformation as stated earlier, is that the people who need to execute the change believe in it, and they own and become the new identity of the organization. We facilitate this by asking everyone to write the story of this change as if looking back after two to five years, when the dream has been achieved. They need to tell the story of how that happened. The changes made. The most important piece here is for them to articulate the role they have played in this successful transition and who they have become. What they let go of as old ways of doing things and tell the readers what new beliefs and processes were embraced.

A book gallery is announced and when all books are completed to some extent, these are displayed with pride. Everyone presents the key message.

They form small groups again and speak of this in greater detail where they can help each other to get more clarity.

Finally, we have each person make their own personal statement of a provocative proposition. Who they have become to get an embodied sense of what is possible for each of them to be.

We have collected some more drenching exercises for your use:

1. Asking the participants to sleep over it and come back the next day or after a week and revisit the dream. We can then experience if the energies have diminished or amplified for that dream.
2. Asking the participants to pretend it has happened and to be that person or that organization that was imagined. We set up a simulated environment where client/s walk and talk as a being part of this brave new world. Using theatre and other methods of embodiment is powerful.
3. Asking clients to articulate the same dream through different channels of expression- audio, visual, and kinaesthetic. This gives a somatic experience for the dream and somatic memory is sometimes stronger than that of the brain.
4. Sharing that dream with five other people and experiencing oneself during the process of sharing and taking feedback on how the other's experienced you during that process can be another powerful way of drenching.
5. Staying in a state of meditation and allowing oneself to fully live that dream is another method of drenching. Here we allow the dream to be fully experienced from all the senses and also connect in the present moment with the dream.

Drenching During Design Stage

In our experience, pausing to explore and clarify the values that will underlie all actions is critical to organization transformation and its sustainability. While developing a shared dream is important, ensuring that the dream is lived through following certain shared values is equally important. The excitement and impatience for action sometimes makes a group ignore this process.

Depending on the size of the system, value clarification and exploration could be done in few hours or might take weeks and months. In one of the large Ai projects that we did, we helped an organization co-create their mission, vision and values. This work took many months to complete and once these were approved by the Board, the leadership wanted us to help them implement actions emerging from the project. We asked them to suspend the action and focus on internalization and institutionalization of the values. As the saying goes "Culture eats strategy for breakfast" we need the culture as an enabler rather than an impediment to strategy execution.

They understood that unless the whole organization is soaked and drenched in these values, real alignment between the organization culture, mission, vision and strategies won't happen. We created a group of story gatherers and guides (called Margdarshak's – Hindi for "one who shows the way"). They were given the assignment to bring values as an integral part of who we are and what we do. They began a series of engagements – town halls, small group meetings, screening of videos, dialogue, listening and interactions as means to help all employees drench into the values and see the link between the values, vision and mission.

The details of this project was published in the Appreciative Inquiry Practitioner (Sankarasubramanyan et al., 2013). This organization recently reviewed and recast their values and embarked on a similar process of Drenching because they saw its critical contribution to their organization transformation.

In Ai summits, we do a shorter version of this process. We have used simulations that bring out value elements critical to the dream. These simulations give an experience to members about how they would go about and execute actions to live the dream. At the end of the simulation, we ask members to reflect on the experience and identify opportunities for personal and organizational transformation with reference to some of the values. Participants do find this valuable since it gives them a here and now experience in a safe space and a chance to take stock of where they are individually and as a system.

Drenching before Action

One of the most memorable exercises that participants speak about even after a decade is what we call the "Appreciate behind one's back" exercise that we do before the closure of an Ai summit. We learned it when some other trainer used it in one of the workshops we attended and we loved it.

The exercise goes as follows:

1. Give each person an A4 size sheet of paper (we use coloured sheets to make it more fun), a strip of masking tape and a marker pen.
2. We request people to help each other paste the paper in the back of the person (sometimes we use a safety pin instead of masking tape).
3. We then announce to the group "We are used to gossiping about others behind their backs. Today we are doing something different. We are going to appreciate them behind their backs. We appreciate them for who they are, what they do, how they contributed to you or the organization and how grateful you are that they are your colleague".
4. We tell them to write as much as they want since we can put more sheets. We tell them not to write their names. We ask them to also draw pictures,

use metaphors, poems and other creative expressions. We also tell them that they could write for a few people or for the whole group.

The groups start tentatively, some of them start writing and others look amused or confused. Slowly the energy starts to flow and it starts to throb and increase like a crescendo. People form a queue or like small trains, one writing for another...many thankyou's will be heard, many squeals of laughter, back slapping and loads of fun.

We give it a good 20–30 minutes till people have completed and checked that they have written for everyone they wanted to. Then we ask them to take out the sheets and read. People smile from ear to ear, some have tears in their eyes, some hug each other, some come and thank us for the experience and all of them see themselves and each other with an appreciative eye.

We debrief the experience and ask them to see how they can now go and act to live their dream with an appreciative eye so that what they do will bring a smile in everyone and they catch each other doing things right.

An interesting thing happens in almost all the Ai summits that we have facilitated. During the exercise, someone will notice that there is no paper behind me and my colleague. They will insist that we stick a paper and they will give us appreciation. We have more than 25 such sheets preserved from various workshops and it is a delight to read them once in a while. We had recently visited the office of a client who had attended the Ai summit with us almost a decade ago and we were happy to see her sheet still prominently displayed in front of her desk. We commented on that and she replied

"Yes, I preserved it across my two jobs and shifting offices! When I have a bad day or I'm generally feeling a bit down, I read it. In an instance, I smile, my mood brightens and I feel better". She added "When I read the paper, the visual of the session flashes back in my memory. I can still see the room and all the people and I even remember most of their names".

Leadership coaching is another important Drench process during the Destiny phase of an Ai based organization transformation. Coaching contributes that the leaders work on their internal voices of cynicism, judgement and fears and develop an open mind, heart and will for the transformation that is unfolding. Many studies have pointed out, leadership can make or break a transformation process (see Chapter 5 for studies on why organization transformation fails) and we have also experienced similar issues in our OD consulting practice. We encourage client leaders to either undergo coaching with us or ask them to raise their concerns related to organization (and personal) transformation with their coaches. In Chapter 6, we have written the story of one of the founders who "discovered" the word Joy as the key value for his transformed organization and embedded the value in everything they do.

Conclusion

We have many more examples of short and long drenching interventions that we have used in our work. You may also know many of them or you now know how to use one of the interventions that you know from a drench perspective.

When we first conceptualized Drench, we saw it as a new stage between Dream and Design. We still see it that way and we also as a process during all the other stages as well before transitioning into the next stage. When we stated this to a colleague, she replied "You are basically saying that we should drench in Appreciative Inquiry as a whole for transformation". We think she said it better than us.

References

Sankarasubramanyan, R., Joshi, W., Jha, S., Vasudevan, P. (2013). The story of transcend. *AI Practitioner*. 15, 1. 50–54.

Stavros, J., Cole, M. (2013). SOARing towards positive transformation and change. *Development Policy Review*. 1. 10–34. www.researchgate.net/publication/259975881_SOARing_towards_positive_transformation_and_change

Chapter 11

Drenching in the Spirit

Appreciative Inquiry as a Spiritual Quest

> **Key Points**
>
> 1. Spirituality and Appreciative Inquiry.
> 2. Indian Spiritual traditions and linkages to Ai Practice.
> 3. Our spiritual quest.

Introduction

Let us define "spirituality" before we go ahead. Many a times, it is wrongly connected to religion, God etc. In our view, spirituality is the relationship between self and the sacred. We see Spirituality as the human pursuit for purpose, meaning and connection. This pursuit could be at an individual, organizational or at a community level and realizes wholeness and transformation.

In one of our organizational transformation assignments, we facilitated a session on internalization and institutionalization of shared values. One of the participants said in that session "Most of us look at how we can demonstrate these values in our behavior at a transactional level. I think Ai asks us to experience values as transformative of our being rather than just our behavior". This was an insight for many of us and we requested this person to explore further. She was well versed in the Indian spiritual traditions and brought out an interesting parallel between Appreciative Inquiry and Spiritual quest. She said that in traditional Indian thought, there are two ways of living – *Preyas and Shreyas. Shreyas* refers living with a focus on transformation or moksha, spiritual growth, peace and lasting happiness. *Preyas,* on the other hand, represents living for what is immediately pleasing and pleasurable, which is more transactional and may not be beneficial in the long term. In order to bring organizational transformation, we need to focus on Shreyas and that is what Appreciative Inquiry asks us to do. In other words,

DOI: 10.4324/9781003538059-14

Appreciative Inquiry can be a spiritual process of organizational transformation when we shift the focus from short term transactional actions to a transformational view.

Paul Gibbons (1999) defines Spirituality in organizations as "Re-orienting the organizational mission and strategy and re-organising the structures and processes in order to achieve goals, through spiritual means". Organizations that are more human centred, environmentally and socially responsible will have a spiritual purpose underlying its work. They see themselves as making money for a better environment and community and not at the cost of it. This could be a big ask for many organizations today that are focussed on generating immediate, short term wealth creation for its shareholders. However, it is an ideal worth pursuing and there are stories of some organizations in the corporate sector that live this way.

Diane Whitney (1999) speaks about four organizing principles of Appreciative Inquiry as a spiritual practice. The four principles are a) spirit as energy, b) spirit as meaning, c) spirit as epistemology and d) spirit as sacred. She says "Something about Appreciative Inquiry leads people to call it spiritual, to describe their experiences as deeply meaningful, energizing and connected to something grander and more universal than themselves"

We have always had the same sense of the Spiritual underpinnings of Ai as Diane Whitney did. It may not have been created with that in mind, but any philosophy that becomes so widely accepted is tapping into something beyond the obvious.

We are students of the Indian spiritual traditions over the past two decades. Interestingly, the Sanskrit word given for this ancient wisdom is *Darsana*. *Darsana* literally means to "see" for oneself. It is the experience of seeing the truth with the mind's eye. Appreciative Inquiry is also *Darsana* since it is also about seeing the world anew with an appreciative eye and honoring that view.

The Spiritual Quest Embedded in Appreciative Inquiry

During one of the training workshops on Appreciative Inquiry, we asked participants to form pairs and share stories with each other about a peak experience in their life when they felt they were at their best, they felt alive, vibrant and connected with themselves and the world. This was an open workshop and most participants were strangers to each other. We told the participants to walk around the room, look at everyone and choose a person whom they feel drawn towards. All the pairs formed quickly except two people who stood in two corners of the room and looked at each other. They both pointed at each other and said "yes" together as if they were searching and found each other.

After 45 minutes, all of them came back for debrief except this pair. One of us had to go searching for them and they were engrossed in each other at the hotel lobby! They reluctantly returned to the room. One of them turned to us and asked "Is Appreciative Inquiry a spiritual practice?". That was a surprise question and one of us asked that person why she says so. She replied "It is very uncanny, when we started telling each other our stories, it felt like my partner was telling mine and I was telling hers. We seem to know each other very intimately even though we have never met before". Her partner chipped in "It feels like we are one spirit in two bodies". Those two participants experienced a deep connection between them through their stories and found a deeper meaning and purpose in their lives.

From an Indian spiritual tradition perspective, they experienced "no-otherness" or non-duality. According to this philosophy, there is only one phenomenon and that is existence, awareness and limitless. This is called Brahman. The world of multitudes is an appearance and we are trapped in this Maya. However, we can experience this oneness in deep meditation and other spiritual experiences, similar to what those two participants had.

In 2013, We saw similarities between Appreciative Inquiry and Advaita Vedanta, one of the most sophisticated of all *Darsanas*. In our excitement and naivety, we presented on this at the World conference in Nepal and followed it by publishing an article in the Ai Practitioner. We say naivety because our approach was simplistic. At a superficial level, the approaches of Appreciative Inquiry and Advaita Vedanta might look very similar. Advaita Vedanta is about recognizing the "One Truth" of all existence; while Ai seeks to discover one hope or dream that can bring together and align the energies of the system in which it is being applied.

We wrote in that paper (Sankarasubramanyan and Joshi, 2013) the following:

Advaita literally means "non-dual". It is a belief that the world is one, and there is only one absolute truth, which is not manifest, called the "Brahman". All that is seen is a manifestation of this truth. It is what allows us to make sense of what is essentially "pure nothingness". Hence nothing is good or bad, all are different manifestations of the same truth.

In Advaita, the way to understand reality is to grasp the "absolute" truth of "oneness" by seeking beyond the obvious. When we grasp the absolute truth, there is no ego as everything we see is only a manifestation of that oneness and truth, a bit like a hologram. When we realize that, we stop judging others and ourselves and connect with the higher consciousness, which is absolute bliss or "Sat Chit Ananda". The dynamic process of inter-action between the manifest world with multiple realities and the Whole or Brahman is depicted in the diagram above. The interaction is based on the four processes of transcendence, emergence, co-creation and con-nectedness. The Brahman emerges in its various forms that bring in the diversity of co-creation. The forms manifest in our experiences as stories and when we inquire into each other's stories, we experience the deep

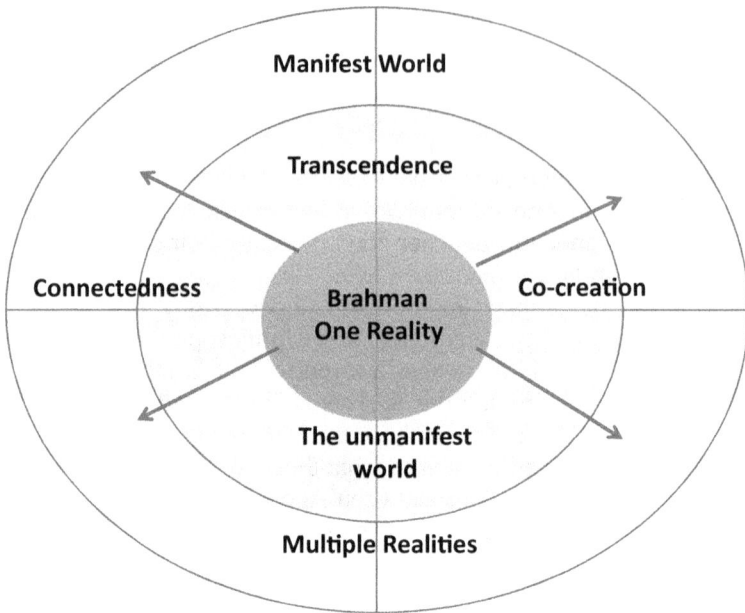

Figure 11.1 T he Advaita philosophy.

connectedness between all forms. This awareness helps us to transcend the forms and connect to the ultimate reality or Brahman.

Please see Figure 11.1 for Advaita philosophy.

As we write this book, decades later, hopefully wiser and better read, we present a fresh take on this. The potential for Ai to be a deeply spiritual quest is undeniable. It taps into individuals, organizations and communities for spiritual transformation. It focuses on the raison d'être, the purpose of its existence which enlivens people. "To Enliven" (Merriam-Webster Dictionary) means to give life, action, or spirit to animate.

Ai awakens the spirit. It allows the system to transcend the current way of seeing, riddled by differences and individual priorities and needs. When we focus on what divides us, the answers can overwhelm. What unites is usually at a different level of consciousness. A common desired future which can only be accessed by the spirit, if we let go of the current way of seeing.

All Indian philosophical traditions give importance to the concept of *Sankalpa. Sankalpa* means resolute intention to achieve a goal. Sankalpa acts as a guide for all forthcoming actions, and allows us to stay focussed on our aspirations. Sankalpa includes three energies – *jnana* (knowledge) *iccha* (desire) and *kriya* (action) Shaktis. When we aspire to transform, we create a dream/ vision for the future. To bring the future to the present and make the dream a reality, we need knowledge, energy and action. This becomes present and available to us when we set our resolute intention (*Sankalpa*) to live the dream. How do we develop the *Sankalpa* for transformation?

Vedanta asks us to follow three steps of *Shravana, manana and nididhyasana*. *Shravana* is listening and understanding. *Manana* is reflection, examination and resolving one's doubts. *Nididhyasana* is contemplation, deeper internalization and becoming one with the truth.

While these Sanskrit words might sound esoteric, this is a universal process of how we learn and transform. Imagine you want to be an Appreciative Inquiry Practitioner. You will learn Ai through reading, attending a training program and so on. This is *Shravana*. You will then have to reflect on your learning and resolve doubts about your understanding of the principles and practices of Ai. You might do this on your own or by speaking to a friend/ coach etc. This is *Manana*. Then comes the crucial stage of *Nididhyasana* where you contemplate on your contrarian tendencies – to be deficit focussed, problem-solving oriented at times. You learn to transform your mind to see abundance and accept a constructionist worldview. These three processes prepares one with the *shaktis* (powers) of *jnana* (power of knowledge) *Iccha* (power of energy) and *Kriya* (Power of application). Once you have done that, you have set the *Sankalpa* for your practice of Appreciative Inquiry. We can apply this process for organizational transformation as well.

Appreciative Inquiry as the 4th Loop of Learning

The concept of double loop learning was first articulated by Chris Argyris (1978). This was further extended to triple loop learning by Romme (1999). The first loop being the basic problem-solving loop, where we correct errors in a system. The second loop of learning is where we go to the assumptions and rules that govern the system and address issues at that level. The third loop is a deeper level where we ask the question "Why does the system exist?" and "What are the implications of transforming this system?"

Another way of putting this is to ask the questions "Are we doing things right?" in the first loop. "Are we doing the right things?" in the second loop, and "How do we decide what's right?" in the third loop (Yuthas et al, 2004).

We believe that Appreciative Inquiry transcends these three loops and asks the question "What do we ultimately want?". We believe that when we choose our future, we transcend beyond the right and wrong and focus on what gives us energy, vitality and freedom. When people in a system come together and choose to focus on what they really want, transformation happens. This is choosing Shreyas over Preyas…choosing the transformational over the transactional. This choice making is spiritual.

We will examine how this fourth loop learning unfolds in an Appreciative Inquiry process:

1. Every system starts by embracing diversities that are various manifestations of what is (incompletely) understood as the social construction of reality of the organization. The system then tries to step through the three loops of learning by trying to build a common view either through consensus or someone/ group deciding what is right.
2. In Appreciative Inquiry, the stages of Define, Discovery and Dream help the system to converge on the ultimate transformation. However, this remains as a possibility till the future is embodied and contemplated in the here and now. This is where Drench plays a significant role. Drench unleashes the spirit and helps the system to sees itself as enlivened by a calling that transcends the differences. Drench helps to discover the indivisible, the oneness.
3. From this new level of consciousness, the design emerges as new forms of the reality...which is again incomplete by themselves but are connected by spirit to the 'one' reality.

The Open and Incomplete circle (Enso) is one of the deepest symbols in Japanese Zen. The circle is the revelation of a world of the spirit without beginning and end. The Zen circle reflects the experience of Drench – perfectly empty yet completely full, infinite, and open to what is emerging and transforming.

Ai Principles and the Process of Transformation

The principles of Appreciative Inquiry are a testament to this process of transformation:

1   **Wholeness:** This principle highlights the Inclusion of every voice without judgement of right and wrong. We believe in the interconnectedness of the world and people. Wholeness also helps us to choose what will bring the best of us all the time without evaluating it as right or wrong. Vedanta says "You are That" meaning that you are that wholeness. This is like the hologram – every bit of it represents the whole.
2   **Heliotropic:** This principle highlights the belief that all living systems move towards growth and life. That which helps living systems to move towards growth is the spirit. Drenching in the discovery of life giving forces and focusing on what we ultimately want help to kindle and awaken this spirit that is present in every living system. In Vedanta it is said that our minds naturally chooses to turn inward towards our core or consciousness when we let go of our worldly desires.

3 **Anticipatory:** This principle highlights that human systems move towards what they imagine of their future. In other words, we create our own future and it becomes a self-fulfilling prophecy. IThe Amritabindu Upanishad says, "Mind is both the energy that is responsible for our bondage and for our liberation". When we anticipate a great future, that happens because the mind directs the spirit to do so.

4 **Poetic:** This principle highlights that organizations are ongoing stories constantly written and rewritten by people based on how they interpret their experience. This principle also reminds us that we choose how to interpret our experiences. The ancient Indian traditions believed that Poetry is our pathway to transcendence and it is inherently linked to our spiritual nature.

5. **Simultaneity:** This principle emphasizes that inquiry and change are not separate and happens simultaneously. This principle is deeply aligned with recognizing the spirit. When we ask questions about something, we manifest it into one level of reality immediately. When it is spoken multiple times by almost the entire organization, we are already aligning the energy in a particular direction. Hence crafting the interview questions is crucial in Appreciative Inquiry. Spiritual practices like meditation and mindfulness often focus on cultivating awareness of the present moment. Simultaneity can be understood as a way to experience the fullness of the present, where past, present, and future are all interconnected. This is also the expected outcome of Drench processes.

6. **Constructionist:** "Words create the world" is a good expression of this principle. Reality is not fixed and is created in the moment based on interactions in any system. This principle says that language is a powerful tool for creating meaning. Diane Whitney (2010) calls this process spiritual resonance. She says,

"The language and metaphors we use to explain events and our experience of them reflect our worldview. For many of us adopt a language at work that portrays the world as a machine dependent upon material input, transformation and output, a machine which enhances economic exchange and accumulation. People are talked about and treated as part of the machine. Much of what makes us human, including our spirituality, gets left out or overlooked in this worldview. A holistic worldview and language invite us to express our spirituality in the workplace".

Being Ai Is to Have a Spiritual Practice

We have realized that the more we drenched in our spiritual practice, the more we embodied the principles of Appreciative Inquiry in our work. We also recognize that in order to be appreciative of the system that we work with, we need to be appreciative of ourselves. In order to believe in the system's potential to transform, we need to believe that about ourselves. Being brought up in a deficit worldview, having been educated in the machine paradigm and been highly successful as problem solvers, we had to completely change our construction of the world to be appreciative. We believe that drenching in Advaita Vedanta and Yoga are pathways that helped us to honor the view, develop an appreciative eye, revere diversity, embrace our dream, nurture the use of "Us" and pause within… all processes of Drenching in Appreciative Inquiry. You may have your own practice.

A participant in one of our workshops asked us for a "to do" list for a budding Ai Practitioner and we said, this and we put this up here to conclude this chapter. We said to him that this is what we strive to be, though not necessarily successful all the time:

1. To be a discoverer with a beginners' mind;
2. To approach every organization, every person as a mystery;
3. To tend to the emerging spirit assiduously and consciously;
4. To allow emergence of the fullness of possibility to blossom in all its glory; and lastly
5. To believe that life is the expression of the divine.

We need to Drench in the spirit as much as the people and organizations that we work with.

References

Argyris, C., Schon, D. (1978). *Organisational Learning: A Theory of Action Perspective.* Boston, MA: Addisson-Wesley.

Gibbons, P. (1999). Spirituality at work, what, why and how?. *AI Practitioner.* 7. 7–9.

Romme, Witteloostuijn, V. (1999). "Circular organizing and triple loop learning". *Journal of Organizational Change and Management.* 12, 13. 439–454.

Sankarasubramanyan, R., Joshi, W. (2013) Advaita and appreciative inquiry. *Appreciative Inquiry Practitioner.* 15, 1. 17–20.

Whitney, D. (1999). Spirituality at work. *AI Practitioner.* 7, 1. 73–88.

Whitney, D. (2010). "Appreciative inquiry – Creating spiritual resonance at the workplace". *Journal of Management.* 7, 1. 73–88.

Yuthas, K., Dillard J., Rogers R. (2004). "Beyond agency and structure: Triple-loop learning". *Journal of Business Ethics.* 51. 229–243. doi: 10.1023/B:B USI.0000033616.14852.82

Chapter 12

Our Drench in the Field

The Beginning

All the greatest and most important problems of life are fundamentally insoluble... They can never be solved, but only outgrown. This "outgrowing" proves on further investigation to require a new level of consciousness. It was not solved logically in its own terms but faded when confronted with a new and stronger life urge.

Carl Jung

I (Sankar) grew up in a world of scarcity. My oldest memory of childhood is my mother telling me that I can't have that toy because we can't afford it. In the 1960s and 70s India was a struggling nation. Rice, Milk and many a staple food were rationed, you had to wait for 10 years to get a telephone connection or buy a two wheeler. A refrigerator or a four wheeler were only for the rich. I was more aware of our family's limitations than endowments.

I remember one day when I was in my sixth grade, I was super excited since I got a 93/100 marks in Mathematics paper, a subject that I was not very proficient in. I ran home to my Mother and told her my marks. Her response was "what about the 7 marks. Why did you lose that?". Like her, I also learned to look for the gaps, deficits and focussed on the analysis of why there is a gap and how to fix the same. I became good at it as I progressed through college and got my Master's degree. Then I started my career in Human Resources Management.

DOI: 10.4324/9781003538059-15

As an HR a Manager, I was used to seeing what is wrong with a person or an organization, conduct a diagnosis and suggest remedial actions that meant restructuring, retrenching or retraining people to become better. The people and the organizations became "better" or at least I felt so, but I also experienced this process as drain on my energies as well as for the people who were involved. However, I continued what I was doing since I didn't know of any other way to make things better!

Over the years I became proficient in Organizational development and got certified as a T-Group (a personal growth model created by NTL, USA) facilitator and started my consulting practice. I found myself doing the same thing – diagnose what's wrong and find ways to fix it, except that I didn't fix it myself, but got the client system/ participants to own up the problem, solutions and commit to fixing it. All changed in 1997 without my knowing it till 2001!

I attended the 50th anniversary celebrations of NTL Institute at Bethel, ME and the whole function was organized as an Appreciative Inquiry Summit. This was facilitated by a team headed by the late Jane Watkins. What unfolded in front of me was magic. I experienced sharing about all that I was proud of pinching myself once a while to check if I'm speaking in my dream or in reality. This was because no one had asked me till then to speak about what I was proud of in myself! I experienced me being appreciated by others and more importantly by me. That was probably when, I shifted seeing from from myself through a scarcity lens to a lens of abundance.

Playing with Appreciative Inquiry

One of my first assignments using Appreciative Inquiry was when I was asked to be a consultant for a large public hospital in Mumbai to help build a mother and child friendly culture in that hospital.

As usual, I spoke to doctors, administrators, nurses and so on to find out what ails the system... and the floodgates were opened! People poured out all that is wrong, bad and morbid about the place. Also they said that they are helpless and can't do anything about it because someone up there or the system was responsible. Every focus group I did generated a huge laundry list of issues and many suggestions for actions. However no one took ownership for any of the actions! I was stuck, helpless and disappointed with the system. When I reflected on what was happening, I had two insights. I realized that I might be getting these responses because I'm asking for them! Secondly, they are open to sharing these with me because I'm respecting and honouring what they said to me. However, I haven't yet helped them to reframe and focus on what is possible rather than identifying the solutions to problems.

I also realized that amongst these outpourings of misery, there were glimpses of statements about how proud they are about their professions, small stories leaked about how they did some good jobs despite all the odds, some appreciation of the good actions by others and so on… This was like the silver lining amongst the clouds.

These small instances helped in changing my belief about the hospital. I began to believe that something works here. I began to respect the staff who have shown tremendous commitment against all odds to help a patient live. I started to look for life here… and found it! The project took a larger turn to include more hospitals and maternity homes and then my co-author/ partner also joined the facilitation team.

We started seeking out stories of what's working, what's make this work worthwhile for them. The moment we asked these questions, the stories began and there was no stopping them! There were stories of joy, of the miracle of life, of wonder of the gift that this profession has given. They were moving, and often there were many tears, but they were about why, despite what seemed like impossible conditions, people continued to excel. That was not all, once the staff had shared this, there was a new energy in the room, suddenly they could also see how much was right with the system as well, and not just what was wrong. It changed the entire perspective of how we had stared viewing the "problem" in the beginning.

Suddenly, none of the problems seemed insurmountable. There were stories where people had managed to overcome the odds, stories of success poured forth…these had never been talked about. Like all hospitals, what got noticed, talked about and acted upon was "failures", when "things went wrong". Even though what went right on a daily basis in a public hospital far outnumbered the wrongs, that was never highlighted. Stories of success never made it to the grapevine, only those of failure. Both the authorities and the people themselves had never focused on how much was being achieved. This changed on the day of the workshop, when they saw their work in a new perspective. It also allowed them to see problems as just that, problems, which can be resolved, and not something that was beyond their control. The reality had changed for them as well as for us.

Two things happened here in terms of Drench processes. When the initial outpourings of misery happened, we honoured and respected what we heard. We held the container for all voices to be heard and honoured. We practiced the first Drench process of "honouring the view" and that helped the group to reframe and focus on what gives life to them and to the system. The Hospital staff developed an "Appreciative Eye" the second process of Drench. Along with them, we developed an appreciative eye for them too.

We experienced for the first time the power of Appreciative Inquiry…and there was no stopping us anymore. This experience was life changing to us as well. Both of us have been so much focused on the problems of our personal lives and that is what we got …more problems! When we honoured those problems and changed the focus to the possibilities in our lives, many things that we were even afraid to think of, or thought it was too unlikely…started happening. When we started looking at our lives differently, life changed!

Deeper Drenching

We have experienced many transformations, both in our lives and in others when we start viewing ourselves with an appreciative eye. Another significant experience was that of a participant in one of our Appreciative Inquiry workshops. This person was a very senior executive with a famous and highly successful retail brand. He had heard and read about Appreciative Inquiry and came to experience it himself. He brought in his critical mind along with his free flowing creativity. In his own unassuming way, he helped to transform himself and the group through his persistent focus on what was possible. He experienced for himself the power of this method in the transformation of the group and the individuals. He also saw possibilities of applying this in his work. When he went back to work, he immediately applied what he learned to transform a very poorly functioning store into one of the most profitable in the chain. He did this, merely by listening to stories of the Staff members about their work, what gave life to that work, what energized them, and how it matched with the company values. This started as a short project and then went on for two weeks, as he heard each employee personally, and was moved by what he heard. Stories of customer care and the value staff placed on it abounded. He then extended this to the executive staff of the store, and could see the different perspectives at the floor and executive level. This allowed them to work together, using this new found energy to help them through. There were unexpected benefits, of personal bonding and rapport with the store staff, and customers as well. The store had a record turnaround. Interestingly, he also documented all the stories into an induction book to be shared when new staff are recruited. This person embraced the dream and his role in bringing the dream to reality.

Another story of someone embracing the dream happened when one of the participants create a collage of pictures for building his personal dream. Later when he analysed his collage, he realized he had an intense desire to complete a Triathalon. He Trained for a year and achieved that in the following year.

In our professional lives, we also embraced our dream of living, practicing and educating others in Appreciative Inquiry. By Pausing within and drenching in the dream, we opened ourselves up to the emerging possibilities. In the past 20 years, we have trained more than a 1000 people on the principles and practice of Appreciative Inquiry. The Academy of HRD (www.academyofhrd. org) was the first to approach us to do that and for five years we conducted many workshops, jointly produced a video and contributed to a book on Appreciative Inquiry published by them. Subsequently, we started announcing workshops under our organization, Changeworks. Then many organizations approached us to train their senior leaders, HR and L&D team members on appreciative Inquiry. In every assignment we have done over the past 20+

years, we brought in some element of Appreciative Inquiry without labelling it as such. We designed sessions using some of the Ai principles, brought in some activities around appreciation and/ helped the groups to reframe and see problems as possibilities.

We believe we nurtured the use of "Us" in our practice and embraced our Ai dream within and helped to manifest the dream in reality.

We also have many years of experience in experiential training and we are certified T-Group Practitioners. T-Group is a methodology for individual and group development, created by the NTL Institute in the United States (www.ntl.org) and adapted to Indian context by the Indian Society for Applied Behavioural Science (www.isabs.org). We have developed many hybrid human process laboratories blending both these methods. We have personally experienced the immense power of both these processes in the groups that we have worked as well as in our own lives. We believe that no transformation can happen on the "outside" unless it happens on the "inside". One of our first experiences of blending Ai and T-Group was way back in 2005 where we offered a program called Appreciative Leadership within an ISABS Event (www.isabs.org).

This program was a true test of the Use of "Us" in staying with our being rather than our doing. The basic construct of the workshop was to focus on the being of the leader and how that contributed to Institutional transformation. With that focus, we as the facilitators and therefore leaders had to be able to stay with our being, fully aware of our presence and its impact on the group. We had to let go of trying to make the desired outcomes of the lab happen and allow us to experience what was emerging and honour the view. The provocative proposition (statement of the Dream) created by the participants reiterated that view. See provocative proposition in Figure 12.1.

Figure 12.1 The provocative proposition.

This provocative proposition statement along with the picture was very significant for the participants as well as for us. The Lion and the emerging chick are both within us and we need to honour and embrace both to be Appreciative Leaders in our work and life. We also need to accept our deficits by fearlessly and actively seeking the "possible". This leads to the emergence of the dormant, unseen and unheard reality which is magical in its transformation. When I look back at our scholarship and practice, we have tried to live this provocative proposition. We have worked with our appreciative side and our shadow side and we have ignited that which was dormant within us.

Pause within and the Possibilities

When we look back at our early engagements using Appreciative Inquiry, they were characterized by high energy, action and movement and less of pause, reflection and staying still. We were inspired by a presentation by Mac Odell at the World Appreciative Inquiry Conference in Nepal (2009) where he offered a 7-D Model that he used in his work in Nepal. The last three D's of this model were "Do it now", 'Dialogue/ Discuss" and "Drums/ Dance". We loved his model and brought in some of those elements in our work. Hence our Ai Summits were great fun, full of action, and participants and us, enjoyed the process.

In 2012, we started working with the International Institute of Education and worked with their Fellows from the Leadership program funded by the Packard Foundation. Here we met two women who were not only great clients, but also companions and facilitators. Cheryl Francisconi and Namrata Jha trusted us with the work, joined us in writing a paper and presenting it at the World Appreciative Inquiry conference at Ghent, Belgium. I believe they helped us hone our scholarship and practice of Appreciative Inquiry through dialogues, reflections and feedback on our work. One of the realizations from those conversations was that while we helped bring tremendous energy through our work, we could do better in channelising and focussing it to embrace and live the Dream.

This brought in a new approach to our designs. We didn't discard what Odell taught us. We integrated it with more pauses, more time to soak in and going slow to go fast. This led to the conceptualization of Drench and incorporating drench practices into our work.

One of the most significant and long-term work of organizational transformation work we have done was with the ACG Group, a large global supplier of products and services to the Pharma industry. In the span of a decade of our association, we facilitated the creation of new mission, vision and values, helping them develop a culture of appreciation in their factories, and worked with the senior leadership in cultural transformation and many more interventions. We were fortunate to have Sunil Jha and Priya Vasudevan who

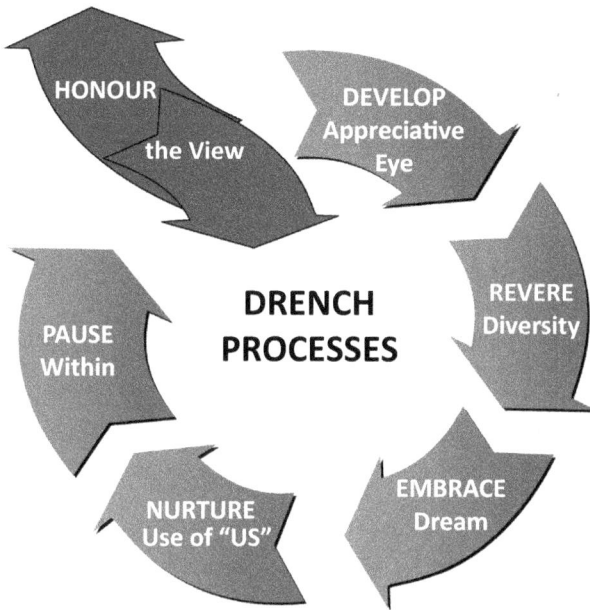

Figure 12.2 Drench process.

trusted us, believed in the philosophy and partnered with all the work we were engaged in with ACG. They also went on to learn Appreciative Inquiry and became practitioners themselves.

Bringing Drench into our awareness helped us to foray into areas where we never imagined we could apply Appreciative Inquiry (see Figure 12.2). We worked on developing safety practices in an appreciative way for a large Oil and Gas company, leadership development of women working with Self-Help Groups in Bihar, building communitive collectives for agriculture communities in Maharashtra, building livelihoods for traditional artisans of Kutch, mainstreaming LGBTQ communities in Mumbai, building student, parent and teacher relationships in schools, culture sensitivity and diversity, embedding Ai in learning and development, developing appreciative HR policies and many more.

We dived deep into all applications and held strongly to the principles of social construction, simultaneity, anticipation, wholeness and the heliotropic principle. We realized that Appreciative Inquiry at the level of principles can be applied to any social system since they are fundamental human principles.

We have also worked with Appreciative Inquiry in difficult situations like restructuring, retrenchment, closing operations and inter-departmental conflicts. All these projects didn't have a happy ending and in some places the system was so much steeped in fear and distrust that we couldn't facilitate the creation of an appreciative climate and anticipating possibilities for the future. However, there were also occasions when despite being disappointed with ourselves, clients came back to us for more work because they saw value in the process.

We did one such difficult project for an organization recently where one of the senior leaders was very much opposed to the process and questioned us throughout our engagement. A month ago, one of us got a LinkedIn contact request from that person. I accepted the request and told him that I was surprised by the request. He immediately called me on the phone and said:

> Yes, I was very upset with both of you when you worked with us. I thought you were asking us to ignore the problems and only look at the positives. I didn't like that. Then it dawned on me that the label of positive and negative are mine and it doesn't belong to what I experience. You were teaching us that…you were teaching us to appreciate what is…this has opened my eyes. Thank you.

Sometimes it takes time for people to honour the view and develop an appreciative eye. We are happy that people do all the time, albeit over a period of time. We trust the process.

Our Inner Search and Appreciative Inquiry

The last decade also brought in more intensity to our inner search for our truth, meaning and purpose. We dived and drenched in Yoga, Vedanta and Buddhist philosophies to understand and contemplate on the reality of the World, God and Self. These journeys also helped to bring a new quality and purpose to our practice of Appreciative Inquiry. We wrote a paper on "Advaita and Appreciative Inquiry" in AI practitioner (2009) which was at the very beginning of our drench. We have a chapter in this book titled the "Spirit and Ai" where we have dived deeper and offered some new understanding to the practice drawn from Indian wisdom traditions.

Our inner search also brought in new meanings to the words 'Appreciate" and "Inquire". The dictionary meaning of "Appreciate" is to value, respect and cherish a situation, thought or a person. In our experience, we really appreciate when we have someone or something in our full awareness. Thich Nhat Hanh says that "When we look at a flower, there is nothing that is not present in the flower. We see sunshine, we see the rain, we see clouds, we see the earth, and we also see time and space in the flower". We really appreciate a flower when we are not only seeing the flower, but we see the whole universe in it, including ourselves. Hence to be Appreciative means to be that awareness in the here and now.

The dictionary meaning of "Inquiry" is to ask, to explore and seek to know. However, we have come to see that the word "Inquire" has a deeper spiritual meaning as expressed by William Blake in his poem, Auguries of Innocence "To see the world in a grain of sand". To see the world in a grain of sand means to inquire in such a way that we see the extraordinary hidden in the ordinary, to find the deep meaning in small things and to break away from the conventional ways of seeing. To embrace wonder and a more profound understanding of what is.

Imagine if we could be like that all the time...to be fully aware and drenched in what we see and see the profound wonder of existence all the time... imagine how we will be and the world will be then. This is the foundational principle of Advaita philosophy which states that we are existence, consciousness and infinite at our core identity...we are the Appreciating Self, we just have to believe it to see it.

In the Now

Some of our recent work is presented in Section 2, Chapters 4 to 8. We have also done many more assignments at a systemic and individual level that are not documented in this book. We continue our quest to educate and give an experience of appreciative living for corporate professionals, students of human resources management and organization development as well as people who work in community and social development. Our belief is that even if 10% of the participants who goes through an appreciative experience apply this way of being in their lives, we have contributed our little bit to transform the world.

We recently offered an Appreciative Inquiry based Coaching process for professional coaches as part of their continuing education credit courses. This was very well received and many more people are wanting us to repeat the same.

The most endearing story from recent times is where the CEO of a large Engineering company learned Appreciative Inquiry from us and personally interviewed a 100+ employees of a newly acquired unit of that organization in a South Indian city. He documented all the interviews and worked with a group of employees to identify themes. He then called everyone, made a presentation of the interviews, themes and asked them "How would you like it if we were to be always this way?". All hands went up and there was a roar of approval. People in the audience broke into conversations organically. He told me later that he was a bit confused about what to do at that time and he remembered my statement "trust the process". After all the chatter stopped in 15-20 minutes and there was silence, he noticed something. All the employees were holding hands and they raised them like a Mexican wave three times. Then one of the employees said to him "We have been watching a lot of football matches lately and they do this wave. This is our way of showing commitment to a new way of being in our organization". We heard recently that this acquired Unit which was meant for domestic market in India has now started delivering globally for the parent organization because of their superior quality of products and services.

Looking Ahead

We believe in magic and miracles. They happen when people really drench into the here and now and soak in their dream. We have done this with our lives and we continue to do so. This book itself is one of the miracles. There is more magic than we can imagine in the world.

Our next work is to drench more in Appreciative Leadership. Watch this space for more stories…

Section 3 Summary

Being, Drenching and Doing

Section 1 of this book focused on the theoretical constructs of Organizational Transformation, Appreciative Inquiry and Drenching. Section 2 informed the reader of our field experiences that reinforced the theories presented in the previous section and brought in new meaning from the drench processes that emerged from those experiences.

Section 3 is an eclectic set of chapters that cover the doing of Drench (Chapter 10- Drench Methods), the spirit of Drench (Chapter 11 – Drenching in the Spirit) and the being of Drench (Chapter 12- Our drench in the field). The order of these chapters indicate how one drenches in the field of Appreciative Inquiry or for that matter how organizational change graduates from transactional to transformational.

As we start a change process, we often engage with change at the level of practices, tools and the ensuing change will be transactional and not sustainable (Chapter 10). However, some of these practices could slowly seep into our everyday lives and we recognize a deeper meaning to these practices and the spiritual side of it (Chapter 11). When we recognize and appreciate the value of the deeper meaning, these practices change their character and become our life principles. This then becomes our way of being and then the transformation is complete (Chapter 12).

The same is true for organizational transformation. Most organizations understand change as a set of new practices and behaviours. By themselves they don't become sustainable till the organization focusses on the underlying values and beliefs that drive those practices and behaviours. When the organization drenches deeply in these values and beliefs some of the practices become a way of life (culture), and they could even they see a spiritual purpose for their existence. This is the source for real transformation.

Another way to understand these chapters is how they keep the "Use of Self" at the centre – be it tools and practices, be it principles or be it a way of life. We, as consultants are the primary instruments in our work and hence the Use of Self as a competence is central to the practice of OD. When an OD practitioner is adept in this competency, they become a powerful instruments for organizational transformation.

Chapter 10 – Drench Methods is a chapter about the tools and methods that we have learned and used in our work. While these tools are extremely useful, we remember a senior colleague once telling us "When you are holding the space as a facilitator, you are all alone and you have to trust yourself. You realize then that there are no other tools available, you are the tool".

The effective use of tools calls for our ability to Use our Self through self-awareness, reflection, diagnosis of the situation and the appropriateness of the tool to be used. Oftentimes, our own impatience to move on and our inability to stay with non-action pushes the client system to move superficially from one stage to another without internalization. Here we strongly recommend that Appreciative Inquiry practitioners must work on understanding themselves, understanding inter-personal and group processes and develop the ability to see themselves as the most important tool for transformation.

Chapter 11- Drenching in the Spirit, brings in the spiritual character and the quest embedded in Appreciative Inquiry that goes beyond the transactional. We have brought in perspectives from many thinkers in the field ranging from Ai practitioners to ancient Indian wisdom. We relate these perspectives with the principles of Appreciative Inquiry.

We are students of the Indian spiritual traditions over the past two decades. Interestingly, the Sanskrit word given for this ancient wisdom is *Darsana*. *Darsana* literally means to "see" for oneself. It is the experience of seeing the truth with the mind's eye. An Appreciative eye is about seeing the world in a non-dual way, without the duality of subject and object, qualities and essence and spatial and temporal. By the Use of Self, we transcend these polarities and experience the oneness of it all while honouring its diverse manifestations.

Chapter 12 is the story of our personal and professional journey in the world of Appreciative Inquiry. We believe that we can't work with clients to help them transform, unless we did that ourselves. We both grew up in a world of scarcity and discovering abundance within oneself has been the biggest and most profound transformation in our life.

Our inner search also brought in new meanings to the words "Appreciate" and "Inquire". The dictionary meaning of "Appreciate" is to value, respect and cherish a situation, thought or a person. In our experience, we really appreciate when we have someone or something in our full awareness. Thich Nhat Hanh says that

When we look at a flower, there is nothing that is not present in the flower. We see sunshine, we see the rain, we see clouds, we see the earth, and we also see time and space in the flower. We really appreciate a flower when we are not only seeing the flower, and we see the whole universe in it, including ourselves.

Hence to be Appreciative means to be that awareness in the here and now. This is another aspect of the Use of Self.

We have been life partners and working colleagues for the past twenty five years. To sustain and enrich both these relationships and live in an Appreciative way has been an opportunity for the Use of Self and the Use of "Us". We are two different people, with different competencies and styles of working and engaging. We also recognize that there is a deep foundation that we both connect into the principles of Appreciative Inquiry and more deeply our spiritual quest and purpose.

At a more practical level, we live the Use of Self when we strive to practice the following, though we may not be successful all the time:

1. To be a discoverer with a beginners' mind
2. To approach every organization, every person as a mystery
3. To tend to the emerging spirit assiduously and consciously
4. To allow emergence of the fullness of possibility to blossom in all its glory and lastly,
5. To believe that life is the expression of the divine

In Closing
Conversations and Contributions from the Field

Appreciative Inquiry is a generative conversation where we focus on what gives life to us. We had such generative conversations with some of our friends who are Appreciative Inquiry scholars and practitioners. We explained the concept of Drench to them, and Priya Vasudevan, Tojo Thatchenkery, Cathy Royal, Sunil Jha, Sushma Sharma and Sundeep Kapila accepted our invitation and offered their valuable perspectives. We have organized their thoughts as reflections about their personal journeys, how they drenched in Appreciative Inquiry, and their take on the future for Appreciative Inquiry.

Priya Vasudevan, Fractional CHRO and OD Consultant, Mumbai, India

Priya was our client when we worked on a a very large organizational transformation process with ACG Group, a global pharma leader in the year 2010. She headed Learning and Organization Development function in that organization. She later moved on to head HR for Liberty General Insurance in India. We related with her as a client, colleague, mentee, and a dear friend.

Priya shared with us that Appreciative Inquiry came at a very important phase in her life. She was in a new job, role and reporting to a new Manager. She felt inadequate in her role, not comfortable with her Manager and was starting to doubt her professional competence. Then she attended an Appreciative Inquiry workshop with the Authors. Priya said:

> "I learned Ai at the right time when I was going through turbulent times. All that I tried didn't help me. My qualities of appreciation and sensitivity were not working. That's when I attended the Appreciative Inquiry workshop. Wasundhara's (one of the authors) presence and her way of being drenched in Ai inspired me".

She continued "I realized from that workshop that Appreciative Inquiry isn't just a theory or a methodology, Appreciative Inquiry gave me a new way of seeing myself and a new way to be. It helped me affirm myself".

DOI: 10.4324/9781003538059-16

Priya spoke about how Appreciative Inquiry positively changed her role. "I started to listen to people, listen to their stories, and invite them to speak stories of their strengths and peak moments. My journey with Appreciative Inquiry began when I stopped focusing on fixing what's broken and started to explore what gives life when we are at our best".

From her experience with her many assignments of organizational transformation, she says this about Appreciative Inquiry and the power of Drench "Transformations don't arrive with a grand announcement. It seeps through slowly and quietly. It comes through when we rediscover pride, develop curiosity, and become fearless and life-affirming...transformations happen when internal resistance changes to resilience".

Priya added that one of her biggest lessons as a change facilitator is to recognize that her role was to hold the space for wisdom to surface and not to guide the group towards a solution. "When we trust the people and the process, when we really appreciate whatever is happening, then we really Drench ourselves in the role of a facilitator". She added "People think that Appreciative Inquiry is being nice and soft. Appreciative Inquiry is gentle but is also deeply rigorous and transformative".

Priya shared with us the story of one of her recent assignments where she led a diagnostic study about the culture in a large hospital in India. She was told by the top leadership of the hospital that there are multiple problems with people, structure, and processes in the hospital. They wanted her to do an "audit" of what is going on and write a report. She listened to them respectfully and told them that while all this could be happening, the system is working and she would like to discover that energy as well. She studied some of the performance indices of corporate hospitals and found that this hospital's performance on some of the matrices was on par with some of the best hospitals.

She shared:

"I got down from the car and I gazed at the hospital building. It was magnificent. I walked inside and found the place exuded positive energy and I said to myself that something life affirming is present here. I forgot all the problems that the leaders told me and found myself asking appreciative questions".

She also shared that the staff opened up when she started asking appreciative questions and later one of them shared with her that they were afraid of her since they thought that she has been sent by the leaders to find out what is wrong with the staff at the hospital. "Defenses came down when they stopped seeing me as an 'Auditor'" she said.

Priya came back from the data collection meetings and she was trying to write her report without much success. She was not synthesizing well – there was too much noise. Her husband suggested – take a break and get back to it later. Priya said:

> I took a break and watched Netflix movies for a while. Then I closed my eyes and ran the movie of my visit to that hospital. I recalled every person, every conversation, every smile and soon I saw myself as a part of that, not separate. I developed a sense of belonging to those people, their stories and that hospital, felt one with them. Then, everything fell in place. This was my Drench.

Priya ended our conversation saying this:

> I didn't realize how much I have drenched in Appreciative Inquiry till recently when I interviewed many successful corporate women leaders for my book *Women of Alchemy* (Vasudevan and Kohli, 2025) (www.shet omorrow.com). They told me that these interviews were life changing for them because of the questions I asked, the way I listened to them, my curiosity to know more about them and the way I responded. I believe Appreciative Inquiry has now become a way of my being.

Tojo Thatchenkery, PhD, Professor, Author and Founder of Appreciative Intelligence Model

We got acquainted with Tojo when we met him and his wife Tessy at the Appreciative Inquiry conference in Orlando, FL in 2007. This acquaintance turned into colleagueship and friendship over the years. Tojo's work in the field of Appreciative Inquiry and his conceptualization of Appreciative Intelligence is well recognized.

Tojo started by sharing the story of his doctoral program at Case Western University with Cooperrider and Srivastav. He had read the seminal article on Appreciative Inquiry by Cooperrider and Srivastav (1987) and he told Suresh that he wants to do his PhD research in Appreciative inquiry. Cooperrider offered him work in the Global Social Change Organization project and he was sent to the Institute of Cultural Affairs headquartered in Chicago, IL. "This was my first drench in Appreciative Inquiry. I travelled with the ICA teams within the US and Europe and learned about them and their work through an Appreciative lens". His thesis was focused on the social constructionist principles as they applied to Appreciative inquiry. His research is built on his earlier work "Organizations as Texts: Hermeneutics as a model for understanding organizational change" (Thatchenkery, 1992) where he pointed out that if we look at an organization with an appreciative eye, we will experience an affirmative reality.

Later when he joined George Mason University, he developed interest in understanding the intelligence that leaders carried, which enabled them to be appreciative leaders. This led to the development of the Appreciative Intelligence model and the publication of his Harvard Business Review recommended book with Carol Metzker – *Appreciative Intelligence: Seeing the Mighty Oak in the Acorn*. Tojo says:

> "Appreciative Inquiry focuses on organizational transformation, at the macro level and Appreciative Intelligence focuses at the micro or individual level. Appreciative Intelligence is the ability to cognitively reframe and see potential in any situation and act on it with success. According to me, Appreciative Inquiry is an exercise using Appreciative Intelligence".

Tojo also shared that he and his colleagues Lindsey Godwin and Brian Whitaker have developed and validated an Appreciative Intelligence scale (https://ais.appreciativeintelligence.com/). Anyone can go to this site and take this test and receive a full description of their results for free.

Tojo shared that he gets his students of the OD and Knowledge Management program to do a capstone project using Appreciative Inquiry. Over 120 projects have been done by students over the past 30 years based on Appreciative Inquiry under his guidance. He hopes to undertake a Meta research on these projects soon.

Tojo's current work is on the Circular Economy and how Appreciatively Intelligent leaders can reframe situations in a way that they can contribute to reuse and sustainability, thereby protecting the environment. He gave an example of how an event management organization is looking at ways to reuse flowers used for functions. He is currently writing a book on the same.

Tojo's take on the future role of Appreciative Inquiry in organizational transformation:

> He said "I see Ai growing in a more customized format, focused on specific organizational areas in a strategic manner. Appreciative Inquiry was earlier used in a general and broad sense and now this focused approach produces better and more tangible results."

Cathy Royal, PhD, Professor and Consultant

We met Cathy at several World Appreciative Inquiry conferences and was always struck by her presence. Her presence brought energy to the room and her voice brought warmth, clarity and humour. One of us got to know her better as fellow members of the NTL Institute Board.

Cathy is well known in the field for her work in quadrant behaviour theory (2013) which she developed when she was with Fielding Institute. Quadrant behaviour theory looks at structural inequalities based on the cultural board that is always at play. One can get details in the paper cited under references.

We began our conversation with Cathy describing her work with black women to rethink their socially constructed identity. She has used Appreciative Inquiry extensively in this work and she sees how Drench is an important aspect for identity development. She said "Identity shift is a meta-cognitive shift and it requires one to reflect deeply". Cathy also said that the quote "if you believe it, you will see it" is very important here and changing this social imprint from a problem-solving perspective to a strength based thinking requires us to soak in it.

Cathy shared her story of her time at Case Western University, studying with David and Suresh. She also spoke about how she was with Tojo at the same University. She said with a smile "I hope David Cooperrider remembers that he signed my dissertation, 35 years ago!". She also reminisced about various meetings she had with other practitioners including John Carter, Charlie Seashore and others in incorporating Appreciative Inquiry into her work on structural inequalities in society. She remembered the contributions of her friend Jane Watkins to the field.

Cathy offered a very interesting and thought provoking perspective on Drench. According to her, Drench has to be at the level of the language and how we use language to construct reality. She spoke about the extensive work she did with the Department of Health and Human Services, USA and the amazing transformation that happened when the language changed from problems to possibilities. She said "There is a space between the "no longer and not yet". When we have left a way of being behind and not yet moved into an affirmative way. This is the space for Drench"

Cathy explained how she uses language in her work. She asks participants to write the "problems" on the left hand column of the paper and ask them to replace the language as a "mystery to be explored" in the right hand column. "Language drives energy and we need to work with that", she said. We both shared how we have learned and been rewarded for using the problem language and hence the difficulty to change and tendency to slip back.

Cathy also proposed that Drench is an important phase when we move from Design to Delivery. This is where power dynamics come in and it is important to bring all voices into the room.

Cathy spoke about how she has brought Appreciative Inquiry and Social Justice work together. She said "Appreciative Inquiry is a platform theory. It can be co-mingled with other theoretical frames. Here we go with Drench… Ai is like water and adapts itself to all spaces". She sees Appreciative Inquiry as the ground and Social Justice as the figure using the Gestalt framework.

Speaking about the future of Appreciative Inquiry, Cathy had the following to say "We are going to have a future, pray we do. The question is what is our preferred future? How do we co-create the world that we deserve to see?". She also shared that Appreciative Inquiry gets a lot of criticism because of lack of clear understanding and there are many other things that people find compelling. Hence, we need to get better at what we do.

Cathy ended this conversation remembering her friend and colleague Louise Diamond who lived her multiple social identities with ease. Louise had a four level model for trust and the highest level was "You will speak my interest even if I'm not there".

Sunil Jha, CHRO and Appreciative Inquiry Practitioner

Sunil Jha is the CHRO for a large global pharma products organization. Sunil is a client, colleague and a friend for over two decades. Sunil's biggest strengths are his presence and his ability to call out what is on his mind without fear. He is demanding at work and kind-hearted and empathetic in relationships. We have experienced his resilience, passion to learn and ability to see potential in every situation.

Sunil first experienced Appreciative Inquiry when we began working as Organization Development consultants in his organization. He drenched in this philosophy and discovered its value and attended a certificate course in Appreciative Inquiry with David Cooperrider from Case Western University.

Sunil started by saying that "Appreciative Inquiry isn't just a methodology. It's a way of seeing, a way of being". He narrated the story of how we began our journey of organizational transformation using Appreciative Inquiry in his organization. This family run Indian organization wanted to be a global leader and this was the context of the transformational journey. Sunil remembers,

> We began our journey with Appreciative Inquiry, not to fix what's broken, but to explore what gives life to our system when we are at our best. We took the best of our past and dreamed of the future that we aspired for.

He continued to describe how we began our first set of appreciative interviews with associates, vendors, clients, families of associates and even the Bankers.

Sunil said:

> "We paused. We listened. We invited stories of strength, hope, and peak moments. Transformation didn't arrive in a grand announcement. It came quietly through voices being heard. Through teams rediscovering pride in their work. Through leaders asking better questions, and cultures becoming more life-affirming than fear-driven.

One must say that within a decade the organization has become the global leader in pharma products and continues to grow and expand its footprints.

We asked Sunil to reflect on his own experiences with Appreciative Inquiry. He spoke first about its impact in his personal life. He believes that living appreciatively has humbled him. "It changed the way I related to my friends and family". He continued "It helped me to hold difficult conversations in a constructive way. It shifted me from reacting to responding and from control to curiosity".

Sunil shared that Appreciative Inquiry helped him to trust people and process and allow the best to emerge. It also helped to remind himself from time to time that people don't resist change, they resist being changed. "It taught me that facilitation is not about guiding people to solutions, but holding space for them to surface their own wisdom".

Sunil ended the conversation saying that contrary to a general belief that Appreciative Inquiry is soft, he believes that Ai is deeply rigorous, human, and transformative because it is built on trusting the wholeness of people and systems.

Sundeep Kapila, Founder of Swasth, and Appreciative Inquiry Practitioner

Sundeep and Garima, started an NGO called Swasth (www.swasth.org) after leaving successful careers in a large consulting firm. Sundeep is an engineer, who consulted in the health sector, started a wellness NGO. He is a certified coach, yoga therapist, a somatic experiencing practitioner, and is currently pursuing his PhD in inverse problems! He is also an Appreciative Inquiry practitioner.

Sundeep began by saying that the word "Swasth" at a generic level means wellness and at a deeper level means "being established in the Self". Swasth as an organization started as a health and wellness clinic and now encompasses physical, mental, emotional, social, and spiritual wellbeing. "We were open to the possibilities as they emerged for us to dive deeper into the Self" Sundeep said and added "we are open to new possibilities now too". Swasth is not only a service provider in health and wellbeing. SWASTH also supports many other NGOs by building a digital health ecosystem and applications.

Sundeep said "We have also expanded into wellness coaching and we are an accredited coaching training institute now" and added "we have built a community of health coaches across the world now and they carry the spirit of Swasth".

The story of our work with Swasth in 2015 is mentioned in Section 2, Chapter 6. During the Drench process, Sundeep had the insight that Joy as a feeling, as a state of being and as an outcome will be the life giving force of this organization and ten years later, Joy is still very much the force that is at the core. We asked Sundeep how they managed to sustain the spirit of our work after a decade. He replied that he and the team that established Joy at the centre of Swasth, spends time with every new employee who joins the organization and shares the story of how Joy has transformed this organization. "Every person, be it an employee or a patient or a participant in our program, experiences us practicing the beliefs that we stand for and that's how a culture is built" Sundeep shared with pride.

Sundeep also shared how Swasth has established a culture of contribution instead of a culture of performance. "We do measure performance very diligently. However, there is a no punishment culture and we appreciate a person's contribution and support the person to excel and contribute more without attaching any negative consequence". He says that this has removed fear from people and there is joy in contributing to the wellness of people. In contrast to 2015 when Sundeep and Garima were speaking to us about expanding number of Swasth Clinics in Mumbai, and other cities, Sundeep says "we no longer measure our success based on these parameters anymore. We are looking at how we build an ecosystem where every person can be situated in their true Self (Swasth) which is always Joyful with a sense of wellbeing".

We asked Sundeep how he lives his appreciative spirit when the world seems to become more oppressive and divided. He had a very interesting take on this. He replied:

It depends on what you are looking for and at what level. When I look at what is happening at the world level, I'm looking at politics, economics, wealth etc. Here I see divisions, anger and fear and lack of safety. When I look at individual persons in our communities or the places I visit, I see the same human spirit of wanting to connect, wanting to contribute, and wanting to experience a sense of wellbeing and joy. I see and focus on that.

Sushma Sharma: Appreciative Inquiry Practitioner, Mentor, Coach

Sushma didn't need to learn Appreciative Inquiry, she naturally lives in an appreciative way. Sushma has been a friend, colleague, mentor and much more to us for the past three decades and more. She is a highly sought after OD consultant and Ai Practitioner in India and abroad.

Sushma started sharing about how she became an appreciative person with a positive mindset. "It was during the time of my college examinations. I was not very confident of writing the Psychology paper and became very anxious. Then it occurred to me that the worst thing that could happen was I could fail and others will say I was not good. It was alright with me and I didn't bother about what others felt. That was the turning point and all my anxiety disappeared. In fact, I did so well in that paper that I got a scholarship" Sushma said with a smile.

Sushma read the book on Appreciative Inquiry and went to NTL Institute (www.ntl.org) and attended the Appreciative Inquiry program with Cathy Royal and Bernard Mohr in the 1990s. "This really appealed and spoke to who I'm and what I believed in. I'm always looking forward to things rather than imagining the worse that can happen. Even when I fail, I look at it as learning. This is my way of being" Sushma shared.

She joined the NTL Appreciative Inquiry Hub as a trainer and they offered the first Ai-Hi lab (Human Interaction Lab with Appreciative Inquiry by NTL Institute). Sushma reminisced those days "I remember I asked one question to a participant 'What is your passion?' and he asked me back 'Do you really want to know my passion?' and I said 'yes'. He shared his passion and then he cried and said "This is the first time someone really asked me for my passion and really listened to me. I never felt so much valued". This became a standard inquiry in all the Ai-Hi labs later.

Sushma believes that language shapes reality and she insists on bringing language that is more life giving and wholistic in her work. "I changed the word diagnosis to sensing, data to stories, and information to metaphors". She also created a new language to describe group processes of forming, storming, forming and performing . She felt that language was very linear and assumes one stage is a pre-requisite for the other. Sushma said

> I also changed the language to "showing, knowing, growing and flowing." Walt Hopkins and I used only this language. When people show up, we get to know them and this begins the process of knowing and when we begin to know each other, we generate flow.

Sushma likes the language of Drench. She believes being drenched in Ai processes enables a person or an organization see value within and to stop looking for validation from outside.

Sushma shared the story of a large Appreciative Inquiry assignment she did for a paint manufacturer in India. She spoke about how she helped them to reframe their problem statement and see the need for a culture transformation. In that project, Sushma started first with a Drench. "I wanted the senior leadership to drench in Ai, so they believe in it and become the change agents. Hence, we started with a three day drench program in Appreciative Inquiry for the top leadership". This workshop resulted in the Leaders doing appreciative interviews of staff in the various offices, collecting stories of success and identifying energies for transformation. These were presented in their annual conference. The leaders then decided to do appreciative interviews with every new employee who joins the organization, thereby sustaining the appreciative culture.

Sushma shared:

> After some years, one of the leaders who had left that organization wrote a book and there was one chapter dedicated to our work. This book was an eye opener for me too. I didn't realize how much impact we had on the system. The whole culture changed subsequent to our interventions and became one of appreciation, focusing on what works and valuing people. The book was called *Be a leader of significance* (2023) and the author was Mosongo Moukwa.

Sushma loves the work of Darya Funches (2022) where she wrote about the three gifts of an OD Practitioner – the gifts of discernment, gift of presence and gift of heart. "I use her work and I have built on it". Sushma opined that these gifts are needed for the new world of Artificial intelligence as well. She said "Discernment is how we decide to use AI, Presence is how we show up with it and Heart is how we build relationships at work". She added that AI can handle all the technical and functional issues at work, much better than people. Now it can free Leaders to focus on building a culture of appreciation, wholeness and connect with people.

Sushma concluded:

> Artificial Intelligence can be our assistantsand not our manager. This is where Appreciative Intelligence of a leader is important. Leaders with Appreciative Intelligence will use the three gifts and use Artificial Intelligence appropriately and build the core life giving forces of people and organizations.

Sushma is presenting a paper on AI and Ai in the IODA conference in September 2025.

Reflections

We experienced these conversations as heartwarming, enriching and feeling reaffirmed in our commitment to an appreciative way of life and work. In all these interviews, the theme was overwhelmingly affirming that Appreciative Inquiry is not a method or a tool, it's a way of life. The transformative nature of Appreciative Inquiry was another theme that people shared from their experiences. This is as true for us, as it is for the people and organizations that have drenched in Appreciative Inquiry over the years.

When we spoke to our interviewees about the future of Appreciative Inquiry, the other AI, Artificial Intelligence was mentioned by all of them. All of them saw immense possibilities of Artificial Intelligence in how it can shape our lives. We spoke about the negative influence of Artificial Intelligence and someone quoted an Appreciative Inquiry saying "what we focus on becomes our reality, what we cultivate, grows". We have a choice to unlock the potential of Artificial Intelligence in such a way that it is human wisdom, powered by a machine.

David Shaked and Vivian Hau in their article "AI's voice for AI" (AI Practitioner, 2024) asked Artificial Intelligence to write the article based on their prompts. They write "We hold the intent to tell Artificial Intelligence that You are welcome here and that you came to the right place". (Inspired by Peter Block's quote "Structure influences behaviour. Design spaces in a way that make you feel 'You are welcome here and you came to the right place").

In that special issue many writers brought in the need to build a trusting relationship between humans and AI and leverage its immense value in helping us do analysis, problem-solving and enhancing productivity. They emphasized that while AI can do all that, human ingenuity, creativity and empathy cannot be replaced by any such Artificial Intelligence.

Tojo also saw an important role for all Appreciative Inquiry practitioners to help train Artificial Intelligence models by asking possibility oriented and life affirming questions. The language models currently used in Artificial Intelligence are mostly deficit and problem-solving focused and we need to bring in the Appreciative language. He said "Every question is an intervention and Artificial Intelligence will answer accordingly, based on whether the question is from a problem-solving perspective or from an appreciative perspective".

Priya Vasudevan offered to so some research on Ai and Ai and write this article which is given in the box below:

Infusing Artificial Intelligence (AI) through Appreciative Inquiry (Ai) in Organizations

Recent research suggests that although around 78% of companies have adopted GenAI in at least one business function over the past two years, and 80% report no significant earnings impact.[1]

Organizations are still tentatively dipping their toes into AI – using tools like Microsoft 365 that enhances individual productivity. The bigger play is in vertical, function-specific applications that offer more targeted value. On another front, organizations have still not embraced Agentic AI that unlocks operational agility and generates new revenue streams. For instance, in call centres, GenAI-driven tasks yield 5–10% improvements, while Agentic AI-driven process reinvention has slashed resolution times by 60–90%.[2]

The primary challenge on the horizon is not technical but human. There is widespread anxiety about AI assimilation triggering job losses. This is compounded by a conventional sequential thinking approach towards AI implementation amongst staff and leaders alike. Appreciative Inquiry (Ai) offers an energizing and transformative approach for AI adoption and overcoming Organisational intertia.. By honouring "the best of what is" and collectively envisioning "what the future could be," through an Ai intervention, – a generative roadmap that integrates human-AI cohabitation could be evolved. The principles of Ai, especially Constructivist, Poetic and Anticipatory principles come to fore in such an intervention. Through application of constructivist and anticipatory principle we could transform social narratives in organization to evocative propositions to unlock the potential of AI to amplify and ease human efforts (vs how many jobs it will replace). This embracing of possibilities by leaders could ultimately lead to generative designing of workflow, revisiting of organization structures and harmonious integration of Agentic AI into the workforce – thus ushering in significant benefits of AI into organizations.

Many people are building a dystopian future image with Artificial Intelligence. We believe that we need to also focus on stories when Artificial Intelligence really worked for us, when the combined power of AI and humans could deliver breakthrough solutions. This will help to build the trust in AI and help us to dream of a future together.

Notes

1 "The state of AI: How organizations are rewiring to capture value," McKinsey, March 12, 2025.
2 "Seizing the AI advantage," Quantum Black AI by McKinsey, June 2025

References

AI Practitioner. (September 2024). International Journal of Appreciative Inquiry. (www.aipractitioner.com)

Cooperrider, D., Srivastav, S. (1987). "Appreciative inquiry in organizational life" in Woodman, R. W. and Pasmore, W. A. (Eds.). *Research in Organizational Change and Development.* Stamford, CT: JAI Press. 1. 129–169.

Funches, D. (Summer 2022). "The three gifts of organization development practitioner" in W. Sikes, B. A. Drexler, and J. Gant (Eds.), *The Emerging Practice of Organization Development.* San Diego, CA: University Associates. 149–164.

Moukwa, M. (2023). *Be a Leader of Significance.* Washington D.C.: LionCrest Publishing.

Royal, C. L. (2013). "Quadrant behavior theory: Edging the center the potential for change and inclusion" in Vogelsang, J., Townsend, M., Minahan, M., Jamieson, D., Vogel, J., Viets, A., Royal, C., and Valek, L. (Eds.), *Handbook for Strategic HR: Best Practices in Organization Development from the OD Network.* Washington D.C.: AMACOM Division of American Management Association International. 182–190. www.jstor.org/stable/j.ctt1d2qzmw.30

Thatchenkery, T. (1992). Organizations as "texts": Hermeneutics as a model for understanding organizational change. *Research in Organization Development and Change.* 6. 197–233.

Vasudevan, P., Kohli, P. (2025). *Women of Alchemy.* Delhi: Vivara Tech Publishers.

Index

For Product Safety Concerns and Information please contact our EU
representative GPSR@taylorandfrancis.com
Taylor & Francis Verlag GmbH, Kaufingerstraße 24, 80331 München, Germany

www.ingramcontent.com/pod-product-compliance
Lightning Source LLC
Chambersburg PA
CBHW070328270326
41926CB00017B/3812

9781032884899